...hat there should be
...dent, autonomous
...cision has been
... in fifteen years.

The Times

...eral Coordinator of
...tion is planning
...rovements in rail-
...el. Among other
...s a dispatch which
...s the ...olition of un-
... place announcers.
... Americans to be
... to which they are
... for the life of them
...he train-guard is
... says The United
...employe who calls
...e he means Ashta-
...fed'' out of his job.
...anguages is recom-
...so cheap and con-
...icate with French
...Italian train-guards
...There ought to be
...lish language for
...ght like to know
...means Forty-sec-
...and when it means
...trains on all our
...bwawa, Umwawa,
...Grrumphf, Zoobz,
...d Mowawa.
...an over-privileged
...d phoneticians.

...en the late Dr. Al-
...ras, with other in-
...ators in the same
...established a con-
...n between cod-
...et rays, it was one
...way in which the
...mistry has recent-
...e immemorial wis-
...thout the slightest
...ns early man got
...t cod liver builds
...fruits and green-
...nswer to scurvy,
...ost ideal of foods.
...distant ancestors
...ly their supersti-
...their permanent
...mber that savages
...y beating on tom-
...e devils of disease,
...d mummy philtres
...But we are not so
...he vast contribu-
...e men and their
...modern pharma-

...of religion have
...ve man's fear of
...it is not so much

In Washington

Mussolini's League Aim Held No Inducement to Us.

By ARTHUR KROCK.

WASHINGTON, Dec. 7.—If one of Premier Mussolini's major objectives in demanding reforms in the structure of the League of Nations is to open the way to United States membership, his effort has made no impression here thus far. Discussion in official and Congressional quarters today of the moves of the Fascist Grand Council developed a unanimity of opinion that nothing can now tempt the United States to join.

A high official, speaking unofficially, said that if the League covenant is lifted out of the Treaty of Versailles, as the Fascists demand, it might be possible for an American administration, with political safety, to engage in greater cooperation with the League. Congress might even be found in a mood to authorize the government to pay for the labor and facilities which now in large measure it accepts from the League gratis. But he did not for a moment believe that the administration would be interested in any form of membership or that American public opinion was ever more opposed to formal League adhesion.

So definite is this impression, so firm this viewpoint, in Washington today that each person this correspondent approached on the subject began the conversation by saying that he had not given much thought to Mussolini's latest activity. From this tower—or cave—of public observation, Europe has seldom seemed more entangled in its own quarrels and difficulties, and the time was never less inviting for the United States to join in them. It is conceded by those here who have major influence in shaping foreign policy that to divorce the covenant from the treaty would be attractive to Russia and to Germany, and that to end the rule whereby the veto of a petty State can prevent the great powers from reaching a decision might bring back Japan. But none of them can see that any of the reforms offer an inducement to the United States to change its policy.

Holds France Dominates League.

The interpretation of one important official may be taken as a sample of the present effect on Washington of Mussolini's moves. He said that, since the retirement of Germany, the League has been dominated by France. Therefore, the inner meaning of the Italian policy is to bring in the absent great powers or those who have served notice of with...

Problems of Recovery

By DR. O...

Professor of Banking and Finance, Harvard Business School

WASHINGTON, Dec. 7.—In the preceding article of this series I called attention to the slight immediate influence which the supply of money at times exerts upon the level of prices. This point is convincingly illustrated in recent experience.

Between 1926 and 1933 the wholesale price index of the Bureau of Labor declined from 100 to below 70. In June, 1926, the stock of money in circulation was estimated at $4,885,000,000. By June of 1933 there had been an increase to $5,720,000,000. During the same period of time there was an increase in the cash reserves of the Federal Reserve Banks from $2,980,000,000 to $3,-813,000,000.

Evidently, if the supply of money, whether in the hands of the people or in Reserve Banks, always exerted a powerful direct influence on prices we ought now to be enjoying a far higher price level than that of seven years ago.

The actual decline in prices during these years is reflected in, and was in part brought about by, a very great reduction in the loans and investments of the banks of the country. In 1926 these loans and investments were in excess of $50,000,000,000. In 1933 they were below $40,000,000,000.

More Banking Activity Needed.

What we need, and indeed what we must have, if prices are to rise to anything approaching the 1926 level, is a very great increase in the loans and investments of the banks of the country, with a consequent increase in the volume of deposits subject to check. In other words, we must look to the creation of conditions which may be expected to bring about this increase, if we are to have a rise in prices through the operation of normal business influences.

Although cash reserves are quite ample to support a greatly enlarged credit structure and, indeed, a credit structure far greater than that of 1926, the banks of the country are not on that account alone in position to make a large increase in loans and investments. This is because full confidence in the banks has not yet taken the place of that widespread lack of confidence in them which compelled the closing of all banks at the beginning of March of ...

the insurance system soon after the ...sage of the Glass-Steagall act las...

Moreover, the conditions for ...into the system have been ma... necessarily severe by those resp... for its establishment. Washingt... urged the banks to extend credi... freely while examiners have bee... jecting existing assets to valu... based upon most pessimistic for... This has exerted a deflationary ... ence unfavorable to the general p... of trade recovery.

System Should Be Widespre...

It is inconsistent with recovery ...to allow any large number of ban... were reopened last March to be ex... from the insurance system. So... or another virtually all of the ban... were opened then must be brough... the guarantee scheme on Jan. 1, ... considerable the burden this m... pose upon the government. The ... ure would be certain to weaken ... other banks now considered reas... solvent.

I feel confident, therefore, that ... last moment whatever governme... is required to enable banks to ... for the insurance system will be ... available. Happily the deflation... fluence incident to the establis... of the insurance system is not ... tinue for many more weeks.

The temporary insurance ... which goes into effect on Jan. ... been limited to deposits not exc... $2,500. The permanent system ... to come into effect on July 1 ne... much further. It provides full ... ance for deposits to $10,000, cover... 75 per cent of a further amount ... $50,000, and 50 per cent for depo... excess of that amount.

In my judgment, it would be w... limit the insurance in the perm... scheme to the $2,500, or some othe... erate amount. It is difficult to di... any public advantage from the ... ance of large deposits. The ... ber of individuals and corpor... who maintain large bank balance... be supposed to be able to make ... telligent choice of a bank.

Masses Need Protection.

The mass of people, on the ... ...nd are not often in a position ...

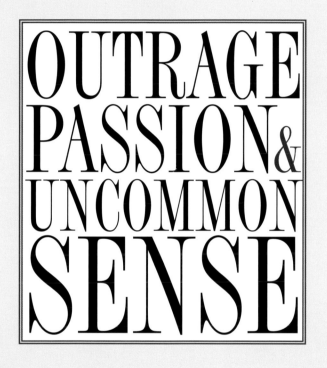

OUTRAGE
PASSION &
UNCOMMON
SENSE

scribe and put down the abhorrent
ng. After what Mr. ROOSEVELT has
w said, the apologists for Governor
LPH of California—to say nothing of
se who applauded his foolish and
ebrand defense of mob murder—
ll be fewer and more ashamed of
emselves.

A fine spirit pervades the rest of the
esident's brief but deeply felt speech.
it he sought to define the aims and
pes of those who are working with
m to bring about not only immediate
overy but a better and more stable
cial order in this country. His rap-
y drawn outline of history might be
ticized. So might his frequent use
so indefinite a phrase as "social jus-
e." But it would be ungracious to
k out minor flaws in what was, on
whole, an inspiring address. It gave
country a vivid impression of a sin-
e man working toward ideal ends
ich he cherishes for the good of all
people. It represents FRANKLIN D.
OSEVELT at his best—and his best is
ry good.

E TREASURY'S NEW FINANCING.

The magnitude of operations in-
lved in financing the public deficit
illustrated by yesterday's announce-
nt of the Treasury's quarterly plans.
less a sum than $950,000,000, in
e shape of one-year loan certificates,
offered for subscription. This amount
by no means unprecedented for a
gle offering. Subscribers were asked
$994,000,000 in the aggregate in
arch of 1932, and for $942,000,000
t March; on each occasion, however,
o sets of short-term loans with dif-
ent maturities were offered, whereas
present offering is all for one ma-
rity. Of the subscription now so-
ited, $727,600,000 may be made in
er short-term certificates, issued
t March and December and matur-
next week; to that extent the trans-
ion will be equivalent merely to a
ar's extension of the indebtedness.
For the new short-term loan the
easury offers an interest rate of 2¼
cent. That represents substantial
rease over the ¼ of 1 per cent borne
the nine months' loan of last Sep-
mber and the ¾ of 1 per cent carried
the similar loan of June. Those bor-
wings were not only for a shorter
m, but were respectively for amounts
74,900,000 and $460,099,000) less
n one-half what is now applied for.
e present rate is considerably below
rates of 4 and 4¼ per cent fixed for
two types of short loans placed on
rch 15. That month's offering, it is
e, was made while the nation-wide
k moratorium was still in force—a
which necessarily required larger
cession from the borrower. But even
the half-year from December, 1931,
March, 1932, rates of 3 to 3¼ per

rights more plainly glimmering, the
stronger the reason for insisting on
borough rights. Besides, Tammany's
regularity is only technical. Its stupidity in bucking against the nomination of Mr. ROOSEVELT and Mr. LEH-
MAN deserved to bring on it the com-
mination of the Bronx sovereign, who
had the wit to choose the winning side.

These battles of the bosses may leave
other than their subjects cold; but
something is due to intelligence, and
Mr. FLYNN often has it. His sense
of humor, moreover, must be highly
developed. Otherwise, he couldn't whip
himself up into so fine a frenzy against
"dictation."

MASS-GIVING.

Considering that all public charities
are finding it difficult to raise money
this year, there is reason to be pleased
with the response thus far to the appeal for the Neediest. Evidently their
cause still has a strong pull upon hearts
and purses. But while the gifts are
coming in gratifyingly—yesterday's
total was somewhat above that for the
same day last year—the number of
contributors seems unhappily to be
falling off. There is, of course, a natural explanation for this. In a time
like the present everybody feels it necessary to husband his resources. It is
also probable that many who have
given generously in other years are
reluctant to send in now a contribution
which must be smaller. But that, we
submit, is a mistaken point of view.
When little can be given, little will be
welcome. In the case of the Fund for
the Neediest, names and numbers
count for a great deal—sometimes
more than money. The spirit of good-
will and cooperation is the main thing.
The list of givers ought to be thought
of as a sort of roll of honor, testifying
to the sympathy and charitable impulse of all who are on it. So it is much
to be desired that none will refrain
from acting on the principle that the
giver, not the gift, is the thing of real
significance, but will forward whatever
amount they can spare, though it be
small.

BRILLIANT BUT DULL

It is now judicially decided that the
"Ulysses" of JAMES JOYCE is not an
obscene or pornographic book. That
will prevail, at least so far as permitting
the work to be imported into the United
States. In the carefully prepared opinion
of Judge WOOLSEY, certain general principles are laid down. It is not fair to
tear a phrase or paragraph from its
context. Since it is a question of intent, the novel must be judged as a
whole. So dealing with it, Judge WOOL-
SEY finds a good deal in "Ulysses" that
is vulgar and offensive, yet does not
fall within the statute relating to obscene publications. There is no delight-

the same property, the situation remains unchanged and "parity" is still
lacking. On the other hand, the Right
may argue that there is no specific limi-
tation on profits in the law and that
power to prescribe codes is to be found
not in the AAA but in the NRA.

The disagreement will probably continue, elsewhere if not in the AAA itself; for it is merely one phase of a
broad difference of opinion between
"conservatives" and "radicals" crop-
ping out at many points within the
Administration. For the present, and
on the immediate issue, the President
has sought a compromise. The bone of
contention between Right and Left—
power to write codes—has been whisked
away from the AAA and restored to
the NRA, from which it was borrowed.

NEW POLAND.

The Polish Minister of Education
said last Summer in Warsaw that citizens of Poland had to choose where
they would spend the small amount of
money they had. "For armaments we
"had to spend. For roads we should
"have spent. Our roads are regrettable.
"But we have educated our children.
"For that we have never ceased to
"spend money." It is in their education in a free Poland that there is hope.
The School Reform Bill of 1932 has as
its objective a seven-year elementary
schooling for every Polish child. The
realization of that purpose, said a
speaker at the celebration, a few days
ago, of the fifteenth anniversary of the
Polish restoration to nationhood, is re-
tarded by the universal crisis but the
nation is unitedly advancing toward it.

One of her poets has said that Poland
is rich in culture and poor in civilization—poor in some of the conveniences
that are accounted essentials in Western countries, but rich in the quality of
her spirit and in "the memory of a
glowing past." The Copernican contribution has put the peoples of the earth
for all time to come under a specific
obligation to Poland. It is conceivable
that the heliocentric theory has had
and will continue to have a real influence upon the evolution of the social
and political life of mankind, as well as
in the development of the physical
sciences. It was in Cracow, the capital
of the Poland which then swept from
the Baltic to the Baltic Sea, that COPER-
NICUS got "his inspiration for discov-
"eries that burst the ancient bonds of
"accepted fact."

Broken and dismembered, Poland was
for a century and a half. And it was
asked, as in the prophecy of EZEKIEL,
"Can these bones live?" But life was
restored, and as PADEREWSKI testified
ten years afterward, it was "the voice
of America" that shook the diplomatic
traditions of the whole world to their
very foundation. The evoking message
of that voice was in the words of

marriage customs. Among the
which the husband brings the w
says, is a shield, a sword or a
and she in turn brings her husb
piece of armor. "Here is the gist
bond between them—that the wif
not imagine herself released fro
practice of heroism, released fro
chances of war. Her fate will
same as his in peace, and in par
risks the same."

Women in mechanized modern
bear arms in the munition worl
chemical factories, but that ma
notion more for the logical Frenc
than the intuitive Germanic min
any rate, it would be the Nazi con
that for purposes of war women
be content to bear the childre
bear the arms.

**Our
Amendment
Rate.**

In the year 1920
illustrating our c
tempo in amendi
United States Co
tion might hav
gested interesting possibilities.
first twelve amendments were a
in fifteen years. There was a pa
sixty-one years, and the group o
Civil War amendments was a
in the space of five years,
There was another long pause of
three years, and two amendme
come tax and popular election
ators—were adopted in a single
1913. It took only seven years
another brace of amendments ca
being, prohibition and woman su
in 1920.

This acceleration if maintained
soon give us a new constit
amendment every year, but in 1
curve turned upward again.
to wait thirteen years for the
pair of amendments—this year's
Duck and Repeal. Sentiment
present moment foreshadows
wait before the next attempt
something to the Organic Law.

THE GIFT.

After these years—with all th
before,
With all that followed after, ca
tween—
Your smile remains, which
jeweled moidore,
Your laughter, which was m
evergreen.

No words return. The beauty
day
You spent beside me; places, gif
friend
We knew together, these ha
away.
Only your smile, your laughter
end.

Earth has known joy and terr
have died,
Women have watched their so
fully grown,
A score of Aprils, rose-and-lila
Have seen their fruit out-fille
flowers blown.

And—miracle of time!—in all th
Each year returns life's dear

OUTRAGE PASSION & UNCOMMON SENSE

MICHAEL GARTNER and the NEWSEUM

HOW EDITORIAL WRITERS HAVE TAKEN ON
THE GREAT AMERICAN ISSUES OF THE PAST 150 YEARS

NATIONAL GEOGRAPHIC

WASHINGTON, D.C.

TABLE OF CONTENTS

CAPTIONS:

PAGE 2: The New York Times' *"Brilliant But Dull"* editorial on the decision by Judge Woolsey to allow James Joyce's Ulysses into the country.
PAGE 4: *Rev. Colley S. Reynolds. His* West Hillsborough *(Fla.)* Times *sought to "become merely the telephone through which its inviting voice may be carried to many listening ears."*

NOTE TO READERS: *The original content of each editorial, including spelling, language and style, has been preserved as much as possible.*

For Carl Gartner (1902–2004) and

Christopher Carl Gartner (1976–1994)

two of the great people

❧

ABOVE: *William Allen White in 1899. "The editor must be the judge of his news. . . . He must take a 'side' in everything," he said.*
OPPOSITE: *H.L. Mencken. "The massed editorial writers . . . seldom produce a new idea, and are almost unheard of when the problems of the country are soberly discussed," he said.*

The editorial staff of the New York Tribune.
Seated, left to right: George M. Snow,
financial editor; Bayard Taylor, correspondent;
Horace Greeley, founder; George Ripley, literary
editor. Standing, left to right: William Henry Fry,
music editor; Charles A. Dana, chief editorial
assistant; Henry J. Raymond, chief assistant.

INTRODUCTION

THE EDITORIAL IS THE SOUL OF THE NEWSPAPER.

Maybe the heart and the soul. ❧ And, on a good newspaper that knows and understands and loves its hometown, or its home country, the editorial is the heart and the soul of the town, or the nation, as well. ❧ "The editor must be the judge of his news, of how it is told, what is recited and what omitted. He must interpret it. He must take a 'side' in everything. Nothing fails so rapidly as a cowardly paper, unless it is a paper that confuses courage with noise."

So wrote a young William Allen White in 1901, a few years after he took over *The Daily Gazette* of Emporia, Kan. We start this book and end it with editorials by White, the first one explaining the role of the newspaper, and the last one defending our freedom of speech.

White is one of the four greatest editorial writers in the history of this nation. The four were men of different generations and different beliefs, but they all reported thoroughly, wrote gracefully and argued passionately. They knew intimately their town — or their nation, or their world — and they were neither blind boosters nor common scolds. They were men who wanted, and made, a better world. Their writings covered a span of nearly 150 years. Besides White, the men are Horace Greeley of the *New York Tribune*, Henry Watterson of *The Courier-Journal* of Louisville and Vermont Royster of *The Wall Street Journal*.

You always knew where they stood.

"If your editorial writer ... 'takes the fence,' thinking of the dangers of antagonizing somebody or other, including the publisher's wife, he can't write anything worth reading and it is not worth while hiring him," the curmudgeonly newspaperman H.L. Mencken told a gathering of editorial writers in 1947. Mencken knew whereof he spoke.

He not only wrote editorials — though he achieved his fame through other writings — he was often the subject of them, perhaps because he wrote in 1923 that "the massed editorial writers of the United States seldom produce a new idea, and are almost unheard of when the problems of the country are soberly discussed."

The *Jackson* (Miss.) *Daily News* once wrote that "Mencken, with his filthy verbal hemorrhages, is so low down in the moral scale, so damnably dirty, so vile and degenerate, that when his time comes to die it will take a special dispensation

OPPOSITE: *William Allen White. "A newspaper has one obligation ... to comment upon the truth as candidly and as kindly as is humanly possible."*

from Heaven to get him into the bottommost pit of Hell."

But Mencken gave as good as he got. After acknowledging that for more than 40 years Henry Watterson "was the most distinguished editorial writer on the American press," Mencken added: "His editorials on foreign politics are empty mouthings of an unintelligent chauvinism. His occasional ventures into economics are pathetic."

Back to that bottommost pit of hell.

Even hell was too good for a Civil War general from the North named Ben Butler, if *The (Nashville) Daily American* editorial page could have had its way. When Butler died in 1893, the *American* wrote: "If there be a future of peace in store for Ben Butler after his entrance upon eternity then there is no heaven and the Bible is a lie. ... Goodbye, Ben! You strutted through a few temporal triumphs; now rest if you can in the brimstone glare of hell fire."

Horace Greeley, the first of the four great editorial writers, was the founder of the *New York Tribune* in 1841 and is generally credited with inventing the editorial page in the 1850s — that is, with putting pieces of opinion on a separate page from the pieces of straight reporting. Until then, newspapers mixed the two, pursuing in the news stories and the editorials an agenda reflected in the partisan names the newspapers bore.

While many newspapers labeled themselves as Chronicles and Tribunes and Mirrors and Registers, others left no doubt where they stood — proudly proclaiming themselves *The Republican*, *The Whig*, *The Independent*, *The Conservative* and, in the case of a weekly newspaper in Osage County, Mo., the *Unterrified Democrat*. (Times change. The *Unterrified Democrat* today lists itself as a Republican newspaper.)

Greeley, a Whig-turned-Republican-turned-Socialist-turned-Democrat, "lifted the American newspaper editorial to the level of a legitimate literary form," Richard Kluger wrote in his history of the *New York Herald Tribune*.

While Greeley had passionate views on nearly every issue of the day, it was abolition that most moved him. His Aug. 19, 1862, editorial, "The Prayer of Twenty Millions," was written in the midst of the Civil War as a letter to President Abraham Lincoln, stating that many of the people who voted for him were "sorely disappointed and deeply pained" that the president had not freed the slaves.

"I write only to set succinctly and unmistakably before you what we require, what we think we have a right to expect, and of what we complain."

Three days later, Lincoln, in the midst of the war, took the time to respond. He began: "I have just read yours of the 19th, addressed to myself through The New-York Tribune. If there be in it any statements or assumptions of fact which I may know to be erroneous, I do not now and here controvert them. If there be in it any inferences which I may believe to be falsely drawn, I do not now and here argue against them. If there be perceptible in it an impatient and dictatorial tone, I waive it in deference to an old friend, whose heart I have always supposed to be right."

He then talked of holding the nation together. Within six months, Lincoln issued the Emancipation Proclamation.

Although there is evidence Lincoln had already made up his mind to issue the Emancipation Proclamation, "The Prayer of Twenty Millions" is, arguably, the most important editorial ever published. (The editors of *The New York Times*, which had at best a sneering relationship with Greeley and the *Tribune*, would disagree. In an editorial praising President Lincoln's response — "He could not have said anything more satisfactory to the country in general" — the *Times* said: "It is in infinitely better taste, too, than the rude epistle to which it is an answer.")

Greeley was "a stubborn spirit … a nobly gifted man … a brave old apostle of freedom," Henry Watterson wrote nearly 50 years after Greeley's death in 1872.

Watterson could have been describing himself. The second of the four great editorial writers, he was for a time a reporter in Washington — he stood next to Lincoln as the president delivered his inaugural address — and then for 50 years, from 1868 to 1918, was editor of *The Courier-Journal*.

"As an orator and statesman he was famous, and as a conversationalist he was renowned," the newspaperman Arthur Krock wrote about Watterson two years after his death. But, "it was as an editorial writer that Henry Watterson attracted and influenced three generations of Americans."

Watterson was the second person ever to win a Pulitzer Prize for editorial writing — he was 78 years old at the time. He never minced words.

"To Hell with the Hohenzollerns and the Hapsburgs," he wrote — again and again — as war broke out in Europe. "I at least have not always been a dummy and have sometimes in a way helped to make history," he wrote a few years before his death, and no reader and no historian could dispute that.

His readers knew where he stood. He called President Grant "an iron-hearted, wooden-headed nutmeg." He hated Prohibition and viewed Carrie Nation as a "crazy Jane," a "poor, old hag." He opposed women's suffrage and wrote that beneath that movement "lies — nay, yawns — an abyss of revolution, menacing not only government and politics, but the whole human species."

William Allen White, the editor of *The Emporia Daily Gazette* in Kansas from 1895 to 1944, is the third of the four great editorial writers. Though he was a worldly man — a biographer of Calvin Coolidge, friend of Herbert Hoover and Wendell Willkie, member of the board of the Rockefeller Foundation and of the editorial board of the Book of the Month Club — he wrote of and for the people of Emporia.

He was folksy. "Parson T.F. Stauffer held his annual coming-out party for his straw hat yesterday afternoon," began an editorial in 1915.

He was personal. "The editor of this paper desires to buy a horse," began another, in 1906.

And he was passionate. "Peace is good. But if you are interested in peace through force and without free discussion — that is to say, free utterance decently and in order — your interest in justice is slight. And peace without justice is tyranny, no matter how you may sugar-coat it with expediency. This state to-day is in more danger from suppression than from violence, because, in the

THE PRAYER OF TWENTY MILLIONS.

To ABRAHAM LINCOLN, *President of the U. States:*

DEAR SIR: I do not intrude to tell you—for you must know already—that a great proportion of those who triumphed in your election, and of all who desire the unqualified suppression of the Rebellion now desolating our country, are sorely disappointed and deeply pained by the policy you seem to be pursuing with regard to the slaves of Rebels. I write only to set succinctly and unmistakably before you what we require, what we think we have a right to expect, and of what we complain.

I. We require of you, as the first servant of the Republic, charged especially and preëminently with this duty, that you EXECUTE THE LAWS. Most emphatically do we demand that such laws as have been recently enacted, which therefore may fairly be presumed to embody the *present* will and to be dictated by the *present* needs of the Republic, and which, after due consideration have received your personal sanction, shall by you be carried into full effect, and that you publicly and decisively instruct your subordinates that such laws exist, that they are binding on all functionaries and citizens, and that they are to be obeyed to the letter.

II. We think you are strangely and disastrously remiss in the discharge of your official and imperative duty with regard to the emancipating provisions of the new Confiscation Act. Those provisions were designed to fight Slavery with Liberty. They prescribe that men loyal to the Union, and willing to shed their blood in her behalf, shall no longer be held, with the Nation's consent, in bondage to persistent, malignant traitors, who for twenty years have been plotting and for sixteen months have been fighting to divide and destroy our country. Why these traitors should be treated with tenderness by you, to the prejudice of the dearest rights of loyal men, we cannot conceive.

III. We think you are unduly influenced by fact that immunity and safety were found on that side, danger and probable death on ours. The Rebels from the first have been eager to confiscate, imprison, scourge and kill: we have fought wolves with the devices of sheep. The result is just what might have been expected. Tens of thousands are fighting in the Rebel ranks to-day whose original bias and natural leanings would have led them into ours.

VI. We complain that the Confiscation Act which you approved is habitually disregarded by your Generals, and that no word of rebuke for them from you has yet reached the public ear. Fremont's Proclamation and Hunter's Order favoring Emancipation were promptly annulled by you; while Halleck's No. 3, forbidding fugitives from Slavery to Rebels to come within his lines—an order as unmilitary as inhuman, and which received the hearty approbation of every traitor in America—with scores of like tendency, have never provoked even your remonstrance. We complain that the officers of your Armies have habitually repelled rather than invited the approach of slaves who would have gladly taken the risks of escaping from their Rebel masters to our camps, bringing intelligence often of inestimable value to the Union cause. We complain that those who *have* thus escaped to us, avowing a willingness to do for us whatever might be required, have been brutally and madly repulsed, and often surrendered to be scourged, maimed and tortured by the ruffian traitors, who pretend to own them. We complain that a large proportion of our regular Army Officers, with many of the Volunteers, evince far more solicitude to uphold Slavery than to put down the Rebellion. And finally, we complain that you, Mr. President, elected as a Republican, knowing well what an abomination Slavery is, and how emphatically it is the core and essence of this atrocious Rebellion, seem never to interfere with these atrocities, and never give a direction to your Military subordinates, which does not appear to have been conceived in the interest of Slavery rather than of Freedom.

end, suppression leads to violence. Violence, indeed, is the child of suppression," said White during a railroad strike in 1922.

White is one of only four persons ever to win Pulitzer Prizes both in journalism and in letters, winning for editorial writing in 1923 and for his autobiography in 1947.

Vermont Connecticut Royster is the fourth of the great editorial writers. Royster guided the editorial pages of *The Wall Street Journal* through the period of its greatest growth, its most independent thinking and its most graceful writing. A Southerner schooled in Greek and Latin, Royster went to college at the University of North Carolina in Chapel Hill, where members of his family had taught for generations. It was there he came under the spell of a philosophy professor named Horace Williams.

"Horace Williams taught me two things that remain with me yet," Royster wrote in 1983, when he was approaching 70 years old. "There's fun to be had in challenging any idea; later I was to be labeled a 'conservative' when in fact I was a radical smashing away at the prevalent political orthodoxies miscalled 'liberal.' Secondly, he taught me that it's only by challenging every idea that you can be sure of what you think, for then you know why you think what you think."

Royster's intellectual rigor, coupled with his graceful writing, produced editorials that were forceful and scholarly in content and lyrical and poetic in style. (To answer your question, yes, his name really was Vermont Connecticut Royster. He was named after a grandfather, whose own father had named all his children after states. The other boys were Iowa Michigan, Arkansas Delaware, Wisconsin Illinois, and Oregon Minnesota. The girls were Virginia Carolina and Georgia Indiana. Royster used to refer lovingly to "Uncle Wis.")

Royster once called a young *Journal* colleague who was leaving New York to edit a newspaper in the Midwest and asked him down for a cup of coffee.

"Will you be writing editorials?" Royster asked.

"Yes," the young man replied.

"Have you ever written an editorial?" Royster asked.

"No," the young man replied.

"Do you know how to write an editorial?" Royster asked.

"I suspect you are about to tell me," the young man replied.

"I am," said Royster. "It's quite simple. Tell the facts. Be clear. Give the other side the space, but give your side the thought."

Another Pulitzer Prize-winning editorial writer, Richard Aregood, put it another way: "I do try to give the poor bastard his due, but I also try to kick him while I'm at it." *The New York Times,* like many newspapers, doesn't even want to give the poor bastard his due. In a note to readers in 2005, editorial page editor Gail Collins wrote: "The goal

OPPOSITE: *Horace Greeley's anti-slavery editorial, "The Prayer of Twenty Millions," prompted a response from President Abraham Lincoln.*

[of *Times* editorial writers] is to convince you, not give you the opposition's best argument." That prompted Gil Cranberg, a retired editorial page editor from Des Moines, to write a letter to the *Times* challenging Collins' "evident belief that addressing the opposition's best argument detracts from your own position. On the contrary, acknowledging 'the other side' signals readers that you took it into account and thus makes your argument more convincing." Cranberg, like Royster and Aregood, is right.

Though no one can match Greeley, Watterson, White and Royster, there were — and are — scores of others who think clearly, report thoroughly (for, as Royster noted, the best editorials are full of facts) and write beautifully. The South, particularly, produced some great editorial writers during the years of civil rights unrest. Ralph McGill of *The Atlanta Constitution* and Eugene Patterson of the *St. Petersburg Times* are two. Both won Pulitzer Prizes for editorial writing — Patterson received his in 1967 while at *The Atlanta Constitution* — but their most eloquent and bravest writings were in personal, signed columns.

Most editorials are not signed, but the anonymity makes them no less graceful, no less forceful. Listen to this, from the *Albany* (N.Y.) *Evening Journal* just after the Supreme Court of the United States in 1857 issued its Dred Scott decision protecting slavery: "Unworthy of the Bench from which it was delivered, unworthy even of the previous reputation of the jurist who delivered it, unworthy of the American people, and of the nineteenth century, it will be a blot upon our National character abroad, and

a long-remembered shame at home. ... It falsifies the most reliable history, abrogates the most solemn Law, belies the dead and stultifies the living — in order to make what has heretofore been a local evil, hereafter a National institution!"

Race has probably been the single issue that has most stirred the passions of editorial writers. Nearly 100 years after the Dred Scott decision, the *Jackson Daily News* was assailing the court over the school-desegregation ruling in Brown v. Board of Education.

"Human blood may stain Southern soil in many places because of this decision but the dark red stains of that blood will be on the marble steps of the United States Supreme Court building," the paper editorialized.

The best editorial writers have that passion — the passion for truth, for freedom, for fairness, for equality.

"There must be a passionate concern for the truth," Virginius Dabney, a onetime editor of the *Richmond Times-Dispatch*, wrote in 1945.

"A big thing missing in lots of editorial pages is passion," according to Richard Aregood, who won the Pulitzer Prize for editorial writing at the *Philadelphia Daily News* in 1985 and who went on to become editorial page editor of the Newark *Star-Ledger*. "I have this feeling that many people writing about stuff don't really care about it. Some don't have the passion. The way most journalists think about editorial pages now, it's kind of a bloodless thing, even a committee thing."

Not so wherever Aregood was working, though. In 1975, when he was at the *Philadelphia*

Daily News, he wrote a 123-word editorial urging the death penalty for a criminal named Leonard Edwards. The last two words: "Fry him."

Editorials must be read to be effective, of course.

"The easiest thing for the reader to do is to quit reading," Barney Kilgore, a newsman who more or less invented the modern-day *Wall Street Journal*, told a young copy editor there in 1960. That's why Aregood's editorials are so effective — nobody can put one down in midsentence.

That's at least part of the reason, too, that Grover Cleveland Hall of the *Montgomery* (Ala.) *Advertise*r won a Pulitzer Prize for editorial writing in 1928. As part of a series of editorials attacking the Ku Klux Klan and its sympathizers, he took on Alabama Sen. Tom Heflin. Titled, simply, "Our Tom," the editorial stated: "A bully by nature, a mountebank by instinct, a Senator by choice. … He is bombastic and blustery." And it ends: "Thus this preposterous blob excites our pity if not our respect." No reader could stop reading that editorial.

The best editorials are as consistent in their beliefs as they are in their writing. Editorials represent the views, the heritage and the traditions of the newspaper itself. By hewing to that line, they allow the readers to use the editorials as a yardstick for their own views and beliefs.

"You can't say one day you think price controls are yummy and the next day they are dumb, to use girls' school parlance. You become part of an institutional personality," wrote Meg Greenfield, the editorial page editor of *The Washington Post* for more than 20 years.

Thus it was that in 1987, seven months after *The Courier-Journal* was sold by the liberal owning family to the Gannett chain, the editorial page sought to reassure readers that while the ownership had changed, the philosophy hadn't.

"This we believe," began an editorial on Feb. 16, 1987. "We believe in the dignity of man. We believe in the sovereignty of nations. We believe in what our Constitution calls the Blessings of Liberty. We believe in human rights and civil rights and equality for all. We believe in governments that help the needy and the poor and the underprivileged and the ill and the young and the helpless so that they, too, can enjoy the Blessings of Liberty. We believe in free trade. We believe in the entrepreneur and the laborer and the free enterprise system that allows open competition in the marketplace. We believe in a military that can defend but will not bully. We believe in freedom to worship, to speak, to write, to assemble. We believe in Kentucky, its heritage and its future. We believe in justice."

Institutional views can change, of course, and sometimes abruptly. After Gannett bought the Jackson, Miss., newspapers, long outspoken foes of integration, the editorial page said: "We were wrong, wrong, wrong." It then called on other Mississippians in public life who previously had embraced segregation to do the same thing. Some did, most didn't.

In 2001, *The New York Times* named a woman as editor of the editorial page, something that surely was beyond the imagination of those editors of a century ago who were so virulently opposed to the women's right to vote. In 1915, the *Times* editorialized: "The grant of suffrage to women is repugnant to instincts that strike their roots deep in the order of nature."

That same year, after New York voters rejected suffrage, the *Times* said: "Open the gates of the franchise, and you open them forever. ... Woman suffrage once in the Constitution, it will remain there. No matter how badly it might work, no matter how sick of it the male and the female electorate might be, it could not be ended."

In a sense, Thomas Paine and Benjamin Franklin were editorial writers, espousing causes with passion and precision, sometimes in newspapers, sometimes in pamphlets. If ever there was an editorial, it was when Thomas Paine wrote, in "The American Crisis," "These are the times that try men's souls. The summer soldier and the sunshine patriot will, in this crisis, shrink from the service of their country; but he that stands it *now* deserves the love and thanks of man and woman."

And ever since the Revolution, through war and peace and crisis and calm, the heirs of Franklin and Paine have been explaining and exploring and expounding issues and ideas for the American newspaper reader. Some, like Hazel Brannon Smith of the *Lexington* (Miss.) *Advertiser*, who attacked racists in her hometown, have been courageous.

Some, like Henry Watterson, have been stirring. (As World War I approached, he wrote: "There are times when feeling must be sent to the rear; when duty must toe the line; when the aversion brave men have for

fighting must yield to the adjuration, 'Give me liberty, or give me death!' That time is now upon us.")

Some, like the anonymous editorial writer for the *New York Herald Tribune* who defended the 1947 blacklisting of Hollywood writers because they refused to testify about their beliefs, have been misguided. (In a letter to the editor, E.B. White, the great essayist, complained: "I can only assume that your editorial writer, in a hurry to get home for Thanksgiving, tripped over the First Amendment and thought it was the office cat.")

Some, like William Allen White, have been homespun. ("Public Notice. Mrs. W.A. White has gone to New York, called there by the illness of her sister. Mr. W.A. White is in Emporia. How about Sunday dinner? This is not only an opportunity, but a duty, as we have said before on many cases of public need. Don't all speak at once, but phone 28 after six o'clock.")

But courageous, patriotic, misguided or homespun, the best editorial writers all know the simple truth that William Allen White told his readers one April day in 1923: "A newspaper has one obligation and one only, to print the truth as far as it is humanly possible, and to comment upon the truth as candidly and as kindly as is humanly possible, never forgetting to be merry the while, for after all the liar and the cheat and the panderer are smaller offenders than the solemn ass."

One footnote: Yes, Virginia, there is a Santa Claus. ❧

OPPOSITE: *Henry Watterson was editor of* The Courier-Journal *for 50 years.*
"He looked like he came out of a Grimms fairy tale," owner Barry Bingham Sr. once said.

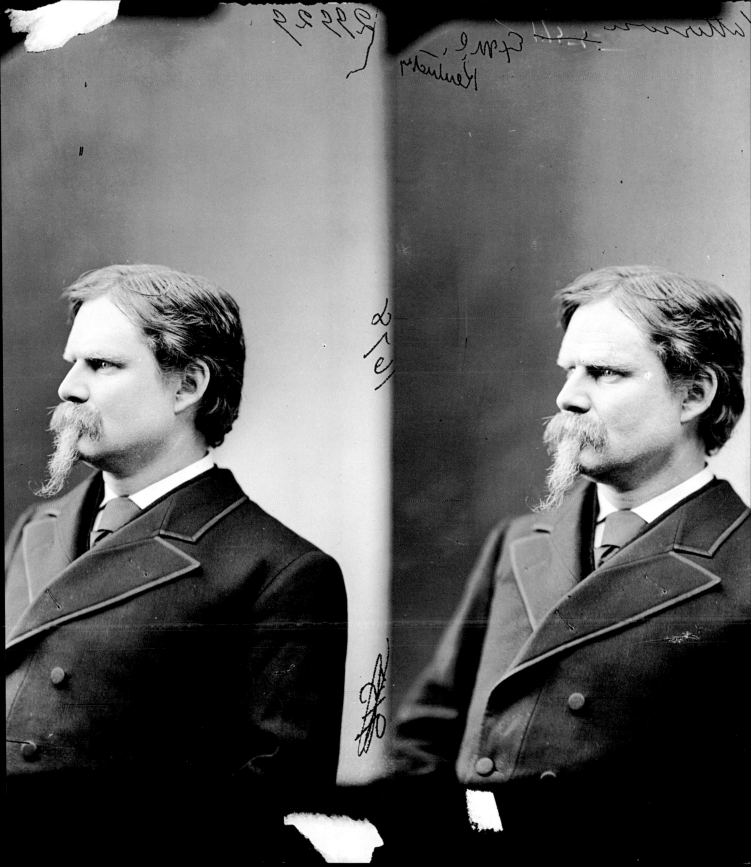

CHAPTER ONE NEWSPAPERING

"IF YOU DON'T WANT IT PRINTED, DON'T LET IT HAPPEN."

That's the motto of the *Aspen Daily News*, a Colorado newspaper founded in 1978, and, stated or unstated, it's the motto that good editors of good newspapers have lived by for generations. ❧ "Editors are only saved from burning at the stake because people don't get together," William Allen White wrote in an editorial in 1901. "Every paper that amounts to anything makes people violently angry. If all the people who are mad at the paper would meet just after the paper is out, there would be enough to hang any editor in the world."

Indeed, offering up opinions every day can be more perilous than White or readers imagined. For while it's one thing to displease the people, it's quite another to displease the boss.

In November of 1966, according to a history of *The New York Times*, Herbert Matthews wrote an editorial about the planned Christmas truce in the Vietnam War. It began: "Kill and maim as many as you can up to 6 o'clock in the morning of December 24 and start killing again on the morning of December 26."

When the publisher, Arthur Ochs Sulzberger, saw that in the early edition, he called the editorial page editor and ordered him to kill it because of its stridency. Instead, a compromise was worked out, and readers of late editions read an editorial that began with what was the second paragraph: "By all means, let there be peace in Vietnam for a few hours or a few days over Christmas and the New Year. It is not much, but it is that much better than uninterrupted war."

If the editor owns the paper, of course, he can write what he wants. Arthur Krock, a great news-paperman of generations past, wrote that Henry Watterson, the editor of *The Courier-Journal* for 50 years in the 19th and 20th centuries, "was the last of the great editors, for the reason that he was the last of those editors who wrote with the power of owner-ship." Krock explained: "A hired journalism, however zealous, however loyal, however entrusted, however brilliant, cannot be great because it speaks through the mist of subordination." (Krock himself was a hired journalist who had a distinguished career in Louisville and at *The New York Times*.)

As if to prove Krock right, Watterson ultimately left the paper after he sold control and then found himself in disagreement with the new owners. He insisted — and his new bosses agreed — that *The Courier-Journal* run an editorial telling the reason for the resignation.

It's no coincidence that three of the four great-est editorial writers were beholden to no one but themselves and their readers. Horace Greeley owned the *New York Tribune*, and White owned *The Emporia Daily Gazette*. Watterson had an ownership interest in *The Courier-Journal*, and the fourth, Ver-mont Royster, worked for *The Wall Street Journal*,

The Aspen Daily News *has straightforward advice about how to keep things out of the newspaper.*

which was then owned by a benevolent family and run by wise executives who had come up through the ranks of the newsroom.

In 1959, when Royster wrote a strong editorial about a State of the Union address, he showed it to Bernard Kilgore, who ran the newspaper. Kilgore refused to read it. "I'll read the editorial in the paper tomorrow," he said.

"The proprietors have put up with my prejudices while by no means always sharing them," Royster wrote later.

When an unhappy reader complained to Kilgore about an editorial by Royster's predecessor, William Grimes, Kilgore responded: "Well, I suppose I might fire him, but how long could I keep any editor if he got fired every time a reader disagreed?"

And it wasn't until a casual lunch more than 20 years after each man had retired that *Des Moines Register* publisher David Kruidenier told editorial page editor Gil Cranberg — both men were then around 80 — that "I don't want you to think there weren't editorials I disagreed with. I just didn't say anything to you about them." Indeed, in all the years they worked together, Kruidenier com-

plained about just one editorial — and that was about the headline.

In "Best Man Lost," Cranberg headed an editorial bemoaning the loss of an incumbent senator that the paper liked and endorsed. Cranberg thought he was just being consistent; Kruidenier thought the headline was overkill and sour grapes, though he clearly agreed with the sentiment.

New owners or new editors regularly have taken quill — or pen, or typewriter, or computer — in hand to share their beliefs and philosophies and to risk, from day one, that burning at the stake that William Allen White wrote about.

When a young Civil War veteran named A.F. Sperry bought a newspaper in Panora, Iowa, in 1865, he changed its name to *The Guthrie Vedette*, and, in the first issue, told readers what to expect.

"Our aim will be to promote the interests of this County; to give the latest news and as much of it as possible; to advocate whatever we believe to be right and necessary, and to present, besides, as good, full and varied miscellany as the limits of the paper, aided by careful selection and condensation, will allow."

More than 100 years later, after the Gannett chain bought the venerable *Courier-Journal* from the Bingham family, who had bought out Henry Watterson 68 years earlier, the new editor felt compelled to reassure readers that the Binghams' liberal philosophy would continue.

"This we believe," began the editorial, and it ran off a litany of beliefs long embraced by the Binghams and their editors. But chain ownership brings a more rapid turnover of editors and publishers, and traditions get lost, heritages muddled, philosophies changed. Thus, yesterday's liberal, family-owned newspaper is today's conservative or middle-of-the-road chain-owned paper, or yesterday's conservative, family-owned paper is today's liberal one.

When the American press was young and major cities had several competing newspapers, editors often used their pages to take a swipe at one another. The decline of that competition led to a similar decline in brashness, perhaps because modern editorial writers try to please a wider audience while still hewing to their editorial line.

When *The New York Times* was launched in the 1850s and gained quick acceptance, Horace Greeley of the *Tribune* noted that the paper appeared to be "conducted with the most policy and least principle of any paper ever started." Greeley took a leave from his newspaper and in 1872 was the Democratic nominee for president, losing to incumbent Ulysses S. Grant. Upon his return to the *Tribune* editorship, the *Times* called Greeley "the man who, intoxicated with the flattery of the base wretches who had been swarming about him,

imagined he had amassed enough 'political capital' by his humiliating office brokerage to be elected President of the United States."

Responding to a Greeley-is-back *Tribune* editorial it mistakenly thought Greeley himself had written, the *Times* went on: "Now that he is contemptuously put aside by the people, [he] appears at the old stand, and hawks his own virtues with unabated vigor. Has he not even yet discovered that the people are not fools, or will nothing shake his faith in that most delusive of all the shams he has publicly supported — himself?"

Earlier, Walt Whitman, doing a stint as an editorial writer on a New York newspaper called the *Aurora*, said of Greeley: "We question whether a man in the empire state entertains so many absurd tenets in religion, such fallacious opinions of government and political economy, such short sighted notions of what are the land's true interests — as this same Mr. Horace Greeley." Yet Whitman and Greeley were on the same side on one of the most important issues of their day — a fight over public aid to Catholic schools.

In 1871, the Republican *New York Times* called the Democratic New York *World* "the most corrupt and degraded journal of the present age," and it wondered in print whether *World* editor Manton Marble was a "turncoat and libeler by turns."

William Grimes, the longtime editor of *The Wall Street Journal*, was more succinct — but almost as nasty — in October 1946 when former Vice President Henry Wallace became editor of *The New Republic*. Headlined "Justice," the editorial read — in its entirety: "Henry Wallace has become editor of The New Republic. We suggest that it serves them both right."

From time to time, editorial writers are called upon to explain, or defend, the general policies of the newspaper. So it was in 1954 that Grimes or Royster, his protégé and successor, wrote an editorial called "A Newspaper and Its Readers." The *Journal* was being criticized for stories giving a peek at what the new-model cars would look like — before the auto industry was ready to disclose that — and for talking about the discounting practices of one auto dealer. Auto dealers and General Motors executives thought such stories were bad for business and bad for the economy.

"A newspaper exists only to provide information for its readers; it has no other reason for being," the editorial said. "It provides that service only so long as it diligently seeks out what is happening and reports it as accurately and as clearly as it can. … When a newspaper begins to suppress that news, whether at the behest of its advertisers or on pleas from special segments of business, it will soon cease to be of any service either to its advertisers or to business because it will soon cease to have readers."

While advertisers sometimes try to pressure newspapers, so do friends of the editor and the publisher.

"The moment I become friendly with a man he wants me to keep his divorce out of the paper," Col. Robert McCormick, the editor and owner of *The Chicago Tribune* said. (McCormick, a biographer noted, "preferred the company of dogs to people and books to dogs.")

But J. Russell Wiggins, the longtime editor of *The Washington Post* who in retirement bought a

"The moment I become friendly with a man he wants me to keep his divorce out of the paper," Col. Robert McCormick of The Chicago Tribune *once said.*

weekly in Ellsworth, Maine, had an answer for that problem similar to the answer offered up by the *Aspen Daily News.*

"A number of citizens recently have asked the editors of this newspaper how to keep out of the paper reports that they have been arrested for driving under the influence, speeding, using drugs illegally, and a few other common offenses," Wiggins editorialized in *The Ellsworth American* in 1979.

"It is very simple," he wrote. "Do not drive under the influence, exceed the speed limit, or use drugs illegally." ❧

INCONSISTENCY

WILLIAM ALLEN WHITE, *The Emporia Daily Gazette,* April 25, 1923

"YOU ARE SO INCONSISTENT," writes a correspondent to The Gazette this morning. "One day you are against Harding and jeer at him and the next day you praise him to the skies. What is the matter with you anyway? Why don't you get a policy and stick to it?"

Exactly — why not be a thick and thin partisan? Why not be for a man or against him? Why not wear a collar? As a matter of fact we do wear a collar. Five thousand subscribers to The Gazette pay us for our honest opinion upon the passing events of the day. They don't pay much, and they don't get much. But what they get is unbiased and as honest as the times will permit.

In a general way The Gazette is Republican, but if the Republican party gets in what seems to be a wrong position, the best duty of a good Republican is to call attention to what seems a wrong position. If a man is right today and wrong tomorrow, say so frankly in each case without malice, and yet heartily. A newspaper has one obligation and one only, to print the truth as far as it is humanly possible, and to comment upon the truth as candidly and as kindly as is humanly possible never forgetting to be merry the while. For after all the liar and the cheat and the panderer are smaller offenders than the solemn ass.

That is why we seem inconsistent to the mind that wears labels and sends out its thinking to be done by party, by church or by groups or cliques or clans or crowds and factions. The fool's jewel of consistency is largely paste! ⚬

SALUTATORY

REV. COLLEY S. REYNOLDS, *West Hillsborough* (Fla.) *Times,* Dec. 4, 1884

THE PROPRIETOR OF THIS PAPER has informed its readers of the change of ownership, and of our appointment to the editorial chair. We greet the readers of the *Times* as kindly as this style of introduction will permit — gladly observing that they have already become a numerous family, and fondly trusting that their numbers will soon increase a hundred fold.

Our object in assuming this position is not to advance some new political, religious or social dogma, neither are we very anxious to appear before the world in the character of a general instructor; but this Gulf coast, or western portion of Hillsborough county, is speaking with a thousand tongues, and demands a translator and transmitter of its utterances. Our paper aims to become merely the telephone through which its inviting voice may be carried to many listening ears. If we can faithfully translate and present to the world the living and actual facts impressed on our mind by long communion with nature in her different moods, as displayed in this peculiar and inviting portion of Florida, we shall be satisfied with our present mission. — We expect, and shall try very hard, to tell the truth; but it will take a long time to tell the whole truth about even this small territory which we especially represent. If any untruth appears in our attempts to describe the country, or set forth its advantages, it will be because eighteen years of intimate acquaintance has not been sufficient to guard our mind against such errors.

It is not expected by the proprietor of this paper, neither does the editor desire, that it should in any way conflict with the interests of any other paper in this county or elsewhere; neither do we expect or desire to bring this section into notice by disparaging any other portion of the State.

It is emphatically our aim to make this a local country paper, leaving our readers as much in want of their leading county and city newspapers as if no such sheet as ours had ever made its appearance. In fact, it will be our pride to foster the interests of our county and State papers whose mission is in a wider field than we propose to occupy.

We therefore ask the kindly aid of our Tampa papers, and of the press throughout the State, in bringing our little enterprise into notice.C.S.R. ❧

REPORTER MR. GANNETT FORGETS A PRIME RULE OF THE TRADE

The Charlotte News, Feb. 19, 1940

Somehow, we have a hunch that we shall not be hiring Mr. Frank Gannett as a reporter when he is through running for the Republican Presidential nomination. We wouldn't be anyhow, of course, seeing that Mr. Gannett, in addition to being a candidate, is the owner of a string of newspapers in New York state. All the same, if he were available as a reporter we should have to think it over seriously before hiring him.

Says Mr. Gannett:

"I have traveled across the country from coast to coast twice in the last six months and have sought to know its sentiments. I make no misleading prophecy when I say that the New Deal will be voted out of power next November whether President Roosevelt heads the Democratic ticket or not."

Which may be so. And may not be. We have no idea. But in any case it seems to us that Mr. Gannett's account of the matter is somewhat less than good reporting. He is quite positive about it, leaves himself no loophole. And yet it is plain to us as newspaper men, ought to be plain to Mr. Gannett as a newspaper man, that in the nature of the case he cannot have got an unbiased view as he passed around.

In the nature of the case the boys he has mainly talked to were sympathizers with Mr.

Publisher Frank Gannett's newspapers remained independent, even when he ran for president in 1940.

Gannett — either Republicans or bitter anti-New Deal Democrats. And all the reports on the other side which he has got must have come through these channels.

It is not a safe way to arrive at dogmatic prophecy.

By the same process, Henry L. Mencken, another newspaperman who ought to have known better, arrived at the considered conclusion that even a Chinaman could beat Mr. Roosevelt in 1936. And what happened? ஐ

A NEWSPAPER AND ITS READERS

The Wall Street Journal, June 16, 1954

ELSEWHERE ON THIS PAGE we publish a number of letters from readers in the auto industry complaining about the publication of two recent news stories.

One of these stories dealt with plans of the various auto manufacturers for their 1955 models. The other reported the sales methods adopted by one dealer to meet competitive conditions in the new car market.

None of these readers challenges the accuracy of either of these stories; indeed, this is stated to be beside the point. But they feel that by the mere act of publication we have done damage to the auto industry in general and to their own business in particular. And since the auto industry is a major one, we are somehow irresponsibly depressing business, spreading unemployment and undermining the economy. Therefore it was wrong for us to publish this news.

The letters are obviously sincere and written from a real sense of grievance. They deserve a considered and sympathetic reply.

The burden of their complaint is that any news of new models before the manufacturers are ready to announce them hurts the sales of current models; if customers know that 1955 models will be better they will postpone purchase. Similarly, news that one dealer is offering some special "bargain" will make other customers demand like bargains and this will damage the new car market.

The burden of their plea is that this newspaper should publish only such news as is approved by the manufacturers, the dealers or their trade associations. This would insure the proper kind of news being printed.

We would like to comment first on the complaint that these two particular stories hurt the auto industry or these dealers' business.

New models have always been news. It has never been a secret that each year the manufacturers are working on plans for improved models next year. With the exception of the war years, changes and improvements from year to year have been standard practice.

OPPOSITE: *Auto dealers and carmakers thought the sneak peek at their new models was bad for business and for the economy.*

It would be an exceedingly ignorant customer who, as he buys this year's model, does not know that next year's will be better; if he were really deterred by this thought he would postpone purchase forever. Our story did nothing to add to this awareness. What we did was to provide some factual information on what to expect. And for the few buyers who might be waiting anyway, our story ought to increase their eagerness by publicizing the fine new products.

Our story on dealer sales methods was simply a report on something that exists. The competitive situation in the new car market would not go away if we refused to mention it. But the news of its effects is both of interest and of value to our readers; it is even of value to one auto dealer to know how another is meeting this situation and boosting his sales.

So we cannot believe that these two stories did any hurt to the automobile industry. They did not make anything happen. They only provided some more information on what is already happening.

But aside from the complaint about these particular stories, there remains the other thought in these letters. It is to the effect that it is a disservice to business to publish information which a particular segment of business doesn't want published. It is an old complaint to this newspaper.

Perhaps the best way to answer it is to note that these letter writers have been readers themselves. They bought and read the paper for information. Would they wish us to print only the banking news approved by bankers, only the steel news approved by steel officials, only the real estate news approved by real estate agents? If we followed that practice would they not soon wonder how much information was not being printed and begin to doubt the usefulness of this newspaper's service?

The fact is that it would be of no use whatsoever. If our readers thought that every story in The Wall Street Journal were censored by the industry or the company which it is covering they would not long have confidence in it. Nor would the situation be any better if we ourselves undertook to censor the news by our ideas of what is "good for business." If we reported only "good" news, readers would not find the paper of value even in their own field.

A newspaper exists only to provide information for its readers; it has no other reason for being. It provides that service only so long as it diligently seeks out what is happening and reports it as accurately and as clearly as it can.

This is particularly so of a newspaper that concentrates on business news. Sometimes what is valuable business news to one reader may be displeasing to another. But in the end the truth about what is happening is the only thing that is of value to anybody.

And when a newspaper begins to suppress that news, whether at the behest of its advertisers or on pleas from special segments of business, it will soon cease to be of any service either to its advertisers or to business because it will soon cease to have readers. ❧

ONE JOURNAL DEFENDS THE RING!

The New York Times, July 12, 1871

THERE WAS ONE DAILY PAPER published in this City yesterday, and one only, which had the audacity to defend the City authorities for the disgrace they have inflicted on the American name. If this statement were made in a crowded meeting, nine-tenths of the audience would at once name the paper that was capable of this disgraceful conduct. They would name the sheet which, a few years ago, started, under a man named Manton Marble, as a "religious organ;" which then became Republican; which was then sold to Fernando Wood and the Democrats; which bitterly opposed the war for the Union, and labored to injure the credit of the country at home and abroad; which sold out to the Young Democracy; which afterward sold out to the Tammany Ring; which was bribed to throw over the candidates of its own party in 1868; which has been false to every principle it ever professed, and to every man it ever pretended to support. In short, the audience

The Tammany Tiger, emblematic of the Boss Tweed ring that controlled New York, stirred editorial writers as well as cartoonists.

THE TAMMANY TIGER LOOSE.—"What are you going to do about it?"

This 1873 Thomas Nast cartoon, which includes a group of leading 19th-century newspaper editors (left and background), criticized the press and Congress for failing to report clandestine stock deals involving a federally subsidized railroad.

would name the New-York *World*, the most corrupt and degraded journal of the present age.

The news of the cowardice of Tweed, Hall & Co. will be received all over the country with anger. The *World* alone rejoices in an incident which fills everybody else with shame. Its degrading apology for its masters we republish in another column. True Democrats will feel a fresh contempt for the journal which professes to represent them, but which in reality does more injury to their cause than all the arguments of their opponents. It might have been thought that no money the Ring could offer would induce any respectable journalist to justify a transaction which is as base as it is pusillanimous. In truth, the organs of the Ring all rebelled yesterday. The *World* alone performed the infamous service ordered of it. If principles had been at stake, it would have felt no compunction about discarding them. The task of denying the words it had used at some former time would have been more welcome to it than any other. But the question was one of money. A man who was poor a few years ago is being made rich by Tweed. He cannot and will not "break with" his benefactor. And thus a journal still read by some Democrats was dragged deeper and deeper into the mire by the unprincipled hand which guides it.

The *World* is, indeed, in the habit of saying that other papers do injustice to Tweed and his friends. The assailants of our City Government are foreigners. Yet it is only a year ago that Manton Marble wrote thus of Tweed:

"We are plundered by him and such as him in all open and public, in all private and dishonest ways. He thrives on percentages of pilfering, grows rich on the distributed dividends of rascality. His extortions are as boundless in their sum as in their ingenuity; streets unopened profit him; streets opened put money in his purse. Paving an avenue with a poultice enriches him; taking off the poultice increases his wealth. His rapacity like the trunk of an elephant with equal skill twists fortune out of the Broadway widening and picks up dishonest pennies in the Bowery. And the system which shields, fosters and prolongs him and his rapacious tribe he refuses to reform altogether, or consents to reform in part only long enough to betray those who believed his word."

Was Manton Marble a slanderer then, or is he a falsifier now? Or is he turncoat and libeler by turns? Now he tells us that any paper which attacks Tweed is "un-American" — for this man, who industriously supplied every enemy of the Union with arguments against his country during the critical years of the war, is suddenly consumed with patriotism. He wishes people to forget that before he had been bribed, he was the first to assail Tweed and his colleagues with the coarsest abuse. Now he is prepared to defend even their most disgraceful acts. What can be the public opinion of a journal which finds cause for pride in the surrender of New-York to an Irish mob, and which is nothing but a channel for the opinions of renegades, Jeremy Diddlers, and superannuated gerund-grinders? ❧

MR. WATTERSON RETIRES

The Courier-Journal, April 2, 1919

M R. WATTERSON RETIRES as Editor Emeritus of The Courier-Journal with this issue.

From 1868 until 1919 its editor, his brilliant, forceful and individual writings on public questions brought fame both to himself and this journal. Desiring to retire last August when control of the newspaper changed hands, he yet was persuaded to remain in the capacity of Editor Emeritus, through which connection he might continue to address the readers of The Courier-Journal while relieved of the active responsibilities of the editorship. He now requests his retirement, finding in conflict his views, opposing the League of Nations, and those of The Courier-Journal, favoring the proposal. His personality will continue to be an inspiration to Courier-Journal workers; his accomplishments, a standard of achievement; his name, one to be praised and loved. He has passed his seventy-ninth birthday. May he pass many another milestone before the world loses him as a companion or letters are deprived of the magic of his pen! 🙣

Henry Watterson "was the last of the great editors, for the reason that he was the last of those editors who wrote with the power of ownership," journalist Arthur Krock wrote in 1923.

BUMS AND SCANDALS

WILLIAM ALLEN WHITE, *The Emporia Daily Gazette,* May 23, 1921

To the Editor of the Gazette ... Sir. Why have you let two big divorce suits go by without a line in the Gazette? Are you shielding them because they are big bugs? Does the fact that a man has money keep his name out of the paper when he runs around with other women and when a poor devil gets drunk you slap his name in the paper?

A Reader

That is a fair question, the answer is this: For 26 years the Gazette has made an invariable rule to keep divorce scandals out of the local news. Also, we have had an invariable rule to print the actual news of divorces, the names of the parties, the causes briefly stated, and the disposition of the children, if any. The community has a right to this news. But the harrowing details that mark the wreck of any home are not news; they are often salacious, sometimes debasing, and always abnormal. We have felt that the wreck of a home is bad enough; but to pry among the wreckage is ghoulish. So readers of the Gazette who want Emporia divorce scandals elaborated should subscribe for some other paper.

Now about the drunk. The man who fills up with whisky and goes about making a fool of himself becomes a public nuisance. If permitted to continue it, he becomes a public charge. The public has an interest in him. Publicity is one of the things that keeps him straight. His first offense is ignored in the Gazette, but his second offense is

As owner of his newspaper, William Allen White was beholden to no one but himself and his readers.

recorded when he is arrested, and no matter how high or how low he is, his name goes in. We have printed this warning to drinkers time and again; so when they come around asking us to think of their wives, and children, or their sick mothers or poor old fathers, we always tell them, to remember that they had fair warning, and if their fathers and mothers and wives and children are nothing to them, before taking, they are nothing to us after taking.

The bum and the divorce are treated always from the standpoint of the community interest. ❧

KEEPING IT OUT OF THE PAPER

J. RUSSELL WIGGINS, *The Ellsworth* (Maine) *American,* March 1, 1979

A number of citizens recently have asked the editors of this newspaper how to keep out of the paper reports that they have been arrested for driving under the influence, speeding, using drugs illegally, and a few other common offenses.

It is the object of this editorial to give to those inquiring readers precise instructions on how they can prevent the publication of these reports in this newspaper or any other newspaper.

It is very simple.

Do not drive under the influence, exceed the speed limit, or use drugs illegally. It is as simple as that.

The publication of the names of persons wrongly alleged to have violated the law may still cause some embarrassment to those completely innocent. That embarrassment does not represent a risk or hazard comparable in seriousness and menace of the dangers of secret arrest, improper detention, and official harassment which may occur without publicity. Publicity is the best protection of the innocent accused against the mistaken suspicions of society; and the best defense of society against improper immunity for those who are guilty of violating the law. There is reason to believe that the fear of publicity may be greater restraint upon illegal behavior than legal punishment.

This newspaper, like most newspapers, has operated many years under the theory that names of minors should not be used for trivial or inconsequential violations of rules or laws, and the court officials of the state are not supposed to release the names of juvenile suspects in these cases.

Recently, many judges have been releasing the names of juveniles involved in more serious crimes, and some newspapers have published these names and this newspaper will do so with the court's advice.

There are other circumstances in which juveniles become involved in incidents that bring their names to public view (where civil actions involve the integrity of public officials connected with juvenile offenses). The reputation of the adults involved is of as much importance to them as the repute of the youngsters is important to them. At this point, all names, in our opinion, become newsworthy.

To summarize: If you wish to keep your name out of the newspaper for speeding, driving while drunk, or improperly using drugs, avoid committing the offenses. That will go a long way toward "keeping it out of the paper." ❧

J. Russell Wiggins was the former executive editor of The Washington Post.

WHAT FOR?

What do you take a Newspaper for?

For all the news?

Read The Tribune.

For able and honest editorials?

Read The Tribune.

For full and accurate market reports?

Read The Tribune.

For the best and sprightliest correspondence?

Read The Tribune.

For news of scientific progress and discoveries?

Read The Tribune.

For the latest educational information?

Read The Tribune.

For the best and purest works of fiction?

Read The Tribune.

For good miscellaneous reading for the family?

Read The Tribune.

For enterprise, intelligence and strength in every feature?

Read The Tribune.

For the fullest and most varied agricultural department of any paper in the country?

Read The Tribune.

Do you want, in short, a complete and well sustained newspaper in which you will never be disappointed, which will do all it promises and more?

Read The Tribune.

THE DAILY TRIBUNE is $10 per year by mail and is delivered by newsdealers for 2 cents per week. Leave your order at the nearest news-stand or at the office of THE TRIBUNE. THE SEMI-WEEKLY TRIBUNE, $3 per year; WEEKLY TRIBUNE, $2.

Horace Greeley gave readers several reasons to buy his New York Tribune.

Horace Greeley

CHAPTER TWO
WAR

Explosions seen from Hickam Field during the Japanese attack on Pearl Harbor.

FIFTH CONGRESS OF THE UNITED

At the Second Session.

Begun and held at the city of *Philadelphia*, in the state *Monday*, the thirteenth of *November*, one thousand and ninety-seven.

An ACT *in addition to the act, entitled "An Act for the punish* ited States."

BE it enacted by the Senate and House of Representatives of the United States of

ll unlawfully combine or conspire together, with intent to oppose any measure or measures of the gove

by proper authority, or to impede the operation of any law of the United States, or to intimidate or pre

overnment of the United States, from undertaking, performing or executing his trust or duty; and

hall, counsel, advise or attempt to procure any insurrection, riot, unlawful assembly, or combinat

tempt shall have the proposed effect or not, he or they shall be deemed guilty of a high misdemeanor, a

ng jurisdiction thereof, shall be punished by a fine not exceeding five thousand dollars, and by im

exceeding five years; and further, at the discretion of the court may be holden to find sureties for his good

t may direct.

Sect. 2. And be it further enacted, That if any person shall write, print, utter or publish, or shall

, or shall knowingly and willingly assist or aid in writing, printing, uttering or publishing any false,

government of the United States, or either House of the Congress of the United States, or the Preside

rnment, or either House of the said Congress, or the said President, or to bring them, or either of them, int

y of them, the hatred of the good people of the United States; or to stir up sedition within the United

posing or resisting any law of the United States, or any act of the President of the United States, done

ted by the Constitution of the United States; or to resist, oppose, or defeat any such law or act; or to aid, e

st the United States, their people or government, then such person, being thereof convicted before any cou

"TO HELL WITH THE HOHENZOLLERNS AND THE HAPSBURGS!"

SO ENDED AN EDITORIAL IN *THE COURIER-JOURNAL* ON SEPT. 3, 1914, THE YEAR WAR STARTED IN EUROPE. THE EDITORIAL WAS WRITTEN BY THE NEWSPAPER'S CO-OWNER AND EDITOR, HENRY WATTERSON, A MAN THEN IN HIS 70S, A MAN WHO BELIEVED IN LIBERTY. THE LINE CONDEMNING THE ROYAL FAMILIES OF GERMANY AND AUSTRIA BECAME HIS BATTLE CRY FOR THE NEXT FIVE YEARS, FIRST AS AMERICA NERVOUSLY WATCHED THAT "WAR TO END ALL WARS"

and then as it entered what we now know as World War I.

A churchman eventually complained that the profanity in the paper was abhorrent. The editor answered in an editorial: "It is our desire to be explicit and we hope we make ourselves reasonably clear, when we say 'to Hell with the Hohenzollerns and the Hapsburgs.' Is that the kind of profanity the *Christian Churchman* abhors? If it is we'll be hornswaggled if we don't repeat it six days in the week and twice on Sundays! There!"

Watterson could be eloquent, and he could be indignant. And, indeed, war moves editors to eloquence and dudgeon, though not always in that order.

What more eloquent line was ever written than the first line of an editorial in *The (Chicago) Press and Tribune* of Dec. 2, 1859?

"John Brown dies to-day!"

And what dudgeon can compare to the first lines of an editorial in the *Los Angeles Times* on April 23, 1943?

"Once or twice since Pearl Harbor, the *Times* has likened the Japanese to rattlesnakes.

"This is to apologize to the rattlesnakes."

It was the rare editorial voice that would not have agreed — at the time — with the sentiments of the *Times*, just as it was the rare editorial voice that would not eventually have agreed with "to Hell with the Hohenzollerns and the Hapsburgs!" But that editorial unanimity disappeared in later wars, in Korea, first, and in Vietnam, especially.

Indeed, 27 years after the *Times* talked about our "nation's wrath [as] a hopeful augury for the intensification of our war effort, at home as well as on the fighting fronts," the newspaper wrote an editorial that began: "The time has come for the United States to leave Vietnam, to leave it swiftly, wholly, and without equivocation."

"As a nation we had no doubt about our purpose [in World War II], a conviction missing in Korea and Vietnam," Vermont Royster, who commanded a destroyer escort in that war, wrote 40

OPPOSITE: *The Sedition Act of 1798 made it illegal to print anything deemed false or scandalous against the U.S. government.*

years afterward. "It's not an exaggeration to say that we believed civilization was at peril, whether that belief was true or false." But Vietnam was different. "If we had won it, that would have settled nothing. If we lost it, as we did, the result would be disaster neither for our own country nor the world. I have no doubt that this want of believed purpose was responsible for the woes it brought."

Thus it was that Royster — veteran and patriot — turned the editorial pages of the *Journal* against a war it originally supported.

"By early 1968," he wrote, "I could no longer resist arguments that as a practical matter the war was a disaster." The *Journal* didn't challenge the motives, it merely thought the war was doomed. "If it had been possible to accomplish the original objective of saving South Vietnam it would have been well worth doing," said the editorial, most of which was written by Royster's deputy, Joe Evans. And it said that "failure would be a stunning blow to the U.S. and the West ... a traumatic experience to have lost a war in which thousands of Americans had died in vain." Yet, the *Journal* said, "the war was not worth any price no matter how ruinous."

Editorial thought follows political thought, or vice versa. So while the Vietnam War divided editorial pages and caused some to change their minds, so it did, too, with politicians and with the country as a whole.

Nowhere was this division more sadly played out than at Kent State University in Ohio, where in May of 1970 four young people were shot to death and at least nine others wounded by National Guardsmen called out to quell anti-war protests on campus. The students had rocks; the guardsmen had bullets.

Suddenly, we were at war with each other — just as in the Civil War some 100 years earlier.

"Is there any possible justification for American Guardsmen firing volleys into a crowd of rock-throwing students?" asked the *St. Petersburg Times*. "Were the members of the National Guard also our young and frightened children? Are we now killing each other for peace?"

Historically, wars have taken freedoms as well as lives.

"In the entire history of the United States, the national government has never attempted to punish opposition to government policies, *except* in time of war," professor Geoffrey Stone writes in "Perilous Times: Free Speech in Wartime." The government of the United States "prohibits political dissent *only* in wartime."

Congress passed the Sedition Act of 1798 as America geared up for war with France; President Lincoln suspended the writ of habeas corpus during the Civil War; Congress passed the Espionage and Sedition acts when the United States entered the First World War; President Franklin Roosevelt ordered about 110,000 Japanese — many of them U.S. citizens — put in "relocation camps" during World War II; McCarthyism and other threats to rights ran rampant during the Cold War; anti-war protesters were prosecuted during the Vietnam War; and the FBI began monitoring public events during the Iraq War, while Congress passed a law allowing agents to, among other things, check to see what books Americans were checking out of libraries.

Sometimes, editorial pages are outraged, sometimes not.

When the Supreme Court ruled that Lincoln had no right to suspend the writ of habeas corpus — that only Congress could do that — the president simply ignored the ruling. *The New York Times* sided with Lincoln.

"A collision of civil and military authority is always to be, if possible, shunned, because the majesty of law must, in all cases, succumb to the necessities of war," the *Times* editorialized on May 29, 1861. "The interposition of [the Court] can only be regarded as at once officious and improper."

Yet when John Brown was hanged, *The (Chicago) Press and Tribune* — sympathetic to his cause — wrote: "As Republicans, maintaining as we do, that neither individuals nor parties in the North have a right to interfere with slavery where it exists under the sanction of positive law in the States, we cannot say that he suffers unlawfully. The man's heroism which is as sublime as that of a martyr, his constancy to his convictions, his suffering, the disgraceful incidents of his trial, the poltroonry of those who will lead him forth to death, have excited throughout all the North strong feeling of sympathy in his behalf, but no where, within our knowledge, is the opinion entertained that he should not be held answerable, for the legal consequences of his act." (Fifty years later, William Allen White wrote that the life Brown gave for his country was "the most precious single treasure ever offered to this union of states.")

Ultimately, of course, wars end, wounds heal, peace prevails and life goes on. And editors take note of that, too.

On Oct. 27, 1920, *The Emporia Daily Gazette* ran a four-paragraph editorial by William Allen White. Headlined "Exit Huns," it said:

"Beginning to-day, the word Hun as applied to Germans is barred from the Gazette. The war is over, and although the United States and Germany have not signed the peace treaty, they are trading together, and are on friendly terms again. So the Gazette has decided to call Germans Germans, and the headline writer may call them 'Teuts' or 'Jerries,' aber nicht Huns!

"However, the star reporter, who heard the German machine bullets whistle in the Argonne, the city editor, who scratched German cooties on the Rhine, and the linotype operator, who drilled his legs off in a balloon school waiting for a chance to get at the Germans, don't like the rule.

"Not that they ever called them Huns — newspapers wouldn't print what they called them — but somehow they can't forget so easily that just pigs is pigs. Huns is Huns, and their natural cussedness shouldn't be forgotten so quickly.

"This is the last shot fired in the big war. Exit Huns!" ❧

THE FATAL FRIDAY

The (Chicago) *Press and Tribune,* Dec. 2, 1859

JOHN BROWN DIES TO-DAY! As Republicans, maintaining as we do, that neither individuals nor parties in the North have a right to interfere with slavery where it exists under the sanction of positive law in the States, we cannot say that he suffers unlawfully. The man's heroism which is as sublime as that of a martyr, his constancy to his convictions, his suffering, the disgraceful incidents of his trial, the poltroonry of those who will lead him forth to death, have excited throughout all the North strong feeling of sympathy in his behalf, but no where, within our knowledge, is the opinion entertained that he should not be held answerable, for the legal consequence of his act. As long as we are a part of the Union, consenting to the bond by which the States are bound together, supporting the constitution and the laws, and using the language and entertaining the sentiments of loyalty, we cannot join in the execration of the extreme penalty which the unfortunate and infatuated old man will suffer. We may question the wisdom of the method by which he is punished — may believe that Virginia would have added to her honor and confounded her enemies, by an act of clemency toward him and his associates — may condemn in unmeasured terms the cowardice and blood-thirstiness which her people have displayed — but when we

John Brown

The life John Brown gave for his country was
"the most precious single treasure ever offered to this union
of states," William Allen White wrote.
The (Chicago) Press and Tribune *called his trial
disgraceful, but defended the legal process.*

question the right of a Sovereign State to inflict a penalty for so glaring and fatal an infraction of her laws, we are advocating disunion in its most objectionable form. For that we are not prepared. We would be glad to avert the axe which hangs over the old man's head, if persuasion and entreaty would do it; but we see no way under Heaven by which, doing our duty as law-abiding citizens, we could counsel the use of force for his rescue, or by which we could join in a crusade against those by whom he has been legally though hastily, and because hastily, shamefully, condemned! We are not debarred, however, the right of praising the inherent though mistaken nobleness of the man, of pitying the fanaticism which led him into his present strait, of regretting that a character which might have been so illustrious in the history of his country, must be loaded with the consequences of his errors.

To our more radical readers these views will be unpalatable; but there are such that Republicans must entertain. When the fanatical action of the South and the accumulated aggressions with which she has affected the North, dissolve the ties that hold the North and South together, and when we no longer owe allegiance to the constitution and laws which the propagandists of Slavery have long trodden under their feet, then we may have reason, upon the broadest principles of human right, to not only bless but aid any work that will assist in the emancipation, by arms if necessary, of every human being on American soil. Until that time comes there is but one course left. That we have pointed out.

We have firm belief that this execution of Brown will hasten the downfall of that accursed system against which he waged war. Throughout all this land, men will not fail to see that there is a conflict between the principles of humanity that have obtained a lodgment in every human heart, and obedience to laws which all have tacitly agreed to support. The shock caused by his death will be more than a nine days wonder. The emotions excited and the reflections provoked by the tragedy, will go to the very foundations of our political structure; and in all parts of the Union men will ask themselves how long this institution which compels men to put to death their fellows like Brown, who act upon motives and for objects that command the approbation of the world, shall be suffered to disgrace the age and the civilization in which we live. The question will reach hearts that have been callous heretofore; and ere many years it will bring the opposing forces which now distract the country — right on the one side and wrong on the other — enlightenment and barbarism — Christianity and Atheism — Freedom and Slavery — face to face for a final conflict. We have no apprehension of the result, whenever it comes. The events of to-day, bring it nearer than it has ever been before since the struggle began at Charlestown, Massachusetts, in 1775. It is our's, as it should have been Brown's to labor and wait! ❧

VAE VICTUS!

Henry Watterson, *The Courier-Journal*, April 7, 1917

"Rally round the flag, boys"
— Uncle Sam's Battle song;

Sound the bold anthem! War dogs are howling;
Proud bird of Liberty screams through the air!"
— The Hunters of Kentucky

It is with solemnity, and a touch of sadness, that we write the familiar words of the old refrain beneath the invocation to the starry banner, the breezy call of hero-breeding bombast quite gone out of them; the glad shout of battle; the clarion note of defiance; because to us, not as to Nick of the Woods and his homely co-mates of the forest, the rather as to the men of '61, comes this present call to arms.

We may feel with the woman's heart of Rankin, of Montana, yet repudiate with manly disdain the sentimental scruples of Kitchin, of North Carolina.

There are times when feeling must be sent to the rear; when duty must toe the line; when the aversion brave men have for fighting must yield to the adjuration, "Give me liberty, or give me death!" That time is now upon us.

Unless Patrick Henry was wrong — unless Washington and the men of the Revolution were wrong, that time is upon us. It is a lie to pretend that the world is better than it was; that men are truer, wiser; that war is escapable; that peace may be had for the planning and the asking. The situation which without any act of ours rises before us is as exigent as that which rose before the Colonists in America when a mad English King, claiming to rule without accountability, asserted the right divine of Kings and sent an army to enforce it. A mad German Emperor, claiming partnership with God, again elevates the standard of right divine and bids the world to worship, or die.

From the beginning the issue was not less ours than of the countries first engaged. Each may have had ends of its own to serve. Nor were these ends precisely alike. At least France — to whom we owe all that we have of sovereignty and freedom — and Belgium, the little David of Nations — fought to resist invasion; wanton, cruel invasion; to avert slavery, savage, pitiless slavery. Yet, whatever the animating purpose — whatever the selfish interests of England and Russia and Italy — the Kaiser scheme of world conquest justified it.

In us it sanctifies it. Why should any American split hairs over the European rights and wrongs involved when he sees before him grim and ghastly the mailed figure of Absolutism with hand uplifted to strike Columbia where these three years she has stood pleading for justice, peace and mercy? God of the free heart's hope and home forbid!

Each of these three years the German Kaiser was making war upon us. He was making war secretly, through his emissaries in destruction of our industries, secretly through his diplomats plotting not merely foreign but civil war against us, and, as we now know, seeking to foment servile and racial insurrection; then openly upon the high seas levying murder upon our people and visiting all our rights and claims with scorn and insult — with scorn and insult unspeakable — at this moment pretending to flout us with ignominy and contempt. Where would the honest passivist draw the line?

Surely the time has arrived — many of us think it was long since overdue — for calling the braves to the colors. Nations must e'en take stock on occasion and manhood come to a showdown. It is but a truism to say so.

Fifty years the country has enjoyed surpassing prosperity. This has overcommercialized the character and habits of the people. Twenty-five years the gospel of passivism, with "business is business" for its text, has not only been preached — indiscriminately

oracularly — without let or hindrance, but has been richly financed and potentially organized. It has established a party. It has made a cult, justifying itself in a fad it has called Humanity — in many ways a most spurious humanity — and has set this above and against patriotic inclination and duty.

Like a bolt out of the blue flashed the war signal from the very heart of Europe. Across the Atlantic its reverberations rolled to find us divided, neutral and unprepared. For fifteen years a body of German reservists disguised as citizens have been marching and counter-marching. They grew at length bold enough to rally to the support of a pan-German scheme of conquest and a pro-German

After World War I, William Allen White barred the word "Huns" from The Emporia Daily Gazette. *"The Gazette has decided to call Germans Germans."*

propaganda of "kultur," basing its effrontery in the German-American vote, which began its agitation by threatening us with civil war if we dared to go to war with Germany. There followed the assassin sea monsters and the airship campaign of murder.

All the while we looked on with either simpering idiocy, or dazed apathy. Serbia? It was no affair of ours. Belgium? Why should we worry? Foodstuffs soaring — war stuffs roaring — everybody making money — the mercenary, the poor of heart, the mean of spirit, the bleak and barren of soul, could still plead the Hypocrisy of Uplift and chortle: "I did not raise my boy to be a soldier." Even the "Lusitania" did not awaken us to a sense of danger and arouse us from the stupefaction of ignorant and ignoble self-complacency.

First of all on bended knee we should pray God to forgive us. Then erect as men, Christian men, soldierly men, to the flag and the fray — wherever they lead us — over the ocean — through France to Flanders — across the Low Countries to Koln, Bonn and Koblens — tumbling the fortress of Ehrenbreitstein into the Rhine as we pass and damming the mouth of the Mozelle with the debris of the ruin we make of it — then on, on to Berlin, the Black Horse Cavalry sweeping the Wilhelmstrasse like lava down the mountain side, the Junker and the saber rattler flying before us, the tunes being "Dixie" and "Yankee Doodle," the cry being, "Hail the French Republic — Hail the Republic of Russia — welcome the Commonwealth of the Vaterland — no peace with the Kaiser — no parley with Autocracy, Absolutism and the divine right of Kings — to Hell with the Hapsburg and the Hohenzollern!" ❧

APOLOGY TO RATTLESNAKES

Los Angeles Times, April 23, 1943

ONCE OR TWICE SINCE PEARL HARBOR, The Times has likened the Japanese to rattlesnakes. This is to apologize to the rattlesnakes.

Compared with self-styled human beings who strike from the dark and slay without provocation or warning, who torture their helpless victims and murder them in cold-blooded defiance of honor and decency, the rattlesnake is one of nature's noblemen.

It is logical to suppose that there are words in the Japanese language which signify the torture and execution of uniformed prisoners of war for having discharged a military assignment. Presumably Japs have frequent need for such expressions. But happily or otherwise, there is none in English. To call it brutal is to insult the so-called lower orders of creation, where such senseless sadism is unknown.

From the practical standpoint of a nation which hopes, regardless of the war's outcome, to continue to exist in an enlightened world, the murder by the Japanese government of the Doolittle flyers was an act of insanity. It has bared to a revolted civilization, as not even Pearl Harbor or the horrors of Nanking and Hongkong did, the caricature of a racial soul, warped, shriveled and distorted, not worth its room in hell.

No nation has ever done itself a worse disservice than Japan has done in this wanton crime. By her own considered act, she has put herself outside the pale of international law, which regulates the world's relations in peace as well as in war. By repudiating her pledges in the Geneva Convention, she has forfeited her own right to protection under that long-time intergovernmental agreement. She has steeled against herself the five-sixths of the world's might which is represented by the United Nations. For

Apology to Rattlesnakes

Once or twice since Pearl Harbor, The Times has likened the Japanese to rattlesnakes.

This is to apologize to the rattlesnakes. Compared with self-styled human beings who strike from the dark and slay without provocation or warning, who torture their helpless victims and murder them in cold-blooded defiance of honor and decency, the rattlesnake is one of nature's noblemen.

It is logical to suppose that there are words in the Japanese language which signify the torture and execution of unarmed prisoners of war for having discharged a military assignment. Presumably Japs have frequent need for such expressions. But, happily or otherwise, there is none in English. To call it brutal is to insult the so-called lower orders of creation, where such senseless sadism is unknown.

From the practical standpoint of a nation which hopes, regardless of the war's outcome, to continue to exist in an enlightened world, the murder by the Japanese government of the Doolittle flyers was an act of insanity. It has bared to a revolted civilization, as not even Pearl Harbor or the horrors of Nanking and Hongkong did, the caricature of a racial soul, warped, shriveled and distorted, not worth its room in hell.

No nation has ever done itself a worse disservice than Japan has done in this wanton crime. By her own considered act, she has put herself outside the pale of international law, which regulates the world's relations in peace as well as war. By repudiating her pledges in the Geneva Convention, she has forfeited her own right to protection under that long-time intergovernmental agreement. She has steeled against herself the five-sixths of the world's might which is represented by the United Nations. For what it may be worth in future ill, she has confirmed the prewar "yellow vermin" estimate of her of even her present Axis partners. She has added her own signature to the warrant for her destruction.

Almost as if so timed, the President's revelation of the Doolittle executions was made within a few hours of a step by the Japanese government which, on its face, seems to hint an attempt at propitiation of the Allies. Like her European associates in their losing war of conquest, Japan would be very glad of a negotiated peace on the status quo basis. If the appointment as Foreign Minister of the anti-militarist Shigemitsu, prewar advocate of rapprochement with Britain and America, is a move in that direction or even for "softening" the war, these objectives have now a chance slimmer, if possible, than ever.

By another coincidence, word of the flyers' fate comes at a time well calculated to put a permanent quietus on the effort to secure the release of the Japanese now under military restraint in this country and their return to the areas from which, for their own safety as well as ours, they were evacuated. If more evidence were needed of the complete untrustworthiness of Japanese, or of their readiness to repudiate no matter what solemn undertaking, Tokyo has supplied it.

It may be a lesson, too, to the sappy sentimentalists who affect to regard these interned enemies as the innocent victims of racial prejudice and who advocate setting what they call a "democratic example" to Japan in the way of superkindness to internees and prisoners of war. The Oriental savage who is our enemy is fortunate, indeed, in having civilized opponents who will not retort in kind. Were Hitler's Germany in our place, 100 Jap prisoners would already have faced firing squads for every one of the Doolittle party executed.

The nation's wrath is a hopeful augury for the intensification of our war effort, at home as well as on the fighting fronts. In our determination to speed a just and terrible vengeance for our martyred men, however, neither overhaste on the part of our commanders nor pressure of public opinion should be allowed to precipitate undue risks. Rage that translates itself into ill-considered, ill-prepared attempts at reprisal merely plays into the hands of the enemy. Japan has already paid heavily in blood and treasure for her enormities; what she has so far suffered is no more than a drop in the bucket of that which we shall ultimately exact from her.

In the meantime, those of us who cannot fight can turn our righteous anger into channels wherefrom flow the planes and ships, guns and tanks, bombs and bullets for Jap extermination.

How mad are you, white-collar workers in nonwar industry and citizens generally? If you really want to help avenge our wantonly slain and do it directly and effectively, double your War Bond purchases and do it now.

How mad are you, munitions makers? Show it practically and immediately by extending yourselves to increase our arms output, without niggling delays over hours and wages, strikes, slowdowns, absenteeism or any other unnecessary interference with our maximum of war production.

Let's not take it out in futile talking. If we do our part, we can safely leave it to the Army and the Navy to do the rest.

Forget the Mudslinging---and Elect Healy

When other and more pertinent issues are absent or obscure, the tendency among some candidates for public office—particularly in contests for such local positions as membership on a City Council—seems to favor a certain amount of mudslinging. This unfortunate political propensity, which includes injection of questionable personalities, was present in several Councilmanic races preceding the April municipal primaries and still seems to be lurking around as a factor in the few remaining Council contests to be settled on May 4.

An example is afforded in the 10th District, where a runoff fight is in progress between Councilman Hampton and Ned R. Healy.

Healy was nominated to oppose Hampton on a platform pledging businesslike handling of public affairs, plus co-operation with the Mayor and fellow Councilmen for the development of a civic betterment program. And he was nominated despite the circulation of a Hampton-sponsored campaign pamphlet accusing Healy of membership in the Communist party. Healy's prompt demand for criminal libel action against Hampton has brought a full and somewhat abject retraction from his adversary, and the community generally will echo Healy's expressed hope that further campaigning in the 13th District will be confined to discussion and consideration of the respective merits and qualifications of the candidates.

The Times did not indorse Healy in the primary campaign, believing that Mrs. Kay Cunningham was better qualified for the post. Healy was nominated, and this newspaper recommends his election, believing he will make a better Councilman than Hampton.

Inquiry concerning Healy's record as a citizen and his views on public issues indicates that he has been strongly pro-New Deal, that he is a liberal and also that he has substantial business sense and integrity. There is nothing to prove him a radical or in any way related to or associated with any subversive group.

The Times does not indorse all of Healy's views on national issues and policies, but this newspaper does feel that Healy will be an honest, sincere and useful member of the City Council. In the opinion of The Times, the latter considerations are most important.

Congress Fiddles While Money Burns Pockets

The recess of Congress until May 3 with the tax problem unsolved is a failure of the legislative process and a plain defeat of the popular will.

Nothing is more certain than that the public is prepared to accept heavier taxation. Nor is anything more certain than that the public wants taxes put on a current basis. The Gallup poll shows that sentiment for pay-as-you-go taxes has now reached 79 per cent as the result of a steady increase. Sentiment for the Ruml plan, though it has decreased somewhat as the result partly of New Deal partisan appeals, still stands at 72 per cent.

... surplus income—in the sense ... on the shoulders of the Democratic majority. It was the Democrats and New Dealers who made the Ruml plan—the only practicable plan so far advanced for collecting current taxes from current income—into a party issue. It is the Democrats who have been unwilling to agree on a compromise. And, finally, it is the Democrats who insist on a recess with no tax program adopted.

Congress has not earned this vacation. Instead of working the Democrats have been fiddling and playing politics, with both eyes fixed on the 1944 campaign and hardly even a side glance toward the welfare of the nation.

Besides failing to enact the income ...

For Freedom!

[Dedicated to St. George, the patron saint of Great Britain, who was put to death April 23, 303, and the anniversary of whose martyrdom thus falls on this Good Friday.]

BY NORREYS JEPHSON O'CONOR

Up from the age of stone and dinosaur
Mankind has striven; through the bloody days
Of tyrants and their slaves, the whip and galley,
And the widespread marsh of men's intolerance,
In which like quicksand their advancing feet
Were caught and hindered: fear and dread
Of unknown forces, and the mockery
Of persecution in the name of Christ.

But ever on the far horizon shone
The gleam of coming light, the distant dream
Without which peoples perish; the flickering flame
Of Runnymede, which burned away the dross
Of generations and became the brilliant glow
That ran through frontier forests to illumine
The hearts of men in Thirteen Colonies.
Sparks from the burning, wafted overseas,
Caught fresh fuel, and the conflagration,
Sweeping along the streets of ancient Paris,
Brought tumbling down a glittering tinderbox
Of temporalities, and spread from there
To nation after nation; while in the heat
Old prejudices, old conceits shriveled;
Men's hearts and minds were changed, as in a furnace
Old substances and textures are made new
And set to serve new uses.
Liberty, equality, fraternity were watchwords;
The restless moved across a continent,
And through lands hitherto unknown.
Glib was the talk of brotherhood; but men
Became enmeshed with things, and were the pawns
In a new game of power whose weapons were
The sources of supply, and gleaming steel
And stone its showy front. Ambitious dreams
Succeeded one another, till at last
Lust led in leash the Hydra-headed beast
Of war and loosed it on the world. Beneath
Its ravening and relentless jaws men found
The folly of the strange companionship
Of flesh and blood and iron; a new desire
Of freedom from this menace filled men's hearts;
War to end war and bring world brotherhood
Became the purpose of the common man.

Yet schemes for power were not slain; once more
They sprang to life, choking like noxious weeds
The lowly flower of understanding that ran
Astray, bending like grain before the reaper
There was distrust of matching mind with mind,
And ever in the background the machine
Stood like the god of some barbaric tribe
To which men civilized still paid half-shamefaced,
Half-unconscious homage. The shadow of the idol
Lengthened, shutting away the spreading sunlight.
Despair gripped men confused by chiaroscuro,
And so they hearkened to the siren call
Of leaders in whom lust for domination
Supplanted selfless thought for human welfare.

So once again the age of slaves and tyrants
Was reborn, with all the cruel sport
Of persecution refined and subtilized
Former defenses were no longer sure.
Concerned, bemused, the guardians of the lights
Of freedom sought to shield the wavering flames
Exposed and bent before cyclonic gusts
Which brought the storm in unexampled fury.

Madly the engines raced across the earth
And down the skies and underneath the sea,
Bringing barbaric ruin in the space of weeks
To many who for years had striven to free
Their countries from the fettering undergrowth
Of outworn forms and customs and beliefs.
One after one the lamps went out; an age
Of darkness came a second time to dim
The brightness that alone can lead the nations
Forward. But when the smoke of battle cleared
The lights were not all gone, and those remaining
...

Those U.S. Flyers!

Today and Tomorrow

By Walter Lippmann

THE DISARMAMENT OF GERMANY

II

It is clear that when we shall have disarmed the German forces now in being, we shall not yet have disarmed Germany. We shall merely have won the power to take measures which deal with the German war potential from which came the Kaiser's army and then Hitler's army, from which could come again another conquering army.

For after the unconditional surrender there will remain the trained formations, the corps of officers, the staff organization, the whole administrative machinery of total mobilization. There will remain, though it be driven underground, the Nazi party machine and the secret police. There will remain also the German war industry with its tools, its know-how, its laboratories, its technicians and its management.

Merely to deprive Germany of her existing stocks of weapons would, therefore, be only a temporary disarmament. Moreover, if this is all we did, it would be in the interest of German militarism to have us do it. For it would provide what the Germans like to call a creative pause. The victorious Allies would find themselves encumbered with immense stocks of obsolescent weapons and of victorious but rapidly aging military commanders. The disarmed Germans would have a fresh start to concentrate on the weapons and the tactics of the next war. This is what happened between 1918 and 1939 when the French army prepared for the last war while the disarmed Germans, as well as the disarmed Russians, prepared for this war.

THE WAR POTENTIAL

If the war potential is intact, a new armed force can be trained and equipped in a period of from three to five years. The war potential is, therefore, our all-important concern. It consists of the general staff, the corps of officers, the bureaucracy and organized industry. Of these elements the most difficult to deal with, because they are the most elusive, are the general staff and the corps of officers. For they will go underground as they did in 1918, and there they will make their plans for the revival of their power. The Allies have no way of watching them and of dealing with them di...

Brady has shown in his book, "Business as a System of Power," is under highly centralized control. It follows that we could demand the surrender of that control. The high command of German industry would, therefore, pass out of German hands, though Germans would remain the junior partners and would enjoy, after partial reparation had been made for the looting and the devastation, the products and the profits of their industries.

We need not argue about the details of Dr. Loudon's method. The basic principle is what matters. It is that for some time to come, for the period of probation, re-education and reorientation, the trustees would determine German industrial policy. They would leave management and operation to Germans. But they would have the final say on the personnel of the management, on contracts, capital investment, imports and exports, credit, finance, pricing, wage policy, dividends, mergers and all foreign connections. This is infinitely more effective than sending inspectors to plants to see whether guns are being secretly manufactured. For only by a control of this kind can Germany be industrially disarmed. Only thus can German industry be prevented from becoming once more the arsenal of the military caste, and in foreign fields the central instrument of German domination, infiltration, espionage and subversion.

BETTER PROTECTION

Industrial control of this type would give the victorious victims of German aggression the means and the motive for standing guard beyond the period, necessarily brief, of occupation and military government. An inducement to continue in firm control of German action will exist because the victims of Germany will have a share in the profits of German industry and will have protection, better than any tariff, against Germany's industrial power. On the other hand, they will not have a motive to destroy German industry and deny to the German people their chance to live. Thus our apparently contradictory war aims can be reconciled. We can disarm Germany. We can police Germany after we withdraw our troops. And we can give the German masses an inducement, even ...

Lee Side o' L...

By Lee Ship...

On Easter Sunday women try
To look the best they can
But some of us would be more spic
If we hadn't so much span.
LOUISE LINDS...

SHARE-THE-SEAT?

Along with the share-the-ride cam... for motorists why not a share-th... campaign for streetcar lines? Yeste... I boarded a car on which 20 persons ... standing, eight being women. About ... the seated persons were men, incl... three husky young soldiers. One of th... diers got up and gave his seat to a ... little blond about 17 years old but no ... the other men could see the women, y... or old. After the car had traveled ... two miles a woman of about 55 ... and said to a woman some years ... senior: "You take this seat now, fo... next mile or so." That particular li... 17 miles long. Some lucky persons ... the car at the station and have sea... the way home, while some others ... to stand nearly all the way. Wou... it be a most courteous and consid... practice if the able-bodied sitters an... standers would change places every ... miles or so?

TEN HUNDRED O'CLOCK

You persons who hate innovations ... changes and think what was good en... for Grandpa is good enough for us ... due for another shock. The 24-hour ... table is coming. All Army schedule... on the 24-hour plan now. If you ... when the Army bus leaves for Muroc ... Base, for example, you are told it le... at ten hundred. That means 10 a.m. E... een hundred would be 6 p.m. Tue... it was announced that a transcontin... airline has adopted the 24-hour time ... and I suspect all railroads and bus ... will be using it soon. The other ... spread it pretty much all over Eu... I was in Belgium when I first ran ... it and thought I simply couldn't u... stand the kind of French they spok... Belgium when I understood the cle... the railway station to say my train ... at 18 o'clock. Soon afterward theate... France and Belgium adopted it. Th... hour timetable is the best way to ... possible mistakes in telegraphic or ... less orders, and I suppose that in A... areas there are times when one ... tell by the sun whether it is a.m. or ... The length of days and nights ch... with the seasons but there are 24 h... in every calendar day, which begi... midnight and lasts till the next mid... There is no logic in splitting it into ... 12-hour periods.

SUPERSENSITIVE FINGERS

More than 100 blind persons are re... ed to be working in one local air... plant. All of them are said to be ke... up with the average standards in the ... they are doing and several are far a... the average.

HUENEME NEEDS MUSIC

Musical instruments for bands an... chestras are getting so scarce that ... of the boys in outlying Army and ... bases who wish to have a little ... of their own are having a hard ... As this column told recently, many ... ries which used to make musical in... ments now are making parts for p... tanks and service radios. Practical... band instruments being produced ar... zen for the armed services. Many ... stores are buying up secondhand mu... instruments and reconditioning th... Tom Diskin, RM3c, Naval Advanced ... Depot, Port Hueneme, writes me tha... morale problem there would be gr... relieved if they could get instrum... for several boys who can play the ... pet, trombone, saxophone, etc., but ... can't get the instruments. If Port ... neme hasn't any more entertainment ... it had last time I was there these ... surely need some music. They can't ... sing blues without some accompani...

PRECEDENCE

I have some doubt that this is a ... story, even though I saw it in the M... Air Base Mirage. But I'll bet no... like it could be printed in a Ge... army paper. The story is that a lieute... snapped at a private: "Is that your ... rette butt lying on the ground th... The private replied: "It's all yours. You saw it first."

Incidentally, K. W. K. has been re... a book of anecdotes of the War Bet... the States. Many of the stories rep... from training camps recently are in ... book.

Prophecy

Editor and Publisher

The Associated Press wire story c... in biggest headlines on Page 1 of ...

Some 110,000 Japanese — many of them American citizens—were put in "relocation camps" at the start of World War II. The San Francisco News dismissed the massive upheaval and stripping of rights as "an interesting and perhaps not too arduous interlude."

what it may be worth in future ill, she has confirmed the prewar "yellow vermin" estimate of her present Axis partners. She has added her own signature to the warrant for her destruction.

Almost as if so timed, the President's revelation of the Doolittle executions was made within a few hours of a step by the Japanese government which, on its face, seems to hint an attempt at propitiation of the Allies. Like her European associates in their losing war of conquest, Japan would be very glad of a negotiated peace on the status quo basis. If the appointment as Foreign Minister of the anti-militarist Shigemitsu, prewar advocate of rapprochement with Britain and America, is a move in that direction or even for "softening" the war, these objectives have now a chance slimmer, if possible, than ever.

By another coincidence, word of the flyers' fate comes at a time well calculated to put a permanent quietus on the effort to secure the release of the Japanese now under military restraint in this country and their return to the areas from which, for their own safety as well as ours, they were evacuated. If more evidence were needed of the complete untrustworthiness of Japanese, or of their readiness to repudiate no matter what solemn undertaking, Tokyo has supplied it.

It may be a lesson, too, to the sappy sentimentalists who affect to regard these interned enemies as the innocent victims of racial prejudice and who advocate setting what they call a "democratic example" to Japan in the way of super-kindness to internees and prisoners of war. The Oriental savage who is our enemy is fortunate, indeed, in having civilized opponents who will not retort in kind.

Were Hitler's Germany in our place, 100 Jap prisoners would already have faced firing squads for every one of the Doolittle party executed.

The nation's wrath is a hopeful augury for the intensification of our war effort, at home as well as on the fighting fronts. In our determination to speed a just and terrible vengeance for our martyred men, however, neither overhaste on the part of our commanders nor pressure of public opinion should be allowed to precipitate undue risks. Rage that translates itself into ill-considered, ill-prepared attempts at reprisal merely plays into the hands of the enemy. Japan has already paid heavily in blood and treasure for her enormities; what she has so far suffered is no more than a drop in the bucket of that which we shall ultimately exact from her.

In the meantime, those of us who cannot fight can turn our righteous anger into channels wherefrom flow the planes and ships, guns and tanks, bombs and bullets for Jap extermination.

How mad are you, white-collar workers in non-war industry and citizens generally? If you really want to help avenge our wantonly slain and do it directly and effectively, double your War Bond purchases and do it now.

How mad are you, munitions makers? Show it practically and immediately by extending yourselves to increase our arms output, without niggling delays over hours and wages, strikes, slowdowns, absenteeism or any other unnecessary interference with our maximum of war production.

Let's not take it out in futile talking. If we do our part, we can safely leave it to the Army and the Navy to do the rest. ❧

THE LOGIC OF THE BATTLEFIELD

Joe Evans, *The Wall Street Journal*, Feb. 23, 1968

We think the American people should be getting ready to accept, if they haven't already, the prospect that the whole Vietnam effort may be doomed; it may be falling apart beneath our feet. The actual military situation may be making academic the philosophical arguments for the intervention in the first place.

Granted, there is an opposite theory, the "last gasp" notion that the weeks-long wave of assaults on cities and hamlets is the enemy's final outburst before greatly decreasing the war's intensity and coming to the bargaining table. Perhaps it will turn out that way, but right now the evidence does not lend the theory much support.

Hanoi is believed to have relatively large numbers of troops still uncommitted in North Vietnam. The Communists appear to be getting ample supplies of weapons from the Soviet Union and Red China. As long as the arms keep coming and there are Vietnamese Communists to use them, you would suppose they could keep up the struggle more or less indefinitely. Thus far, at least, they are showing with a vengeance their ability to sow destruction and demoralization everywhere.

Meantime the present South Vietnamese government, never very impressive, looks worse and worse. Most important, the government can't protect the people even in the heart of the cities. The Saigon-U.S. effort to secure villages and woo villagers to the government side has been brought to a halt. This is a government and a nation in chaos;

how long can it go on? The failing, it should be stressed, is not in U.S. will or valor, but basically in something lacking in Vietnam itself.

As for the U.S. military undertaking, the current tactic is sad to see: The wholesale destruction of towns and cities in order to "save" them, killing or making homeless refugees out of thousands more civilians. While it is certainly true that an American commander has to destroy a building or a town if he considers it necessary for his soldiers' safety, the scale on which it is going on is hardly endearing the U.S. or Saigon to the populace.

Hence the question: Are developments on the ground making hash of our original, commendable objectives?

The U.S. went in to keep South Vietnam out of Communist hands. But no matter what our forces do, they can't seem to do that. If practically nothing is to be left of government or nation, what is there to be saved for what?

The U.S. also went in to demonstrate to Communist China that it couldn't get away with this kind of indirect aggression and that it hadn't better try direct aggression either. But the Communists are getting away with it; they are putting the mighty U.S. through a wringer, and they may be encouraged to try more of it.

Should such be the upshot, that the U.S. abandons the effort not because it "should" do so but because its purposes have become irrelevant in the light of events on the battlefield and of Vietnamese politics, let no one blink the fact that it will be a disaster. It will be a stunning blow to the U.S. and the West in the larger struggle with international communism. At home it will be a traumatic experience to have lost a war in which thousands of Americans died in vain.

The only thing is that continuing in circumstances so unprepossessing could be a worse disaster. If it had in fact been possible for the U.S. to intervene three years ago and accomplish, at reasonable cost, the objective of saving South Vietnam, it probably would have been well worth doing. But since it seems increasingly doubtful that the original purposes can any longer be achieved, the logic of the battlefield suggests that the U.S. could get forced out of an untenable position.

We don't know that the possibility is being squarely faced in Washington; it seems rather unlikely. The Administration insists that the Communist drives are failing of their aims, which Senator Fulbright describes as "wholly irrational, a fantastic analysis." President Johnson seems more firmly committed to Vietnam than ever.

Now stubbornness up to a point is a virtue, but stubbornness can also go beyond the realm of reasonableness. We believe the Administration is duty-bound to recognize that no battle and no war is worth any price, no matter how ruinous, and that in the case of Vietnam it may be failing for the simple reason that the whole place and cause is collapsing from within.

Conceivably all this is wrong; conceivably the Communists are on the brink of defeat and genuine peace talks are about to begin. It doesn't look

that way, and as long as it doesn't everyone had better be prepared for the bitter taste of a defeat beyond America's power to prevent. ❧

The Vietnam War divided editorial writers just as it divided the nation. "We think the American people should be getting ready to accept, if they haven't already, the prospect that the whole Vietnam effort may be doomed," The Wall Street Journal *wrote in 1968.*

CHILDREN UNDER FIRE

St. Petersburg Times, May 6, 1970

WE BRING THEM INTO THE WORLD AS AN ACT of love.

The first thing they learn is the comforting, dependable presence of another human being.

Sometimes they are rough, inconsiderate, aggressive and selfish.

We teach them responsibility for their actions.

We tell them violence begets violence. We show them that sound relationships are built on trust and respect.

We teach them to love their fellow men.

We take them to Sunday School and church, where they learn that God is Love.

"Red and yellow, black and white, all are equal in his sight."

We send them to schools where they learn about Man's violent history.

We teach them that all must obey the law, strong and weak, rich and poor, president and average citizen.

We ask them to make the world a better place. We ask them to become involved.

We tell them we want peace.

We say the world's future rests on their shoulders.

They are America's children, four of whom were shot to death on the campus of Kent State University by a volley of Ohio National Guard gunfire.

They were using the campus as a sanctuary, said Ohio's Gov. James A. Rhodes and candidate for the U.S. Senate.

They are idealistic. Would the older generations want them any other way?

Many of them feel deeply that the Vietnam War is unjust and immoral. They don't want to die, or have their friends die, or kill, or have their friends kill, in an immoral war. Would the older generations really want them to act otherwise on a belief so fundamental?

They are desperate. Under four presidents, the violence in Indochina has grown steadily larger. President Johnson was elected on a platform of peace. He made the war bigger and 41,000 young men died in a war never declared by law. There were protests in Congress. There were marches on Washington. Many young people worked in the election of 1968. Richard Nixon promised them peace and an end to the war. This week he expanded it into Cambodia without consulting or even informing Congress.

What can we do, many young people are asking. Would we want them not to ask?

There are radicals among the young. They advise violence. They say tear down and burn. Most American students know that is wrong. They learned their early lessons too well. But many of them also are more desperate than ever over a war that keeps growing, over earnest pleas that seem always to fall upon deaf leaders.

"This should remind us all once again that when dissent turns to violence it invites tragedy."
— *Statement about Kent State issued on behalf of President Nixon.*

"The people voted for Nixon so we could get out of this mess. Now we're involved in two wars instead of one."

— *Soldier in Charlie Company,*
2nd Battalion of the 7th Cavalry in Cambodia.

Gov. Rhodes ordered the National Guard into Kent State, after serious rioting, to protect life and university property.

Members of the Guard are supposed to be well-trained in riot control. After the excesses of the Detroit riots, many dollars and hours have been spent in crowd-control training. Procedures are precise and detailed. Exercising restraint is the responsibility of all who uphold the law. At the University of Maryland, Guardsmen carrying no ammunition dispersed a crowd of 2,000 the same day.

Is there any possible justification for American Guardsmen firing volleys into a crowd of rock-throwing students? Were the members of the National Guard also our young and frightened children? Are we now killing each other for peace?

"The greatest honor history can bestow is the title of peacemaker. This honor now beckons America — the chance to lead the world out of the valley of turmoil, and onto that high ground of peace man has dreamed of since the dawn of civilization. If we succeed, generations to come will say of us now living that we mastered our moment, that we helped make the world safe for mankind. This is our summons to greatness. I believe the American people are ready to answer this call."
— *President Nixon, Jan. 20, 1969, Inaugural Address.*

"When will we learn that guns don't solve anything?"   — *Mother of a dead student*

They were using a campus as a sanctuary, but they are not an enemy. They are our children, our past, and our future. ❧

Four young people were shot to death by National Guardsmen on the campus of Kent State in Ohio.

The young son of the slain John F. Kennedy salutes at his father's funeral procession.

CHAPTER THREE

DEATH

CARRIE NATION

"IT'S ABOUT TIME FOR LEONARD EDWARDS TO TAKE THE HOT SQUAT."

THAT WAS THE START OF AN EDITORIAL IN THE *PHILADELPHIA DAILY NEWS* BY RICHARD AREGOOD ABOUT A CONVICTED MURDERER — A "PIECE OF HUMAN CRUD." ❧ "FRY HIM." ❧ THAT WAS THE END OF THE EDITORIAL. ❧ DEATH HAS LONG BEEN FODDER FOR EDITORIAL WRITERS. THE FAMOUS AND THE INFAMOUS, THE NOTED AND THE NOTORIOUS SELDOM GO TO THEIR GRAVES WITHOUT SEND-OFFS ON THE EDITORIAL PAGES. AND A MAN NEEDN'T BE

a convicted murderer to bring out the wrath in the editorial writers. They often speak ill of the dead.

When Carrie Nation died in 1911, Henry Watterson wrote, "Poor, old hag!" and compared her to Meg Merrilies, the gypsy in Sir Walter Scott's "Guy Mannering."

When Civil War Gen. Ben Butler died in 1893, *The* (Nashville) *Daily American* said hell was too good for him.

When H.L. Mencken died in 1956, the *Miami Beach Sun* said, "In his final years, he was a shriveled old man, and if unbeknownst to himself he possessed a soul, it was shriveled too."

When Frank Munsey, an owner of newspapers, died in 1925, William Allen White remembered him as a man with "the morals of a money changer and the manners of an undertaker."

And when Francisco Franco died in 1975, Richard Aregood wrote — in an editorial headlined "Adios, Dictator" — "They say only the good die young. Generalissimo Francisco Franco was 82. Seems about right." (Later, Aregood noted that "in retrospect,

that 'seems about right' looks unnecessary.")

But death also moves editorial writers to eloquence.

"What tongue can speak, what pen write, or what words express the deep, deep feeling of sorrow and anguish that swells every loyal bosom; and what mind can comprehend the deeper *vengeance* that steels every loyal nerve, and makes every loyal mind to resolve that the fiendish crime shall be avenged a thousand times in traitor blood," wrote W.S. Burke on the assassination of Abraham Lincoln in 1865. Burke was editor of a small newspaper in Iowa, *The Daily Nonpareil,* in Council Bluffs.

And death moves editorial writers to patriotism.

"In this hour of mourning and of gloom, while the shadow of an awful and unparalleled calamity hangs over the land, it is well to remember that the stability of our government and the welfare of our country do not depend upon the life of any individual, and that the great current of affairs is not to be changed or checked by the loss of any man however high or however honored," began the final paragraph

---

OPPOSITE: *Carrie Nation. "She seems to have done very well in the business of saloon-smashing and hatchet-selling,"*
Henry Watterson wrote in The Courier-Journal *of Louisville. "Poor, old hag! Peace to her ashes."*

in the *New York Times* editorial on the assassination. "In nations where all power is vested in single hands, an assassin's knife may overthrow governments and wrap a continent in the flames of war. But here the People rule, and events inevitably follow the course which *they* prescribe. Abraham Lincoln has been their agent and instrument for the four years past; Andrew Johnson is to be their agent for the four years that are now to come. If the people have faith, courage and wisdom, the result will be the same."

Similarly, when John F. Kennedy was assassinated in 1963, *The Washington Post* wrote at the end of its editorial:

"If those who crushed out his life had any sane and serious purpose to derange or destroy the Nation he served, they will be disappointed. The great government of this country, under the leaders appointed to succession, will go forward in all its domestic and foreign purposes, guided by men with heavy hearts, but with firm hands."

If there were an anti-Pulitzer Prize, a prize for the worst editorial of the year, it clearly would go every year to a writer who bored his readers with a personal editorial — about cosmic thoughts while waiting in line to buy a movie ticket; about idle musings while driving across Montana; about a mother-in-law or a dog or the not-so-cute utterances of a 3-year-old.

Yet every once in a while, a personal editorial can be moving and meaningful. Such an editorial was "Mary White."

Mary White was William Allen White's teenage daughter. She was nearly 17 years old in 1921 when she died after being struck by a limb while riding a horse. Mary was "a scrapper," William Allen White said in his autobiography. "The tom-boy in her, which was big, seemed to loath to be put away forever in skirts," her father's editorial said. "She was a Peter Pan, who refused to grow up."

The editorial, a matter-of-fact obituary stitched with love, is impossible to read without shedding a tear — and smiling a smile. It was reprinted by newspapers across the country. When White himself died, the Associated Press obituary noted the editorial on Mary White and said it was "now regarded as a classic."

White himself, in his autobiography, said, "Probably if anything I have written in these long, happy years that I have been earning my living by writing, if anything survives more than a decade beyond my life's span, it will be the thousand words or so that I hammered out on my typewriter that bright May morning under the shadow and in the agony of Mary's death. Maybe — when one thinks of the marvels of this world, the strange new things that man has discovered about himself and his universe, it could well be true — maybe in some distant world among the millions that whirl about our universe, Mary will meet her mother and me and, just as she grinned and looked up at her mother that evening when we climbed the mountain in Colorado, with her hand around my finger, she will grin: 'Daddy and I have had an adventure.'"

By the time that autobiography reached print in 1946, White himself had died. ❧

OPPOSITE: *Robert F. Kennedy (left) and Sen. John F. Kennedy confer at the International Brotherhood of Teamsters hearings in 1957.*

THE BEAST IS DEAD

The (Nashville) *Daily American,* Jan. 12, 1893

OLD BEN BUTLER IS DEAD! Early yesterday morning the angel of death acting under the devil's orders, took him from earth and landed him in hell. In all this Southern country there are no tears, no sighs and no regrets. He lived only too long. We are glad he has at last been removed from earth and even pity the devil the possession he has secured.

When Grant died, it was with the respect and esteem of the Southern people. When Sheridan died, all the harm he did our cause during the bloody contest of more than a quarter of a century ago was forgotten and his seeming cruelty had grown to be held as love of country and his terrific assaults as great generalship. When old Tecumseh Sherman passed away, the people whom he devastated and robbed of property and precious lives were pleased to forget the bonfires he made of our cities, the path of death he cut to the sea, and they now hold him up as one who loved well his country and was cruel only to be true.

But with Ben Butler it is different. His stay in the South was a curse to our people and his dead body cannot shake the estimate formed of his character when he sat in New Orleans as a military satrap upon the lives and property of defenseless men and women.

We have no love for him, and praise of any kind, solely because he is at last dead, would be the veriest hypocrisy from Southern people.

"It should be a day of merry-making," The *(Nashville)* Daily American *editorialized when Civil War Gen. Ben Butler died.*

There is nothing in his whole life to excite our admiration. When it is said that he was possessed of great intelligence and undaunted energy all that is to his credit has been said.

He was a truckling demagogue whose selfishness amounted to pollution; he was an autocrat who used power to wreak personal revenge; he was mean and malignant, a hangman from prejudice, the insulter of women, a braggadocio, a trickster and a scoundrel whose heart was as black as the smoke from the coals that are now scorching his soul.

If there be a future of peace in store for Ben

Butler after his entrance upon eternity then there is no heaven, and the Bible is a lie. If hell be only as black as the good book describes it then there are not the degrees of punishment in which some Christians so firmly believe. He has gone, and from the sentence which has already been passed upon him there is no appeal. He is already so deep down in the pit of everlasting doom that he couldn't get the most powerful ear trumpet conceivable to scientists and hear the echoes of old Gabriel's trumpet; or fly a million kites and get a message to St. Peter who stands guard at heaven's gate.

In our statute books many holidays are decreed. It was an egregious oversight that one on the occasion of the death of Ben Butler was not foreordained. It should be a day of merry-making. The "Beast" is dead. The tymbals should beat and the tin horn should get in its exultant work. Butler has gone where he can issue no more orders making the rape of Southern women a gala pastime. He has gone where there are no more spoons to be stolen. He has gone where it is not in his power to order hanged Southern gentlemen for alleged treason against Butlerism.

Good-bye Ben! You strutted through a few temporal triumphs; now rest if you can in the brimstone glare of hell fire. You laughed twenty-five years ago, when you branded your offensive personality upon the memories of your superiors; now smile if you can when powerless and sunk so low as to be beyond the sympathy of even Christian men and women. ❧

THE GREAT DEAD

The (Council Bluffs, Iowa) *Daily Nonpareil,* April 17, 1865

"A prince and a great man is this day fallen in Israel."

THE GREAT CONQUERER, death, has claimed for his victim the chief man of the world. The mighty captain of the hosts of Freedom and the great champion of human Liberty, has fallen, by the hand of the assassin! The nation is insulted, humanity is contemned. The voice of lamentation goes out from the Capitol, and the heart of the nation throbs in echo.

What tongue can speak, what pen write, or what words express, the deep, deep, feeling of sorrow and anguish that swells every loyal bosom; and what mind can comprehend the deeper *vengeance* that steels every loyal nerve, and makes every loyal mind to resolve that the fiendish crime shall be avenged a thousand times in traitor blood. With aching hearts the people mourn the dead President not only as a great and good ruler, but as a near and dear friend; the fall of other rulers would be regretted as national calamities, but the grief of this occasion is deeper and broader; the affections of his countrymen had entwined themselves about Abraham Lincoln with a more than paternal tenderness, and he is mourned as at once our leader and father;

cut down in the prime of life, in the full vigor of manhood, and when he had reached the very pinnacle of earthly greatness.

But had his days been prolonged to more than the allotted time of man he could have risen no higher — he had attained the highest summit to which mortal man is permitted to ascend; and in the full tide of his glory, when his generous heart was just ready to extend mercy beyond justice, in the forgiveness of the enemies of himself, of his country and of liberty, he receives the summons to "come up higher." What a strange and remarkable fitness was there, too, in the time chosen by the assassin for his fiendish work; on the anniversary of the day upon which the Saviour of mankind was slain, the savior of his country was laid a sacrifice upon the altar of Liberty, to seal with his blood, the decree of his people, — "All men shall be free!"

But in the midst of our sorrow we have reason to be thankful that the affairs of the government will pass into the hands of a tried, true, and faithful patriot. The mantle of Lincoln will rest without dishonor upon Andrew Johnson. And may the God of Lincoln be the guide and support of the new President; as the illustrious dead was ever ready to humbly recognize the hand of Almighty Providence in directing the affairs of the nation, may the living never lose sight of the fact that the Lord God Omnipotent reigneth. ❧

REST IN TRUST

WILLIAM ALLEN WHITE,
The Emporia Daily Gazette, Dec. 23, 1925

FRANK MUNSEY, the great publisher, is dead. Frank Munsey contributed to the journalism of his day the talent of a meat packer, the morals of a money changer and the manners of an undertaker. He and his kind have about succeeded in transforming a once noble profession into an 8 per cent security.

May he rest in trust! ❧

Frank Munsey became famous — and, to William Allen White, infamous — for building a media empire.

OPPOSITE: *"What tongue can speak, what pen write, or what words express, the deep, deep, feeling of sorrow and anguish that swells every loyal bosom,"* The *(Council Bluffs, Iowa)* Daily Nonpareil *editorialized after President Abraham Lincoln was assassinated.*

OUR PRESIDENT IS DEAD

The Washington Post, Nov. 23, 1963

Anguish and unbelief, sorrow and depression, dismay and alarm sweep over the Nation in vast waves of shock as the dreadful news from Texas penetrates the consciousness of the country.

The mind does not readily accept the terrible truth. It is unwilling to comprehend the consequences of this desperate and deplorable act. It is unready to believe that in an instant, a life so filled with expectation of future triumphs and achievements so swiftly could be extinguished.

This calamity is not unprecedented in the country's life, but no precedent can prepare the public mind for this sort of disaster. This kind of violence is alien to a land where political differences are often great but where essential respect for the office and person of the President precludes even the thought of physical offense against him.

No one will be willing to believe that this act could have been committed by anyone governed by a normal mind in a rational state. Our politics, our differences and our divisions are not those out of which so foul a deed could arise. It must be put down to madness.

The country, in the wake of this misfortune, must take up the burden now lifted from his young shoulders. If those who crushed out his life had any sane and serious purpose to derange or destroy the Nation he served, they will be disappointed. The great government of this country, under the leaders appointed to succession, will go forward in all its domestic and foreign purposes, guided by men with heavy hearts, but with firm hands. ❧

"The great government of this country, under the leaders appointed to succession, will go forward,"
The Washington Post *editorialized about the death of President John F. Kennedy.*

YES, THE CHAIR

RICHARD AREGOOD, *Philadelphia Daily News*, Nov. 21, 1975

IT'S ABOUT TIME for Leonard Edwards to take the Hot Squat.

Edwards, for those who haven't been following his worthless career, has been convicted of two murders. He's awaiting trial on another murder and the rape of a 14-year-old girl.

He's 29 years old. Hopes of rehabilitating this piece of human crud are doubtful. It's even wildly optimistic to use the word doubtful.

The last time Edwards was freed, it was on bail pending appeal of an overly generous third-degree murder conviction. He had just stabbed somebody to death and justice, in all its majesty, had found him guilty.

Edwards then went out and killed somebody else.

His second murder jury was right. He's not worth the upkeep.

Fry him. ❧

MARY WHITE

WILLIAM ALLEN WHITE, *The Emporia Daily Gazette*, Aug. 15, 1921

THE ASSOCIATED PRESS reports carrying the news of Mary White's death declared that it came as the result of a fall from a horse. How she would have hooted at that! She never fell from a horse in her life. Horses have fallen on her and with her — "I'm always trying to hold 'em in my lap," she used to say. But she was proud of few things, and one was that she could ride anything that had four legs and hair. Her death resulted not from a fall, but from a blow on the head which fractured her skull, and the blow came from the limb of an overhanging tree on the parking.

The last hour of her life was typical of its happiness. She came home from a day's work at school, topped off by a hard grind with the copy on the High School Annual, and felt that a ride would refresh her. She climbed into her khakis, chattering to her mother about the work she was doing, and hurried to get her horse and be out on the dirt roads for the country air and the radiant green fields of the spring. As she rode through the town on an easy gallop she kept waving at passers-by. She knew everyone in town. For a decade the little figure with the long pig-tail and the red hair ribbon has been familiar on the streets of Emporia, and she got in the way of speaking to those who nodded at her. She passed the Kerrs walking the horse, in front of the Normal Library, and waved at them; passed another friend a few hundred feet farther on, and waved at her. The horse was walking, and as she turned into North Merchant Street she took off her cowboy hat, and the horse swung into a lope. She passed the Tripletts and waved her cowboy hat at them, still moving

PHILADELPHIA DAILY NEWS

An afternoon newspaper published by
Philadelphia Newspapers, Inc.
400 N. Broad St., Philadelphia, Pa. 19101
854-2600

GILMAN SPENCER
Editor

PAUL JANENSCH
Managing Editor

MATT GETLIN
Senior Vice President

In Our Opinion

Another Zinger

Just when you start thinking there's nothing more ridiculous those arrogant yo-yos who set policy for the Federal Bureau of Investigation could have done, another zinger comes up.

While the crime rate was soaring, while politicians were vying with one another for the most outrageous illegality, the FBI was on the job — trying to drive people crazy.

Agents worked hard to disrupt the civil rights movement — to the point of trying to break up marriages with anonymous letters. That was for the lower-ranking figures. They saved the best for the Rev. Dr. Martin Luther King.

The FBI worked hard to discredit and disturb Dr. King, even to the point of urging (again anonymously) that he kill himself. He was constantly wiretapped and observed. Agents tried to prevent his meeting with the Pope. They brainstormed various nasty tricks to be tried. They even had their own man ready to be "a new national Negro leader."

That stuff isn't just patronizing and insulting. It's illegal.

It's not enough just to cluck about the abuses.

The idiots who ran this program should not be permitted to hide in the bureaucracy. They should be fired and replaced by real FBI men — the kind who catch criminals.

Adios, Dictator

They say only the good die young. Generalissimo Francisco Franco was 82. Seems about right.

Hold That Raise

The Philadelphia Electric Co. says it needs another $95 million from its customers to cover loans and make up for a year's delay on the approval of a whittled down $105 million rate hike okayed only 10 months ago.

Under the proposed rate hike, the seventh since 1969, the "typical" homeowner's monthly bill will increase $2.26 — from $25.60 to $27.86. PE also wants PUC approval of a scheme to cut rates for off-peak users willing to spend $300-$350 to install time clocks on their power lines.

It is asking all this of a commission of three members. Gov. Shapp has nominated Michael Johnson, a Bryn Mawr labor leader, and Helen B. O'Bannon, a Pittsburgh economist, to the PUC, but the state Senate has yet to approve them.

Nominee Johnson has described utility customers as "captives," and in this case, that's just what they are. Philadelphia Electric's customers are entitled to the input of Johnson and Ms. O'Bannon on this latest PE rate increase request. The Senate should make sure they're seated in time to help decide it.

Window Dressing

There were pictures of Vice President Rockefeller at the Liberty Bell, embracing Gov. Shapp, a Democratic Presidential contender, and reveling in a reception at the Second Bank of the United States.

And then there were all day hearings — a Medicine Show — called the White House Public Forum on Domestic Policy. Among others, it heard Elkins Wetherill, of the Philadelphia-Baltimore-Washington Stock Exchange, plead for less Federal regulation. And it heard Herb Denenberg call for a "Presidential Hotline" to dispense consumer information nationally.

And, after it was over, Rockefeller acknowledged that he'd heard it all before. No doubt he has. That's why it seems ludicrous to stage a traveling roadshow with the sole intent of gathering material for President Ford's

In Your Opinion

Don't Add Up

The only thing Rizzo showed the intellectuals in this city is that they are outnumbered. His house does matter. For any hard-working "intelligent" person would want an explanation as to where his tax money is going. God doesn't need to bless Rizzo. He's already blessed with your tax money and he has enough well paid guards to keep him safe from the terror that is rampant in this city. Like I say, nothing for nothing equals nothing, and dumb for dumb equals you and an undignified politician. —Enlightened

Start At Home

Mr. Ford said we should tighten our belts. He could start with himself by donating his salary to charity like JFK did. He could have done without his expensive swimming pool as he is never in the White House to use it. This unelected man is running all over the world. He has more security people with him than he has audiences. Handshaking, back slapping and baby kissing will not give him votes —M. W.

Cretin Ph.D.

Larry Fields: I nominate you for NOW's "Barefoot and Pregnant" Award. You'd have been right at home in the 18th Century. You made a crack about Edie Huggins, Buddy, you have this cretin philosophy that women should venture no further than the kitchen or bedroom. Your column mirrors your midget mentality. —T. D.

Unequal

Will someone please inform Chuck Stone that Philadelphia's wards aren't equal in population? Most of his election analyses seem based on

Imagine It

Disgusted Father: You're just as sick as any rapist who walks the street. I don't even wish rape on my worst enemy. I've been there . . . twice. I can sympathize with you. Guaranteed it's the most awful experience of a lifetime. If you think you're bitter about the experience, just try to imagine how your daughter feels. You can't, because there are feelings about the incident that she will keep inside of her for the rest of her life. I know how she feels. —Been There

Found Money

Where was the $50 million deficit Moak now speaks about before the election? Seems his eyesight was failing pretty bad before election. Now that it's improving he suddenly sees a deficit. By the time the true picture floats to the top of the cesspool he'll be basking in the sunshine someplace on the fat pension he will be getting at the expense of the taxpayers. —Allen Humphrey

No Room

Bill Wansek: I agree with you about Patricia Hearst. However, the one I feel sorry for is Stephen Weed. That little brat ruined the guy's life. Little Miss Moneybags seems the type who uses the people who love her. Patty loves Patty, I'm afraid, and that leaves no room for anyone else. Hope she gets what she deserves —Mrs. Terry Donnelly

Helped Her

Recently I was in Lankenau Hospital for eye surgery. During my stay there a nurse was very kind, considerate and most helpful. I

Forget It

Marian Bowman: Whether I burn your flag is a matter of personal concern. I have my own beliefs and I'm not going to change them because someone disagrees. For your information I'm not on relief. I work and pay taxes. If I came here just to make some of what you call your American bucks, I could have returned to Puerto Rico a long time ago. I have a job that pays pretty good money, and I'm here because I want to be here. If that makes you or anyone else unhappy, that's too bad. —Doris Sonato

No Joke

Blackbirds today, black folks tomorrow. Kentucky, Tennessee and Illinois plan to slaughter 65 million blackbirds. The Daily News captions says, "Bye Bye Blackbirds." Everything's a joke. White America, wake up and stop this senseless slaughter of native wild life. I call on all conservationists to help outlaw hunting and stop government sponsored "legal" killing of Americans' wild life. —Black Conservationist

Set Back

Just read Chuck Stone's piece. A Wallace-Rizzo ticket is all we need. Forbid that we'd set civil rights and liberties back 200 years. It's enough like voting Mussolini and Hitler from their graves. White America even more so that there are people who will vote for them. —Won't Vote For Fascists

He's Laughing

Just read your story in the paper about George Schwartz becoming President of City Council. I told my ma, Rizzo would either force me laugh. Rizzo wants to turn us into a Italian Mafia city. Ethel Allen, Rizzo wants to be

NEWS

An afternoon newspaper published by
Philadelphia Newspapers, Inc.
400 N. Broad St., Philadelphia, Pa. 19101

854-2600

Editor

PAUL JANENSCH
Managing Editor

NATT GETLIN
Senior Vice President

In Our Opinion

Yes, the Chair

It's about time for Leonard Edwards to take the Hot Squat.

Edwards, for those who haven't been following his worthless career, has been convicted of two murders. He's

Edwards

awaiting trial on another murder and the rape of a 14-year-old girl.

He's 29 years old. Hopes of rehabilitating this piece of human crud are doubtful. It's even wildly optimistic to use the word doubtful.

The last time Edwards was freed, it was on bail pending appeal of an overly generous third-degree murder conviction. He had just stabbed somebody to death and justice, in all its majesty, had found him guilty.

Edwards then went out and killed somebody else.

His second murder jury was right. He's not worth the upkeep.

Fry him.

Murder Inc.

A thinking person can feel crazy just reading the newspapers any more.

Here's William Colby, the head of the CIA, defending his men who plotted doing in various heads of foreign governments when they weren't using their time spying on Americans.

Don't let anybody know their names, says Colby. It may subject the would-be murderers to attacks by "unstable and extremist groups."

So?

The people these clowns were trying to kill can't be expected to show a lot of sympathy.

After all, they were already exposed to attack by the "unstable and extremist" CIA.

You play the game, you take your chances.

Beautiful Planning

Philadelphia architects and engineers have designed a beautiful plan to take the politics and the customary 5 percent payoff out of the process of selecting designers for public buildings. But, they're going to need our help.

The plan is to gather the signatures of 20,000 Philadelphians in support of a City Charter amendment establishing an Architects/Engineers Selection Board in the Department of Public Property. The board would have seven members—none of whose firms would do city business while they served. They would recommend three choices to the commissioner, who would then choose the winner.

The Selection Board will bring the selection of designers out from behind closed doors, says Samuel Crothers 3d, president of the Philadelphia Chapter of the American Institute of Architects. "We want the entire selection brought out in the open and this is the only way."

To dramatize their plea, the planners have wrapped their 17th and Sansom Sts. headquarters in a giant billboard. Beginning Dec. 5, they will seek signatures at Centre Square Plaza, 15th and Market Sts., and out in the neighborhoods.

The new method isn't perfect, but this is one time we

FREDDY WANT-A-LOT

WANT$ YOUR$

In Your Opinion

Insider

The Liddonfield Homes project in Northeast Philadelphia is hidden from the outside. Walk inside and you find graffiti-covered walls, drunken dropouts, racial strife, destruction, and a manager who seems to be blind to the entire situation. People in the vicinity should voice their concern before the situation gets worse. —K. H.

Get Pregnant!

Girls, did you know welfare will support, feed and clothe you and your baby for absolutely nothing? Just get pregnant and come on down to DPA. Why get married? It's cheaper this way. Just live with your boyfriend and the three of you can enjoy the comforts of a nice home. Don't worry, welfare will never find out because they don't check into it. —Unfortunately Sterile

How Can She?

Why aren't these hustlers screened before putting them in office? Edward Lee did a job on Philadelphia, now he puts his sister in office so she can skim off the top. With three kids how can she do the job if it is so time consuming? Another rip-off? Wake up you dummies in Philadelphia. —Reader

Why Not?

Ironside: If Frank Rizzo is any kind of a man, and the great man he thinks he is, he wouldn't try to change the City Charter to run for governor. Why not give up the position of mayor and run like any other man? —Take a Chance

Cosmetician

I agree with Larry Fields. Edie Huggins should go back to emptying bed-

Shocked

I read the Daily News every day. Basically it keeps you fairly well informed. I read the article by Larry Fields, and it shocked me that a responsible reporter could write what he did about Edie Huggins. I watch her show every morning and I don't think there's anything amateurish about it. —Mrs. R. Lowry

Shameful

It's a shame this world has an ignoramous such as Mrs. Corinne Griffen, who believes blacks are the least beautiful of all races. Mrs. Griffen must be blind. If she were to open her eyes she'd see there are beautiful people in all races, not just in physical features, but in every aspect of their being. —Rosetta Thurmond

Bed Panned

I can't believe Larry Fields is a man. He insulted every nurse, whether white, black, male or female when he wrote that he about Edie Huggins. I hope he never needs to be hospitalized. If I had a bedpan full of feces I'd throw it in his face. I hope you've fired him by the time you receive this letter. —Jeanette Sheppard, RN

Non-Winner

I've been living in Philadelphia for 40 years and I'm an honest, hard working woman. I'm confused. No one, but no one ever wins at these lotteries in the ghetto. The money in the suburbs. And the money of the poor people they play?

Not Up to Us

The plug should not be Karen Quinlan. Maybe there is a hope that she will come out of it. At least they'll know they tried to keep her

Gotta Be

Chuck Stone has got ... in doubt, the worst ... read. He puts down all ... didn't vote the Bowser ... Bowser was black, got a ... mayoral ... Rizzo won by ... would have a ... against them. Maybe ... for mayor next ... personally ... Rizzo is ...

Human Prey

There's truth ... sportsmen in their ... of wild game. A ... is said at the ... search of human ... Supreme Court ... of the body-part ... for victims of ... get to the rights ... If the headlines ... acquire a large ... Democracy ...

Not Oriented

It's so rotten the ... elected president of ... remnants of Watergate ... lesbian in a minority ... her. The lesbian ... remnants of Watergate ...

Philly Farm

Richard Aregood's short editorials in the Philadelphia Daily News *got right to the point.*

Ingestible

Larry ... while he did Edie ...

gaily north on Merchant Street. A Gazette carrier passed — a High School boy friend — and she waved at him, but with her bridle hand; the horse veered quickly, plunged into the parking where the low-hanging limb faced her, and, while she still looked back waving, the blow came. But she did not fall from the horse; she slipped off, dazed a bit, staggered and fell in a faint. She never quite recovered consciousness.

But she did not fall from the horse, neither was she riding fast. A year or so ago she used to go like the wind. But that habit was broken, and she used the horse to get into the open to get fresh, hard exercise, and to work off a certain surplus energy that welled up in her and needed a physical outlet. That need has been in her heart for years. It was back of the impulse that kept the dauntless little brown-clad figure on the streets and country roads of this community and built into a strong, muscular body what had been a frail and sickly frame during the first years of her life. But the riding gave her more than a body. It released a gay and hardy soul. She was the happiest thing in the world. And she was happy because she was enlarging her horizon. She came to know all sorts and conditions of men; Charley O'Brien, the traffic cop, was one of her best friends. W.L. Holtz, the Latin teacher, was another. Tom O'Connor, farmer-politician, and Rev. J.H.J. Rice, preacher and police judge, and Frank Beach, music master, were her special friends, and all the girls, black and white, above the track and below the track, in Pepville and Stringtown, were among her acquaintances. And she brought home riotous stories of her adventures. She loved to rollick; persiflage was her natural expression at home. Her humor was a continual bubble of joy. She seemed to think in hyperbole and metaphor. She was mischievous without malice, as full of faults as an old shoe. No angel was Mary White, but an easy girl to live with, for she never nursed a grouch five minutes in her life.

With all her eagerness for the out-of-doors, she loved books. On her table when she left her room were a book by Conrad, one by Galsworthy, "Creative Chemistry" by E.E. Slosson, and a Kipling book. She read Mark Twain, Dickens and Kipling before she was 10 — all of their writings. Wells and Arnold Bennett particularly amused and diverted her. She was entered as a student in Wellesley in 1922; was assistant editor of the High School Annual this year, and in line for election to the editorship of the Annual next year. She was a member of the executive committee of the High School Y.W.C.A.

Within the last two years she had begun to be moved by an ambition to draw. She began as most children do by scribbling in her school books funny pictures. She bought cartoon magazines and took a course — rather casually, naturally, for she was, after all, a child with no strong purposes

---

OPPOSITE: *Mary White was nearly 17 when she died in 1921. "She hungered and thirsted for righteousness. . . . She was a Peter Pan, who refused to grow up," William Allen White wrote of his daughter.*

— and this year she tasted the first fruits of success by having her pictures accepted by the High School Annual. But the thrill of delight she got when Mr. Ecord, of the Normal Annual, asked her to do the cartooning for that book this spring, was too beautiful for words. She fell to her work with all her enthusiastic heart. Her drawings were accepted, and her pride — always repressed by a lively sense of the ridiculousness of the figure she was cutting — was a really gorgeous thing to see. No successful artist ever drank a deeper draught of satisfaction than she took from the little fame her work was getting among her schoolfellows. In her glory, she almost forgot her horse — but never her car.

For she used the car as a jitney bus. It was her social life. She never had a "party" in all her nearly seventeen years — wouldn't have one; but she never drove a block in the car in her life that she didn't begin to fill the car with pick-ups! Everybody rode with Mary White — white and black, old and young, rich and poor, men and women. She liked nothing better than to fill the car full of long-legged High School boys and an occasional girl, and parade the town. She never had a "date," nor went to a dance, except once with her brother, Bill, and the "boy proposition" didn't interest her — yet. But young people — great spring-breaking, varnish-cracking, fender-bending, door-sagging carloads of "kids" — gave her great pleasure. Her zests were keen. But the most fun she ever had in her life was acting as chairman of the committee that got up the big turkey dinner for the poor folks at the county

home; scores of pies, gallons of slaw, jam, cakes, preserves, oranges and a wilderness of turkey were loaded in the car and taken to the county home. And, being of a practical turn of mind, she risked her own Christmas dinner by staying to see that the poor folks actually got it all. Not that she was a cynic; she just disliked to tempt folks. While there she found a blind colored uncle, very old, who could do nothing but make rag rugs, and she rustled up from her school friends rags enough to keep him busy for a season. The last engagement she tried to make was to take the guests at the county home out for a car ride. And the last endeavor of her life was to try to get a rest room for colored girls in the High School. She found one girl reading in the toilet, because there was no better place for a colored girl to loaf, and it inflamed her sense of injustice and she became a nagging harpie to those who she thought could remedy the evil. The poor she had always with her, and was glad of it. She hungered and thirsted for righteousness; and was the most impious creature in the world. She joined the Congregational Church without consulting her parents, not particularly for her soul's good. She never had a thrill of piety in her life, and would have hooted at a "testimony." But even as a little child she felt the church was an agency for helping people to more of life's abundance, and she wanted to help. She never wanted help for herself. Clothes meant little to her. It was a fight to get a new rig on her; but eventually a harder fight to get it off. She never wore a jewel and had no ring but her High School class ring, and never asked for anything but a wrist watch. She refused to have her hair up; though she was nearly 17. "Mother," she protested, "you don't know how much I get by with, in my braided pigtails that I could not with my hair up." Above every other passion of her life was her passion not to grow up, to be a child. The tom-boy in her, which was big, seemed to loath to be put away forever in skirts. She was a Peter Pan, who refused to grow up.

Her funeral yesterday at the Congregational Church was as she would have wished it; no singing, no flowers save the big bunch of red roses from her Brother Bill's Harvard classmen — Heavens, how proud that would have made her! and the red roses from the Gazette force in vases at her head and feet. A short prayer, Paul's beautiful essay on "Love" from the Thirteenth Chapter of First Corinthians, some remarks about her democratic spirit by her friend, John H.J. Rice, pastor and police judge, which she would have deprecated if she could, a prayer sent down for her by her friend, Carl Nau, and opening the service the slow, poignant movement from Beethoven's Moonlight Sonata, which she loved, and closing the service a cutting from the joyously melancholy first movement of Tschaikowski's Pathetic Symphony, which she liked to hear in certain moods on the phonograph; then the Lord's Prayer by her friends in High School.

That was all.

For her pall-bearers only her friends were chosen; her Latin teacher, W.L. Holtz — her High

William Allen White. "If anything survives more than a decade beyond my life's span, it will be the thousand words or so that I hammered out . . . in the agony of Mary's death," he said.

School principal, Rice Brown; her doctor, Frank Foncannon; her friend, W.W. Finney; her pal at the Gazette office, Walter Hughes; and her brother Bill. It would have made her smile to know that her friend, Charley O'Brien, the traffic cop, had been transferred from Sixth and Commercial to the corner near the church to direct her friends who came to bid her good-bye.

A rift in the clouds in a gray day threw a shaft of sunlight upon her coffin as her nervous, energetic little body sank to its last sleep. But the soul of her, the glowing, gorgeous, fervent soul of her, surely was flaming in eager joy upon some other dawn. ❧

CLOSED

The riderless horse at President John F. Kennedy's funeral procession. The famous and the infamous, the noted and the notorious seldom go to their graves without send-offs on the editorial pages.

CHAPTER FOUR
RACE

*The Rev. Martin Luther King Jr. addresses a rally
of marchers in Selma, Ala., in 1965.*

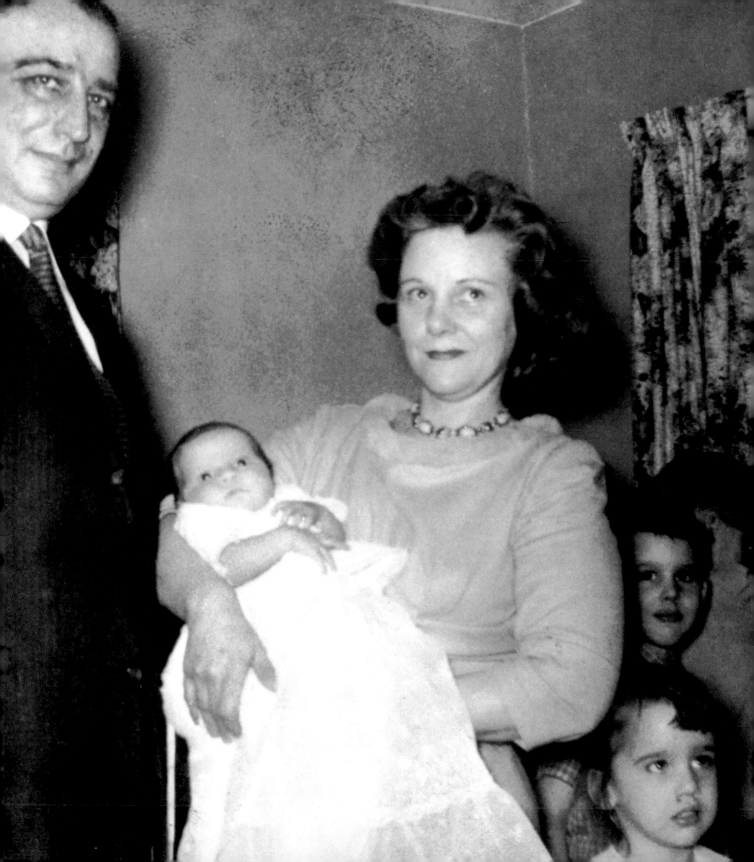

"THESE PEOPLE ARE CRACKPOTS."

"THESE PEOPLE" WERE THE FREEDOM RIDERS WHO ARRIVED IN JACKSON, MISSISSIPPI, ON MAY 24, 1961, HOPING TO DESEGREGATE CAFETERIAS AND BUS-STATION RESTROOMS. THE ASSESSMENT OF THEM WAS IN A FRONT-PAGE COLUMN IN THE *JACKSON DAILY NEWS*. IT WAS WRITTEN BY EDITOR JIMMY WARD, A SEGREGATIONIST WHO MINCED NO WORDS. IN EDITORIALS AND COLUMNS, HE HAD CALLED THE NORTHERNERS "IDIOTIC AGITATING NITWITS" AND "ABNORMAL mammals," and he questioned whether they belonged in jail, a mental hospital, or the zoo.

Race has forever stirred the passions of editorial writers, moving them to bile or eloquence. Horace Greeley's greatest editorial — a critical letter to President Lincoln sixteen months after the start of the Civil War — was about freeing the slaves. It prompted a heartfelt response from the President and, not long thereafter, his issuance of the Emancipation Proclamation. It is, perhaps, the most powerful editorial ever published — and it came from the pen of a man who just a few years earlier was defending the South's right to secede.

"If the Cotton States shall become satisfied that they can do better out of the Union than in it, we insist on letting them go in peace," he wrote in 1860. "The right to secede may be a revolutionary one, but it exists nevertheless. …We must ever resist the asserted right of any State to remain in the Union and nullify or defy the laws thereof; to withdraw from the Union is quite another matter."

The *Albany* (N.Y.) *Evening Journal* was poetic in its despair when the Supreme Court in 1857 ruled in the Dred Scott case that slavery was all right in America. The (Milledgeville, Ga.) *Federal Union* was just as strong in its defense of the decision. And Greeley was unsparing in his withering assessment of Roger Taney, the Chief Justice who wrote the decision:

> "When we are ready to surrender sense and reason, conscience and intellect, and all pretension to mental and physical freedom; when we are ready to beslaver Bombast with praise, and to write the panegyric of the little Napoleon; then, and not till then, will we get on our knees to Roger Taney."

Nearly 100 years later, passion again gripped editors as the Supreme Court ruled that the nation's schools must be desegregated.

"Neither the atom bomb nor the hydrogen bomb will ever be as meaningful to our democracy as the unanimous declaration of the Supreme Court that racial segregation violates the spirit and the letter of our Constitution," the *Chicago Defender* editorialized on May 18, 1954. "This means the beginning of the end of the dual society in American life and the … segregation which supported it."

The same day, the *Jackson Daily News* ran an editorial entitled "Bloodstains on White Marble

OPPOSITE: *Civil rights worker Viola Liuzzo was killed by a sniper's bullet while driving a freedom rider between Selma and Montgomery, Ala.*

Steps." It said, in part: "Human blood may stain Southern soil in many places because of this decision, but the dark red stains of that blood will be on the marble steps of the United States Supreme Court building. ... White and Negro children in the same schools will lead to miscegenation. Miscegenation leads to mixed marriages, and mixed marriages lead to mongrelization of the human race."

Scores of reporters and editors who saw and covered the civil rights movement — from papers North and South — came away with the idea that democracy must always be fought for, that freedom is fragile, and that in times of crisis the press must be bold and brave.

Thus it was that a handful of Southern editors and editorial writers — Ralph McGill in Atlanta; Hazel Brannon Smith in Lexington, Miss.; Eugene Patterson in Atlanta and St. Petersburg; Ira B. Harkey Jr. in Pascagoula, Miss.; Harry Ashmore in Little Rock; Lenoir Chambers in Norfolk, Va.; Buford Boone in Tuscaloosa, Ala.; J. Oliver Emmerich Sr. in McComb, Miss., and Hodding Carter Jr. in Greenville, Miss. — took calm but courageous stands as they tried to lead the South as well as explain it, and often those calm and courageous stands helped keep their towns relatively calm and peaceful during these times.

Of the 11 Pulitzer Prizes for editorial writing awarded between 1957 and 1967, seven were awarded for civil rights editorials written by Southern editors — Boone, Ashmore, McGill, Chambers, Harkey, Smith and Patterson. Carter had won one earlier.

Equality wasn't something these men and women came to suddenly. In 1937, Hodding Carter ran a photo of the great black track star Jesse Owens, upsetting many readers of the Greenville paper.

"We'll print it again when we feel like doing so," Carter responded in an editorial. "We fail to see anything traitorous to the white race in acknowledging the accomplishment of a negro boy." Carter continued: "Get this straight, everyone of you. We were brought up on a Louisiana farm. To our knowledge, every member of our family, as far back as any of you in Greenville can trace that mythical attribute called ancestry, have been of the South, have fought for it, and have loved its ideals and its foibles as well. But we personally have never felt so unsure of our status as a white man that we had to bully a negro, to return courtesy with rudeness, or to make him think that he was a despicable beast who could sense neither kindness nor gratitude nor trust."

Similarly, in 1952 the Greenville paper began using courtesy titles — Mr. or Mrs. — when referring to blacks.

But the editorial pages were anything but bold and brave — or even attentive — when the government rounded up more than 100,000 Japanese living in America and sent them off to internment camps during the early years of World War II. Most were U.S. citizens. Those papers that did comment did so approvingly, with *The San Francisco News* dismissing the massive upheaval and stripping of rights as "an interesting and perhaps not too arduous interlude."

"Japanese citizens, alien and native-born alike, have, on the whole, taken their evacuation orders in good spirit, and for that they deserve a word of praise," the *News* editorialized on April 8, 1942. "They are in a position to assert rights guaranteed them by the Constitution, but with most sensible unanimity they have recognized that certain privileges must be suspended in times of national danger. That, we frankly admit, reflects a high order of intelligence on their part. ... By fostering this helpful attitude within their own groups they can do much to make the whole experience an interesting and perhaps not too arduous interlude in the lives of all concerned."

The *Los Angeles Times* gave not a passing nod to the rights of the Japanese who were American citizens: "The time has come to realize that the rigors of war demand proper detention of Japanese and their immediate removal from the most acute danger spots," it editorialized in January of 1942. "It is not a pleasant task. But it must be done and done now. There is no safe alternative."

As William Allen White knew, there is, of course, an alternative to racism or classism or any other *ism*. And that is equality.

"The white man considers any colored man — black, brown, red, yellow or maroon — as an animal," White wrote in 1922. "The anthropological conceit of the white man is ponderous, unbelievable, vastly amusing to the gods."

He was commenting on the jokes that would be made because blacks planned to start a country club in New Jersey, and "something exquisitely funny seems to excite the white race when

The issue of slavery was part of President Abraham Lincoln's inaugural address in 1861.

it sees the colored race doing things which are ordinary parts of the day's work and play to the white people. It is as though the elephant should drive an auto, or a horse play the piano." But then he asked: "What's the joke if he [someone other than a white man] develops the same desires and aspirations that we do, and who in God's name are we, anyway?" ❧

JESSE OWENS' PICTURE

HODDING CARTER JR., (Greenville, Miss.) *Delta Star,* July 16, 1937

BY INDIRECT CHANNELS the report has come to us that this newspaper has recently received unfavorable local comment because (1) it printed negro sprinter Jesse Owens' picture; (2) it carried a feature story of Nelson street, which is Greenville's Beale street, and (3) it has on occasion given prominence to stories in which negroes appeared in a commendable light. Such criticism has been lumped into the general charge of "nigger loving."

Perhaps we should overlook this matter. We do not think that it represents the viewpoint of the overwhelming majority of Greenville's citizens, for we have the impression that most of us here are civilized. Then too, vicious gossip, like any other rank weed, flourishes in the heat. Maybe these recent torrid days are blameable.

However, the weather affects us too, so here goes.

Jesse Owens is a remarkable athlete, the winner of more Olympic firsts than any other American. His picture has appeared at some time or other in every newspaper of which we have knowledge. This week Mound Bayou, a dusty all-negro village in Mississippi, which has done a pretty good job of running itself for fifty years, had as its guest this negro athlete. And so we printed his picture. We'll print it again when we feel like doing so. We fail to see anything traitorous to the white race in acknowledging the accomplishment of a negro boy, and in giving a helping hand of publicity to a little town which

The photograph of Jesse Owens that appeared in the Delta Star. *"We fail to see anything traitorous to the white race in acknowledging the accomplishment of a negro boy," the paper said.*

is proud that for seventy-five years it has tried to follow the white man's ideal of good citizenship and self-government.

Nelson street, as we have said, is Greenville's Beale street. It is a miniature of that Memphis thoroughfare, and Harlem's Lennox avenue. It is undeniably one aspect of southern life, humorous, colorful, cheerful, barbaric. Have we white people shut our eyes to Beale street and Harlem? We have not. We've made the savage beats of their music ours; their rhythmic dances are intimated in our ballrooms and country clubs; their slurring syllables, transmitted to us from our cradles to our graves, appear on our tongues as the "Southern accent" so cherished by Dixie belles visiting Nawth, and certainly more pleasant than the harsh nasalness of east and mid-west. Their crooning slang is repeated every time Southerners get together for anything from a game which we call African dominoes to a discussion of the cotton outlook.

We admit the crime of printing in this newspaper, stories about negroes other than of their misdemeanors and brutalities. Dr. Carver, that fine old Tuskegee scientist, who has done as much for Southern agriculture as any other man, recently was honored by the State of Mississippi. We printed the story and editorialized upon it. Would you have us publish only crime and police court news of negroes — and omit the white offenders to boot? Does that encourage our negroes to live decently and honorably? We have attacked the murderous blot of lynching in the South. But we have also fought the anti-lynch bill so ardently espoused by a Democratic president whose background is not the South. Do these stands violate the taboo? When the negroes of Greenville banded together in the spring flood panic and offered their services, we gave the humble gesture full credit. Should we have taken their aid for granted?

Get this straight, everyone of you. We were brought up on a Louisiana farm. To our knowledge, every member of our family, as far back as any of you in Greenville can trace that mythical attribute called ancestry, have been of the South, have fought for it, and have loved its ideals and its foibles as well. But we personally have never felt so unsure of our status as a white man that we had to bully a negro, to return courtesy with rudeness, or to make him think that he was a despicable beast who could sense neither kindness nor gratitude nor trust.

Here in the Delta we make our living, in the ultimate analysis, from the negro. He tills our fields. His ready spending of his scant funds has built our business sections, and maintained our economic balances. All of us have not always been fair to him in our dealings. Is it more degrading to be honest with him than to cheat him? Is it more revolting to try to instill in him a pride in his worthwhile actions than to — hush, hush — make him think that his race is fit only for mockery by day and concubinage by night?

We're not apologizing. We're pitying. The object of our pity is the hypocrisy expressed by what we know is an indefensible minority of a lovable town which we have made our home. ✺

THE OPINION OF CHIEF JUSTICE TANEY

Albany (N.Y.) *Evening Journal,* March 10, 1857

WE PRINT TO-DAY a sophistical, dogmatic, muddy, and extreme Pro-Slavery document, which future historians will speak of as the present age speaks of the edicts of Jeffries and the Star Chamber. Unworthy of the Bench from which it was delivered, unworthy even of the previous reputation of the jurist who delivered it, unworthy of the American people, and of the nineteenth century, it will be a blot upon our National character abroad, and a long-remembered shame at home. It declares that the slaveholder may take his Slaves and hold them in any Territory under Federal control, and that neither Congress, nor the Territorial Government, nor the People, have the power now or hereafter to forbid him. It declares that the Constitution, though established "to secure Liberty," nowhere protects the existence of Freedom, and though it never mentions the word "Slave," everywhere legalizes Slavery! The monstrous absurdity of the argument, is only equalled by the astounding revolution it seeks to effect in our jurisprudence. It falsifies the most reliable history, abrogates the most solemn Law, belies the dead and stultifies the living, — in order to make what has heretofore been a local evil, hereafter a National institution! ❧

Chief Justice Roger Taney (left) and Dred Scott. Wrote Horace Greeley: "When we are ready to surrender sense and reason, conscience and intellect, and all pretension to mental and physical freedom; when we are ready to beslaver Bombast with praise, and to write the panegyric of the little Napoleon; then, and not till then, will we get on our knees to Roger Taney."

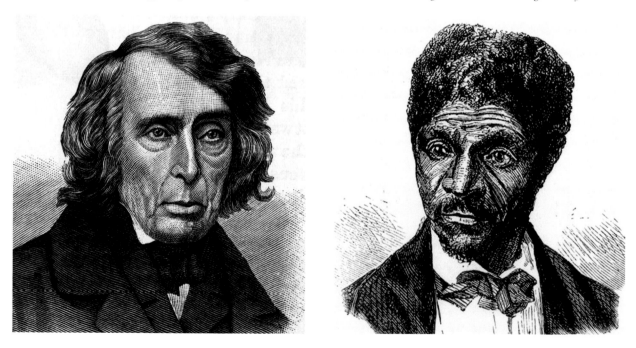

THE ISSUE MUST BE MET

(Milledgeville, Ga.) *Federal Union*, March 31, 1857

THE LATE DECISION of the Supreme Court of the United States, in the Dred Scott case, will bring the enemies of the South face to face with the Constitution of their country. They cannot escape the issue presented — the observance of the laws of the land, or disunion. They can no longer dodge under such pretexts as "bleeding Kansas." That harp of one string has played its last tune, and must now be hung up. Or, if continued to be used by the reverends Henry Ward Beecher and Theodore Parker, it will not call forth the responses it was wont to do in the flush times of "bleeding Kansas." Many of the followers of these infidel preachers are not the fools or fanatics their conduct would seem to indicate. They acted upon principle, many of them, in their opposition to the repeal of the Missouri Compromise; and their zeal for free Kansas was excited to the highest pitch, by the lying agents of the Free State Party. But it is a quite different question now. The leaders of the Black Republican Party are denouncing the decision of the very Tribunal to which they had appealed, and are endeavoring to excite among the people of the North a bitter hostility to it. They will endeavor to organize a party on the basis of opposition to the decision of a majority of the Court in the Dred Scott case. But, fanatical as the people of New England are, they will hesitate to enter the ranks of a political party, organized for the express purpose of overturning a decision of the Supreme Court of the United States. Some of our Southern editors deprecate the agitation to which this decision will give rise. But let it come. The fury of the storm has passed. The treasonable conduct of the leaders of the Black Republican party will be rebuked at their very doors. The issue they have raised will be met by the true-hearted, Constitutional, law-abiding men of the North, and thousands who followed Fremont and "bleeding Kansas," will find themselves allied with the Union men of the country, in sustaining the determination of the Supreme Court in the Dred Scott case. ❧

SUPREME COURT OF THE UNITED STATES.

No. 7.—DECEMBER TERM, 1856.

DRED SCOTT, (A COLORED MAN,)

vs.

JOHN F. A. SANDFORD.

Argument of Montgomery Blair, of Counsel for the Plaintiff in Error.

STATEMENT OF THE CASE.

This is a suit brought to try the right to freedom of the plaintiff and his wife Harriet, and his children Eliza and Lizzie. It was originally brought against the administratrix of Dr. Emerson, in the circuit court of St. Louis county, Missouri, where the plaintiff recovered judgment; but on appeal to the supreme court of the State, a majority of that court, at the March term of 1852, reversed the judgment; when the cause was remanded it was dismissed, and this suit, which is an action of trespass for false imprisonment, was brought in the circuit court of the United States for the district of Missouri, by the plaintiff, as a "citizen" of that State, against the defendant, a "citizen" of the State of New York, who had purchased him and his family since the commencement of the suit in the State court.

The defendant denied, by plea in abatement, the jurisdiction of the circuit court of the United States, on the ground that the plaintiff "is a negro of African descent, his ancestors were of pure African blood, and were brought into this country and sold as slaves," and therefore the plaintiff "is not a citizen of the State of Missouri." To this plea the plaintiff demurred, and the court sustained the demurrer.

Thereupon the defendant pleaded over, and justified the trespass on the ground that the plaintiff and his family were his negro slaves; and a statement of facts, agreed to by both parties, was read in evidence, as follows: "In the year 1834, the plaintiff was a negro slave belonging

The Supreme Court decision of 1857, "a sophistical, muddy, and extreme Pro-Slavery document."

By the President of the United States of America

A Proclamation.

Whereas, on the twenty-second day of September, in the year of our Lord one thousand eight hundred and sixty-two, a proclamation was issued by the President of the United States, containing, among other things, the following, to wit:

"That on the first day of January, in the year of our Lord one thousand eight hundred and sixty-three, all persons held as slaves within any State or designated part of a State, the people whereof shall then be in rebellion against the United States, shall be then, thenceforward, and

THE PRAYER OF TWENTY MILLIONS

Horace Greeley, *New York Daily Tribune,* Aug. 20, 1862

To Abraham Lincoln, *President of the United States*:

Dear Sir: I do not intrude to tell you — for you must know already — that a great proportion of those who triumphed in your election, and of all who desire the unqualified suppression of the Rebellion now desolating our country, are sorely disappointed and deeply pained by the policy you seem to be pursuing with regard to the slaves of Rebels. I write only to set succinctly and unmistakably before you what we require, what we think we have a right to expect, and of what we complain.

I. We require of you, as the first servant of the Republic, charged especially and preëminently with this duty, that you EXECUTE THE LAWS. Most emphatically do we demand that such laws as have been recently enacted, which therefore may fairly be presumed to embody the *present* will and to be dictated by the *present* needs of the Republic, and which, after due consideration have received your personal sanction, shall by you be carried into full effect, and that you publicly and decisively instruct your subordinates that such laws exist, that they are binding on all functionaries and citizens, and that they are to be obeyed to the letter.

II. We think you are strangely and disastrously remiss in the discharge of your official and imperative duty with regard to the emancipating provisions of the new Confiscation Act. Those provisions were designed to fight Slavery with Liberty. They prescribe that men loyal to the Union, and willing to shed their blood in her behalf, shall no longer be held, with the Nation's consent, in bondage to persistent, malignant traitors, who for twenty years have been plotting and for sixteen months have been fighting to divide and destroy our country. Why these traitors should be treated with tenderness by you, to the prejudice of the dearest rights of loyal men, we cannot conceive.

III. We think you are unduly influenced by the counsels, the representations, the menaces, of certain fossil politicians hailing from the Border Slave States. Knowing well that the heartily, unconditionally loyal portion of the White citizens of those States do not expect nor desire that Slavery shall be upheld to the prejudice of the Union — (for the truth of which we appeal not only to every Republican residing in those States, but to such eminent loyalists as H. Winter Davis, Parson Brownlow, the Union Central Committee of Baltimore, and to *The Nashville Union*) — we ask you to consider that Slavery is everywhere the inciting cause and sustaining base of treason: the most slaveholding sections of Maryland and Delaware being this day, though under the Union flag, in full sympathy with the Rebellion, while the Free-Labor portions of Tennessee and of Texas, though writhing under the bloody heel of Treason, are unconquerably loyal to the Union. So emphatically is this the case, that a most intelligent Union banker of Baltimore recently avowed his confident belief that a majority of the present Legislature of Maryland, though elected as and still professing to be Unionists, are at heart desirous of the triumph of the Jeff. Davis conspiracy; and when asked how they could be won back to loyalty, replied — "Only by the complete Abolition of Slavery." It seems to us the most obvious truth, that whatever strengthens or fortifies Slavery in the Border States strengthens also Treason, and drives home the wedge intended to divide the Union. Had you from the first refused to recognize in those States, as here, any other than unconditional loyalty — that which stands for the Union, whatever may become of Slavery — those States would have been, and would be, far more helpful and less troublesome to the defenders of the Union than they have been, or now are.

IV. We think timid counsels in such a crisis calculated to prove perilous, and probably disastrous. It is the duty of a Government so wantonly, wickedly assailed by Rebellion as ours has been to oppose force to force in a defiant, dauntless spirit. It cannot afford to temporize with traitors nor with semi-traitors. It must not bribe them to behave themselves, nor make them fair promises in the hope of disarming their causeless hostility. Representing a brave and high-spirited people, it can afford to forfeit anything else better than its own self-respect, or their admiring confidence. For our Government even to seek, after war has been made on it, to dispel the affected apprehensions of armed traitors that their cherished privileges may be assailed by it, is to invite insult and encourage hopes of its own downfall. The rush to arms of Ohio, Indiana, Illinois, is the true answer at once to the Rebel raids of John Morgan and the traitorous sophistries of Beriah Magoffin.

V. We complain that the Union cause has suffered, and is now suffering immensely, from mistaken deference to Rebel Slavery. Had you, Sir, in your Inaugural Address, unmistakably given notice that, in case the Rebellion already commenced were persisted in, and your efforts to preserve the Union and enforce the laws should be resisted by armed force, *you would recognize no loyal person as rightfully held in Slavery by a traitor*, we believe the Rebellion would therein have received a staggering if not fatal blow. At that moment, according to the returns of the most recent elections, the Unionists were a large majority of the voters of the Slave States. But they were composed in good part of the aged, the feeble, the wealthy, the timid — the young, the reckless, the aspiring, the adventurous, had already been largely lured by the gamblers and negro-traders, the politicians by trade and the conspirators by instinct, into the toils of Treason. Had you then proclaimed that Rebellion would strike the shackles from the slaves of every traitor, the wealthy and the cautious would have been supplied with a powerful inducement to remain loyal. As it was, every coward in the South soon became a traitor from fear; for Loyalty was perilous, while treason seemed comparatively safe. Hence the boasted unanimity of the South — a unanimity based on Rebel terrorism and the fact that immunity and safety were found on that side, danger and probable death on ours. The Rebels from the first have been eager to confiscate, imprison, scourge and kill: we have fought wolves with the devices of sheep. The result is just what might have been expected. Tens of thousands are fighting in the Rebel ranks to-day whose original bias and natural leanings would have led them into ours.

VI. We complain that the Confiscation Act which

you approved is habitually disregarded by your Generals, and that no word of rebuke for them from you has yet reached the public ear. Fremont's Proclamation and Hunter's Order favoring Emancipation were promptly annulled by you; while Halleck's No. 3, forbidding fugitives from Slavery to Rebels to come within his lines — an order as unmilitary as inhuman, and which received the hearty approbation of every traitor in America — with scores of like tendency, have never provoked even your remonstrance. We complain that the officers of your Armies have habitually repelled rather than invited the approach of slaves who would have gladly taken the risks of escaping from their Rebel masters to our camps, bringing intelligence often of inestimable value to the Union cause. We complain that those who *have* thus escaped to us, avowing a willingness to do for us whatever might be required, have been brutally and madly repulsed, and often surrendered to be scourged, maimed and tortured by the ruffian traitors, who pretend to own them. We complain that a large proportion of our regular Army Officers, with many of the Volunteers, evince far more solicitude to uphold Slavery than to put down the Rebellion. And finally, we complain that you, Mr. President, elected as a Republican, knowing well what an abomination Slavery is, and how emphatically it is the core and essence of this atrocious Rebellion, seem never to interfere with these atrocities, and never give a direction to your Military subordinates, which does not appear to have been conceived in the interest of Slavery rather than of Freedom.

VII. Let me call your attention to the recent tragedy in New-Orleans, whereof the facts are obtained entirely through Pro-Slavery channels. A considerable body of resolute, able-bodied men, held in Slavery by two Rebel sugar-planters in defiance of the Confiscation Act which you have approved, left plantations thirty miles distant and made their way to the great mart of the South-West, which they knew to be in the undisputed possession of the Union forces. They made their way safely and quietly through thirty miles of Rebel territory, expecting to find freedom under the protection of our flag. Whether they had or had not heard of the passage of the Confiscation Act, they reasoned logically that we could not kill them for deserting the service of their lifelong oppressors, who had through treason become our implacable enemies. They came to us for liberty and protection, for which they were willing to render their best service: they met with hostility, captivity, and murder. The barking of the base curs of Slavery in this quarter deceives no one — not even themselves. They say, indeed, that the negroes had no right to appear in New-Orleans armed (with their implements of daily labor in the cane-field); but no one doubts that they would gladly have laid these down if assured that they should be free. They were set upon and maimed, captured and killed, because they sought the

---

FOLLOWING PAGES: Frank Leslie's Illustrated Newspaper *of 1857 and the* Chicago Defender *of 1945. "Neither the atom bomb or the hydrogen bomb will ever be as meaningful to our democracy as the unanimous declaration of the Supreme Court that racial segregation violates the spirit and the letter of our Constitution," the* Defender *wrote in 1954.*

FRANK LESLIE'S
ILLUSTRATED

NEWSPAPER

—VOL. IV.]   NEW YORK, SATURDAY, JUNE 27, 1857.   [

STS AND TRAVELLERS.

py to receive personal narratives,
ncluding adventures and incidents,
n who pleases to correspond with

opportunity of returning our thanks
as artistic correspondents through-
y, for the many sketches we are
ving from them of the news of the
they will spare no pains to furnish
gs of events as they may occur.
emind them that it is necessary to
, if possible, by the earliest convey-

DRED SCOTT—HIS FA-
NCIDENTS OF HIS LIFE
ON OF THE SUPREME

ling in the Fair grounds at
nd engaged in conversation
ainent citizen of that enter-
he suddenly asked us if we
ke to be introduced to Dred
expressing a desire to be thus
gentleman called to an old
as standing near by, and our
ratified. Dred made a rude
our recognition, and seemed
notice we expended upon
und him on examination to
looded African, perhaps fifty
with a shrewd, intelligent,
face, of rather light frame,
re than five feet six inches high.
xpressed a wish to get his portrait (we had made

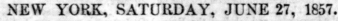

ELIZA AND LIZZIE, CHILDREN OF DRED SCOTT.

have it taken. T
explained to Dred
should have his li
illustrated paper o
ruled his many obj
to grow out of a su
he promised to be a
day. This appointm
Determined not to
an interview with
lawyer, who prompt
introduction, expla
was to his advanta
taken to be engrav
also directions whe
domicile. We foun
culty, the streets in
being more clearly d
the city than on t
finally reached a w
protected by a balco
description. Appro
saw a smart, tidy-lo
thirty years of age,
assistants, was busy
tion, "Is this whe
we received, rather
swer, "Yes." Upo
home, she said,

"What white r
for?—why don't w

efforts before, through correspondents, and failed), and
asked him if he would not go to Fitzgibbon's gallery and

own business, and let dat nigger 'lone f
steal dat nigger—dat are a fact."

WORLD'S GREATEST WEEKLY

Chicago Defender

NATIONAL EDITION

Vol. XLI, No. 18 — THIS PAPER CONSISTS OF TWO PARTS — PART ONE — CHICAGO, ILL., SATURDAY, AUGUST 18, 1945 — Price 10 Cents ★★

MINNESOTA HISTORICAL SOCIETY

NEGRO SCIENTISTS HELP PRODUCE 1ST ATOM BOMB

Halt Purge Of GIs In Combat Units

By EDWARD B. TOLES
(Defender War Correspondent)

RHEIMS, France — Purging of volunteer Negro infantrymen from combat units into kitchen and labor outfits was halted here this week.

Vigorous protests by the front-line Negro troops against being assigned to pots and pans brought a stop to the transfers.

Ranking army officers told encamped Negro soldiers at the Camp San Francisco reinforcement center near historic Chateau Thierry that they would remain combat troops. All further transfers to service outfits would be distinued, the assembled men were told.

No mention was made of what disposition would be made of volunteers already transferred to service units.

The latest action, coming on the heels of the atom bomb, the Russian war declaration, and the Japanese surrender offer, may still be changed with the new events, but it is thought, said one camp officer, that Negro infantrymen would be transferred to Negro combat engineer battalions now being redeployed through the States.

Three divisions with whom Negro infantrymen fought have already arrived in the States, the Negro members having been carefully withdrawn.

At Camp San Francisco, I talked with many of the 400 former infantrymen from the 1st, 2nd, and 99th divisions mixed among the 2,000 others, all having under 85 points, including combat artillerymen from the 333rd, 999th, 349th and 686th now awaiting assignment to service units.

Refusals to accept service duty and heated protests went all the way to supreme headquarters from Negro infantrymen, they told me at the two camps I visited.

Hit Jim Crow

"We volunteered from service units as a protest against Jim Crow and have demonstrated our abilities. Now we ask that we continue with the infantry units that we fought with up front. Even the white soldiers in these units couldn't understand why we left," said Sgt. Bruce Wright, Fordham law school graduate from New York whose Bronze Star with a Purple Heart cluster that glistened as he gestured meaningfully while we talked.

Said Sgt. Happy Peters of the 1st Division, 5335 South Parkway, Chicago: "I want to fight, not to labor."

How they came from their infantry division near Bamberge, Germany, with no knowledge of of what they were going to do and how long they had remained in a reinforcement depot was told to me by Sgt. Willie Noland, 6216 St. Lawrence avenue, Chicago, who said: "Even after an officer had told us that we still would remain combat troops, seven men were ordered assigned to a trucking company. When they refused to go, their assignments were cancelled and termed mistakes." They were Albert Hartzog, New York; Robert Mabry, Pittsburgh; Jay C.

See HALT PURGE, Page 6, Col. 1

Dustin' off the NEWS

By LUCIUS C. HARPER

THERE ARE SOME BILBOS AT WORK IN OUR ARMIES

THAT ALL the Bilbos are not confined principally to the U.S. Senate, nor are they isolated in Mississippi, but some of their ilk are safely tucked away in our military forces where they can crush our spirit and impede our progress without outside interference, is strikingly indicated in a personal letter to this column from 600 men of "D" Companies of the 17th, 56th and 66th Armored Infantry Battalion of the 12th Armored Division.

L. C. Harper

This group of heartbroken, spirit-crushed soldiers, who, having served their country bravely and conquered the enemy, fell victim to a greater enemy (race prejudice) operating so successfully within their own ranks and behind their backs. Here is how "military Bilboism" has wrecked the hopes and aspirations of our black heroes. Their case is not singular; it has become rather typical in the widespread Jim Crow system in our armed forces, fighting ironic-are six hundred of the several thousands of Negroes who volunally, for Democracy. Here it is:

Dear Mr. Harper:

We, of whom this letter concerns, teered to come to the infantry during the month of December 1944 (which is now history) and which was, indeed, one of the most disastrous months in American military annals. We who had long wanted to quit our trucks, shovels, winches, and numerous other labor battalions, for a rifle and a foxhole, were given the opportunity to satisfy the long cherished desire of almost every Negro soldier in service units: to actually fight for our country. Now, we know the army had no idea of the response they were to get from its most unorthodox offer of allowing Negro service troops to volunteer as infantry re-inforcements.

Gen. B. O. Davis, himself, spoke to us when we arrived at Noyon, France, for additional training be-

Open First Negro VFW Post In Dixie

BIRMINGHAM—(ANP) — Birmingham last week became the first southern city to legally establish a Negro post of the Veterans of Foreign Wars, Archie Williams, founder, announced.

The new post is named the Julius Ellsberry post, in honor of the Birmingham sailor who was the first citizen from Jefferson county to give his life for his country in World War II.

Joe Donaburg, state commander of the VFW, E. C. Spangerburg, state chaplain, and George D. Keiley, past commander, officially

TWO-FRONT PUPPY

Private Lloyd E. Berry of Chicago, Illinois (center) a member of the Quartermaster corps who recently arrived in the Pacific theatre directly from the Italian front, carries his unit's mascot, "AWOL." AWOL is claimed to be the first mascot to serve on both major fronts. As of this date no one has tallied AWOL's points, and he apparently isn't bothered by the oversight.

Jap Peace Brings Unemployment Threat For Millions Of Negroes

(Defender Washington Bureau)

WASHINGTON — Japan's offer to surrender this week gave Negro America the unemployment jitters.

The war's sudden end may be the beginning of the worst period of unemployment ever faced by Negro Americans, it was felt here among official circles.

Without a workable Fair Employment Practice Committee and with the coming cut-backs in industries, the cancellation of war contracts will especially be felt among Negroes in industrial centers such as Detroit, Chicago and Los Angeles.

While Washington officials conservatively predict that the nation's unemployment may exceed 6,000,000 in 30 days, no estimate as to the percentage of Negro layoffs has been attempted.

Shipbuilding Hit

However, the large number of Negro war workers in the shipbuilding industry will face the first mass layoffs in the nation.

The cancellation of $4,000,000,000 in war contracts by the army and navy, including $1,200,000,000 for 92 warships, has already displaced a huge number of Negro workers who were among the last to be employed in this industry.

In the shipbuilding industries, it is on the West Coast that Negroes who have migrated from South to furnish the war workers in plants from San Francisco to Los Angeles will suffer the greatest setbacks.

War Manpower officials on the West Coast are already urging that thousands of the war workers soon to leave shipyards and aircraft least fifty per cent of the white workers, however, have indicated they will return to their old homes in the Middle West, South and East.

Meanwhile added to the unemployment spectre is the development of racial tension which is expected to be increased when outbreaks reach their peak.

The San Francisco CIO Council reporter indications of mounting racial tensions and requested Edmund G. Brown, district attorney, and Robert W. Kenny, State attorney general, to investigate.

The council cited several instances of discrimination not only against Negroes, but against Chinese-Americans and Nisei. Officials here admit that wtih unemployment widespread, race discrimination may be expected to increase.

Much of the shock of sudden wholesale cutbacks have been softened in some of the shipyards in the San Francisco Bay area. Steps already taken switching the Bay area yards, where upwards of 40,-

See JAP PEACE, Page 6, Col. 2

Half Million Join In Bud Billiken Picnic

(See Photos on Page 15)

By ALBERT G. BARNETT

Conquering heroes of World War II came home from the far-flung battle fronts of the world Saturday, to receive the wild acclaim of more than a half-million people at the Chicago Defender Bud Billiken Club's 16th annual parade and picnic.

With more than 10,000 persons in the colorful pageant, marching to the tunes of a score or more bands; with 30 gaily-colored floats adding a touch of pomp to the three-mile procession—and with one float—a replica of the flag-raising on Iwo Jima, having six with countless thousands more leaning from window sills, from roof-tops, atop viaducts and waving and shouting from any vantage point that gave clear point of vision.

In the vanguard and sitting on top of an open coupe as he acknowledged the plaudits of the throng, was David W. Kellum, city editor of the Chicago Defender and nationally known as Bud Billiken, who was the general director of the Bud Billiken Club's 16th annual parade.

Crack Bands Feature Parade

In the line-of-march there were units of the U. S. Army including a detachment and band from Camp Ellis, Ill., the crack band from Great Lakes Naval Training Station, a battalion of soldiers from the Eighth Illinois Reserve Militia

Canadian Court Orders Hotel To End Jim Crow

Negro Couple, Barred From Dining Room, May Sue Hostelry

QUEBEC, Que.—Jim Crow crossed the border into Canada last week and was promptly bounced out again.

The Canadian courts ordered the Chateau Frontenac, famed Quebec hostelry, to allow Dr. George Dows Cannon, prominent New York physician, and his wife, complete access to all facilities in the hotel.

The Negro couple had previously been barred from the main dining room and bar of the well-known hotel.

Dr. Cannon registered on July 29, planning to vacation until Aug. 1 in Quebec, the only walled city in North America. On Aug. 1, however, he and his wife were denied entry into the dining room. The following day this restriction was extended to include the bar.

The doctor consulted a lawyer and applied for an injunction against the management. The citizens of Canada's seventh largest city watched with interest, for Canada is generally considered more racially democratic than her neighbor to the south.

An interlocutory injunction was granted Dr. Cannon Aug. 7. Hotel officials were ordered to serve the couple in the main dining room and to allow them complete access to all other parts of the hotel that are public.

The injunction was effective until 5 p.m., Thursday.

Dr. Cannon may also seek damages from the hotel, but whether legal proceedings have been instituted has not yet been revealed.

Chicago Major Takes Bar Exam In Italy

Maj. Raymond A. Watkins of Chicago, now serving as judge advocate of the 92nd division in Italy, took his Illinois Bar exam there with only an army manual for pre-examination cramming.

Maj. Watkins is a veteran of the old 8th Illinois National Guard, served with the 370th when war was declared and until it became part of the 92nd division.

Ph.D.'s For 2 At Iowa

IOWA CITY—(ANP)—At the summer convocation, Wednesday, the University of Iowa conferred the degree of doctor of philosophy upon two Negroes — Nick Aaron Ford, former professor of English at Langston university, and Milton Gordon Hardiman, professor of romance languages at Lincoln university, Mo.

MATH EXPERT

J. ERNEST WILKINS

Youthful math wizard who worked at the University of Chicago in developing the first atomic bomb. He won renown several years back when at the age of 19 he became the youngest Ph.D. in the nation.

Frauleins Meet Negro Troops—And Like 'Em

BERLIN—Fraulein is now fraternizing with the most non-Aryan race on earth.

And apparently she loves it.

When Georgia-born George Bass drove a six-ton quartermaster truck into Berlin this week a mild revolution took place among the Berlin blondes and ex-Nazi gigolos who stood about and stared.

"Schwarze Amerikaners" gasped the Berlin girls, which is German for "black Americans," and there was a pell mell rush to see if what the Fuehrer had said about Negroes was true or false.

Bass and his group of some dozen GIs strode into the Femina cabaret on the afternoon of Aug. 11, lined up at the bar and ordered "cocktails" — an innocuous pink drink without a trace of alcohol.

And soon on the old stamping grounds of Adolph Hitler they were dancing wth the prettiest and blondest barmaids and habitutes in the house.

The appearance of colored soldiers here has caused an unexpected sensation. Apparently the Berlin frauleins have forgotten all their Aryan inhibitions at the sight of the giant colored non-Aryans with their well-fitting uniforms and flashing smiles.

"He always was a favorite with the girls," said Mrs. John Leslie of Chicago, an aunt of Bass, who heard of the incident through a Chicago newspaper.

Aid Secret Experiment At Chicago

Many Negro [...] Get Jobs At [...] Atom Bomb [...]

By RICHARD D[...]

Crack Negro [...] helped produce [...] bomb that made [...] ask for peace.

Discovery of th[...] shattering atomic [...] speeded by Negro scie[...] ing full-time on the [...] of atomic power at the [...] of Chicago and Colum[...] sity, it was revealed [...] week.

At Chicago, a hand-p[...] of Negro physicists, c[...] mathematicians joined [...] key workers on the [...] billion dollar project [...]

Some indication of th[...] played was given at Ch[...] officials estimated that [...] of the project fifteen [...] the key scientific wo[...] Negroes.

At Columbia, Dr. [...] Knox, veteran researc[...] headed a group of Neg[...] who worked on the r[...] experiment.

Lists Scientists

While full details o[...] war secret are withhe[...] tary security, the Defe[...] ed the names of color[...] at Chicago who have [...] portant roles in dev[...] terrifying new weapon[...]

Checked with Univ[...] cials, the following h[...] on the atom project s[...] ginning:

Edward A. Russel[...] Moddie Taylor, chem[...] Delaney, chemist; Ben[...] chemist; J. Ernest Wilk[...] matician and Jasper [...] physicist.

It was research d[...] laboratories of Chicago [...] possible the construct[...] huge atomic bomb pl[...] Ridge, Tenn., and Richl[...] Wash., the War Depa[...] vealed.

In Washington, the [...] power Commission an[...] of War Information [...] that a large percentage [...] at the Oak Ridge plan[...] groes who had been re[...] many cities throughout [...] for secret work on th[...]

Work at Knoxville

It was learned that [...] Negroes held highly t[...] sitions in the vast plant [...] ville, Tenn. An exact [...] of work done by Neg[...]

See NEGRO, Page 6, C[...]

DOROTHY GREETS DISABLED VETS

benefit of that act of Congress which they may not specifically have heard of, but which was none the less the law of the land—which they had a clear *right* to the benefit of—which it was *somebody's* duty to publish far and wide, in order that so many as possible should be impelled to desist from serving Rebels and the Rebellion and come over to the side of the Union. They sought their Liberty in strict accordance with the law of the land — they were butchered or reënslaved for so doing by the help of Union soldiers enlisted to fight against Slaveholding Treason. It was *somebody's* fault that they were so murdered—if others shall hereafter suffer in like manner, in default of explicit and public direction to your generals that they are to recognize and obey the Confiscation Act, the world will lay the blame on *you*. Whether you will choose to hear it through future History and at the bar of God, I will not judge. I can only hope.

VIII. On the face of this wide earth, Mr. President, there is not one disinterested, determined, intelligent champion of the Union cause who does not feel that all attempts to put down the Rebellion and at the same time uphold its inciting cause are preposterous and futile—that the Rebellion, if crushed out tomorrow, would be renewed within a year if Slavery were left in full vigor — that Army officers who remain to this day devoted to Slavery can at best be but half-way loyal to the Union — and that every hour of deference to Slavery is an hour of added and deepened peril to the Union. I appeal to the testimony of your Embassadors in Europe. It is freely at your service, not at mine. Ask them to tell you candidly whether the seeming subserviency of your policy to the slaveholding, slavery-upholding interest, is not the perplexity, the despair of statesmen of all parties, and be admonished by the general answer!

IX. I close as I began with the statement that what an immense majority of the Loyal Millions of your countrymen require of you is a frank, declared, unqualified, ungrudging execution of the laws of the land, more especially of the Confiscation Act. That Act gives freedom to the slaves of Rebels coming within our lines, or whom those lines may at any time inclose—we ask you to render it due obedience by publicly requiring all your subordinates to recognize and obey it. The Rebels are everywhere using the late anti-negro riots in the North, as they have long used your officers' treatment of negroes in the South, to convince the slaves that they have nothing to hope from a Union success — that we mean in that case to sell them into a bitterer bondage to defray the cost of the war. Let them impress this as a truth on the great mass of their ignorant and credulous bondmen, and the Union will never be restored — never. We cannot conquer Ten Millions of People united in solid phalanx against us, powerfully aided by Northern sympathizers and European allies. We must have scouts, guides, spies, cooks, teamsters, diggers and choppers from the Blacks of the South, whether we allow them to fight for us or not, or we shall be baffled and repelled. As one of the millions who would gladly have avoided this struggle at any sacrifice but that of Principle and Honor, but who now feel that the triumph of the Union is indispensable not only to the existence of our country but to the well-being of mankind, I entreat you to render a hearty and unequivocal obedience to the law of the land.

Yours, Horace Greeley.

PRESIDENT LINCOLN'S LETTER

ABRAHAM LINCOLN, *New York Daily Tribune*, Aug. 25, 1862

Hon. Horace Greeley:

Dear Sir: I have just read yours of the 19th, addressed to myself through The N.Y. Tribune. If there be in it any statements or assumptions of fact which I may know to be erroneous, I do not now and here controvert them. If there be in it any inferences which I may believe to be falsely drawn, I do not now and here argue against them. If there be perceptible in it an impatient and dictatorial tone, I waive it in deference to an old friend, whose heart I have always supposed to be right.

As to the policy I "seem to be pursuing," as you say, I have not meant to leave any one in doubt.

I would save the Union. I would save it the shortest way under the Constitution. The sooner the National authority can be restored, the nearer the Union will be "the Union as it was." If there be those who would not save the Union unless they could at the same time *save* Slavery, I do not agree with them. If there be those who would not save the Union unless they could at the same time *destroy* Slavery, I do not agree with them. My paramount object in this struggle *is* to save the Union, and is *not* either to save or destroy Slavery. If I could save the Union without freeing *any* slave, I would do it; and if I could save it by freeing *all* the slaves, I would do it; and if I could do it by freeing some and leaving others alone, I would also do that. What I do about Slavery and the colored race, I do because I believe it helps to save this Union; and what I forbear, I forbear because I do *not* believe it would help

"Every hour of deference to Slavery is an hour of added and deepened peril to the Union," Horace Greeley wrote in "The Prayer of Twenty Millions."

to save the Union. I shall do *less* whenever I shall believe what I am doing hurts the cause, and I shall do *more* whenever I shall believe doing more will help the cause. I shall try to correct errors when shown to be errors; and I shall adopt new views so fast as they shall appear to be true views. I have here stated my purpose according to my view of *official* duty, and I intend no modification of my oft-expressed *personal* wish that all men, everywhere, could be free.

Yours, A. Lincoln.

MR. LINCOLN TO MR. GREELEY

The New York Times, Aug. 24, 1862

Mr. Lincoln to Mr. Greeley — The President's response to Mr. Greeley's public letter, addressed to him last week, is explicit enough, and settles one or two disputed points as to Mr. Lincoln's opinions and policy. His one and paramount object in the war is "to save the Union" — to save it with or without Slavery, under one set of circumstances or another, or by one agency or another, but at all events to save it somehow. His simple platform is "The salvation of the Union." To this end his whole policy looks, and whatever he does or fails to do is with reference to its bearings upon this one great point. He could not have said anything more satisfactory to the country in general.

The letter, like all Mr. Lincoln's literary attempts, exhibits the peculiarities of his mind and style; but the logical sequence and precision, and the grammatical accuracy of this, is greatly in advance of any previous effort. It is in infinitely better taste, too, than the rude epistle to which it is an answer. ❧

THEIR BEST WAY TO SHOW LOYALTY

The San Francisco News, March 6, 1942

Japanese leaders in California who are counseling their people, both aliens and native-born, to co-operate with the Army in carrying out the evacuation plans, are in effect, offering the best possible way for all Japanese to demonstrate their loyalty to the United States.

Many aliens and practically all the native-born have been protesting their allegiance to this Government. Although their removal to inland districts outside the military zones may inconvenience them somewhat, even work serious hardships upon some, they must certainly recognize the necessity of clearing the coastal combat areas of all possible fifth columnists and saboteurs. Inasmuch as the presence of enemy agents cannot be detected readily when these areas are thronged by Japanese the only course left is to remove all persons of that race for the duration of the war.

That is a clear-cut policy easily understood. Its execution should be supported by all citizens of whatever racial background, but especially it presents an opportunity to the people of an enemy race to prove their spirit of co-operation and keep their relations with the rest of the population of this country on the firm ground of friendship.

Every indication has been given that the transfer will be made with the least possible hardship. General DeWitt's order was issued in such a way as to give those who can make private moving arrangements plenty of time to do so. All others will not be moved until arrangements can be made for places for them to go. They may have to be housed in temporary quarters until permanent ones can be provided for them, but during the summer months that does not mean they will be unduly uncomfortable.

Their property will be carefully protected by the Federal Government, their food and shelter will be provided to the extent they are not able to provide it for themselves, and they will be furnished plenty of entertainment and recreation. That is not according to the pattern of the European concentration camp by any means.

Real danger would exist for all Japanese if they remained in the combat area. The least act of sabotage might provoke angry reprisals that easily could balloon into bloody race riots.

We must avoid all chance of that sort of thing. The most sensible, the most humane way to insure against it is to move the Japanese out of harm's way and make it as easy as possible for them to go and to remain away until the war is over. ❧

Japanese-Americans en route to an internment camp. "The only course left is to remove all persons of that race for the duration of the war," said The San Francisco News.

OVERPLAYING THEIR HANDS

Jimmy Ward, *Jackson Daily News*, May 24, 1961

THERE IS A DEEP LYING SUSPICION now that there is far more to the deliberately provoked agitation in Alabama than just the immediate spectacle of the "freedom rider" puppets.

And presence of United States Marshals to protect the announced law-breaking, pre-arranged, outright flaunting of constituted authority by a chosen group, lends even more credence to the belief that the federal government not only gave their blessing, but actually encouraged this outrage.

This, coupled with the bitter struggle of integrationists and political opportunists in Congress who are desperately trying in every conceivable way to make the federal school aid bill a downright blackmail against the South.

Unless the South agrees to prostitute its school system to government-enforced integration, then there will be no federal aid to schools.

The determined opposition to such a dictatorial pressure has caused those proponents of such despicable political maneuvering to attempt anything including their financial blessing and pledge of federal protection for such notoriety as that gained by the "freedom riders."

Thus far, the national indignation now being expressed over the Alabama incidents has been just what these political opportunists have wanted to show that the South is what they have called it all the time in their ranting and raving.

However, some of the more curious aspects of this scandalous performance, which had national attention days before it was carried off, have now begun to appear to the more level-headed and law-minded public: The usurpation of state and local authority by federal marshals, with the not-so-hidden threat of further domination by alerted federal troops; the continued pronouncement that these riot-inciting professionals would have complete federal government protection; the quick and hysterically loud support by the usual subversive law-hating elements.

Even some of the national TV commentators who have been so prone to gleefully kick at the South and slant their comments to favor the agitators are now wondering.

Others are wondering too, and we not only venture to say, but definitely predict that instead of the questionable condemnation of the South so calculatedly expected by these power-grabbing elements, the very opposite will ensue.

If such outlawry is to be condoned and supported by the federal government, then there be no need for the FBI, federal courts or state law enforcement agencies since any subversive element may violate the law under the guise of being discriminated against. ⮞

OPPOSITE: *A hospitalized freedom rider who was beaten at a bus terminal in Montgomery, Ala.*
"These people are crackpots," Jackson Daily News *editor Jimmy Ward said.*

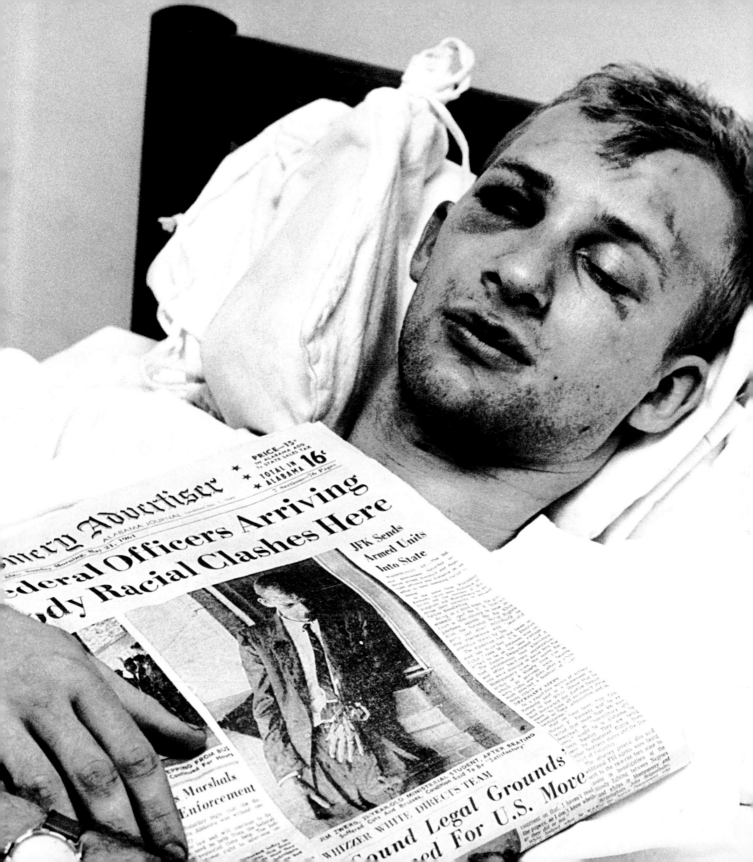

ARREST OF BOMBING VICTIM IS GRAVE DISSERVICE

Hazel Brannon Smith, *Lexington* (Miss.) *Advertiser,* May 16, 1963

It is not moral or just that any man should live in fear, or be compelled to sleep with a loaded gun by his bedside.

Holmes County Deputy Sheriff Andrew P. Smith's action in arresting a 58 year old Negro farmer, Hartman Turnbow, for fire bombing his own home, has come as a numbing shock to the people of Holmes County.

It is a grave disservice to our county and all our people in these days of increasing racial tension and strife.

White and Negro citizens of Holmes County alike simply could not believe that something like this could happen in our county, that a man and his wife and 16-year-old daughter could be routed from sleep in the small hours of the morning and be forced to flee their home literally in terror, only to be shot at by intruders outside — then to have the head of the family jailed the same day for doing the dastardly deed by an officer sworn to uphold the law and protect all citizens.

The only evidence presented against the aged Negro man at the preliminary hearing was testimony given by Deputy Smith and that was only an account of the bombing and shooting incident, as reported by Turnbow, to him. Mr. Smith added his own opinions and suppositions, as did County Attorney Pat M. Barrett, who prosecuted the case. As a result the man was bound over under $500 bond for action by the Holmes County Grand Jury in October.

Mr. Barrett, who said he was "not a demolition expert" nevertheless told the Court that "it just couldn't have happened. There is no way on God's earth for that situation over there to have happened like he said it happened."

Four other Negroes, who had been arrested the same day in connection with the same case, were released for lack of evidence. Not one shred of evidence was presented against them. But they had been held in jail five days and five nights.

This kind of conduct on the part of our highest elected peace officer has done serious injury to relations between the races in Holmes County — where we must be able to live in peace and harmony, or not live at all.

It is distressing that no statement has come from Mr. Smith saying that he is continuing his investigation. Perhaps he is. We hope so.

But irreparable damage has been done, and let no one doubt it.

We have always taken pride in being able to manage our affairs ourselves. When we become derelict in our duty and do not faithfully execute our obligations, we may rest assured it will be done for us.

FBI agents and U.S. Justice officials have already made an exhaustive investigation of this bombing and shooting incident.

A suit has already been filed against Deputy Smith, Mr. Barrett and the District Attorney, stating these Negroes were arrested "on false and baseless charges," which were in effect an effort to coerce and intimidate Negro citizens of Holmes County and get them to cease voter registration activity.

The Federal suit asks for a permanent injunction to prohibit these officers from interfering with voter registration activities, including the prosecution of the charges now filed against Turnbow, who attempted to register to vote here April 9, and Robert Moses, director of SNCC, a voter registration project.

This kind of situation would never have come about in Holmes County if we had honestly discharged our duties and obligations as citizens in the past; if we had demanded that all citizens be accorded equal treatment and protection under the law. This we have not done.

But if we think the present situation is serious, as indeed it is, we should take a long, hard look at the future.

It can, and probably will, get infinitely worse — unless we have the necessary character and guts to do something about it — and change the things that need to be changed. ❧

A NEGRO GOLF CLUB

WILLIAM ALLEN WHITE, *The Emporia Daily Gazette*, July 28, 1922

At Westfield, N.J., a negro golf club has been established and a 9-hole course laid out. A negro colony there seems to warrant the golf course. The item that this course is laid out will cause a million giggles to sizzle across the country. Cartoonists will make funny pictures of it. Vaudeville artists will do sketches about it. Something exquisitely funny seems to excite the white race when it sees the colored race doing things which are ordinary parts of the day's work and play to the white people. It is as though the elephant should drive an auto, or a horse play the piano.

The reason for this risibility of the white man at the black man's human activities is obvious and it is no credit to the white man. He thinks it is funny to see the black man doing things that normal human beings do, because the white man does not think of his dark-skinned fellow traveler on the planet as a human companion. The white man considers any colored man — black, brown, red, yellow or maroon — as an animal. The anthropological conceit of the white man is ponderous, unbelievable, vastly amusing to the gods. Why should not the black man play golf if his economic status gives him leisure for golf? Why should he not have a motor car and a country house if he can afford it? Why giggle at the normal activities of men whose skin differs from our own?

Something of the same psychological reason is behind the fact that we middle-class people make merry over the fact that the worker in the mines and shops and furnaces wears a silk shirt or rents a house with a bath or rides to work in a car. Why shouldn't he? Is he an elephant doing stunts? Is he a horse playing the piano? What's the joke if he develops the same desires and aspirations that we do, and who in God's name are we, anyway? ❧

Civil rights marchers in Memphis. Of the 11 Pulitzer Prizes for editorial writing awarded between 1957 and 1967, seven were awarded for civil rights editorials written by Southern editors.

William Jennings Bryan on the campaign trail. William Allen White's editorial "What's the Matter With Kansas?" played a role in Bryan's losing run for president against William McKinley in 1896.

CHAPTER FIVE

POLITICS

"WHAT'S THE MATTER WITH KANSAS?"

WILLIAM ALLEN WHITE HAD THE ANSWER. ❧ IN 1896, POPULISM WAS GAINING A HOLD IN THE COUNTRY, AND WILLIAM ALLEN WHITE WANTED NONE OF IT. SURE OF HIMSELF AND FULL OF HIMSELF, THE YOUNG EDITOR VIEWED POVERTY AS A SIGN OF LAZINESS, THOUGHT CAPITAL FAR MORE IMPORTANT THAN LABOR, AND HAD NOT AN OUNCE OF SYMPATHY FOR THE UNLUCKY OR THE UNSCHOOLED OR THE UNSUCCESSFUL. ❧ THOSE WERE AMONG THE PEOPLE, THE common men, who were for Democrat William Jennings Bryan in the presidential campaign against Republican William McKinley. Bryan urged the free coinage of silver to increase the supply of money to help the common man, and he criss-crossed the country giving a speech that ended: "Having behind us the producing masses of this nation and the world, supported by the commercial interests, the laboring interests, and the toilers everywhere, we will answer their demand for a gold standard by saying to them: You shall not press down upon the brow of labor this crown of thorns, you shall not crucify mankind upon a cross of gold."

It was a powerful message, and it attracted lots of folks in Emporia. One afternoon, as the immaculately dressed White headed back from the post office, "a crowd of Populists tackled me," White recalled in his autobiography. "They surrounded me. They were older men — men in their forties and fifties and sixties — and I was twenty-eight. They were shabbily dressed, ... They were struggling with poverty and I was rather spick-and-span, particularly offensive in the gaudy neckties for which I have had an unfortunate weakness. Anyway, they ganged me — hooting, jeering, nagging me about some editorial utterances I had made. I was froggy in the meadow and couldn't get out, and they were taking a little stick and poking me about. And my wrath must have flamed through my face. Finally I broke through the cordon and stalked, as well as a fat man who toddles can stalk, down the street to the office … and sat down to write for Monday's paper an editorial, and I headed it, 'What's the Matter With Kansas?' And … it came out pure vitriol."

Vitriol and sarcasm. It was a paean to capital, an insult to populists.

"Oh, this is a state to be proud of! We are a people who can hold up our heads. What we need here is less money, less capital, fewer white shirts and brains, fewer men with business judgment, and more of these fellows who boast that they are 'just ordinary old clodhoppers, but that they know more in a minute about finance than John Sherman'; We need more men … who hate prosperity, and who think that because a man believes in national honor, that he is a tool of Wall street. We have had a few of them; some 150,000   but we need more."

The editorial caused a sensation. It was reprinted widely, and the McKinley campaign spread more than a million copies of it hither and yon in its winning effort. (Bryan carried Kansas, and the Democrats, derided by White, carried

OPPOSITE: *Dodge City, Kan., peacekeepers in 1890.*

WILLIAM J. BRYAN.
Compliments of The New York Journal

The Nebraska Democrat's populist message helped him win the state of Kansas in the 1896 presidential campaign.

could never swell up," his wife said around that time. "He has already swelled beyond the dimensions of any ordinary fame."

(Henry Watterson also opposed Bryan. Watterson was in Switzerland during much of that 1896 campaign, but he sent a telegram to his partner — a telegram *The Courier-Journal* printed — that said: "Another ticket our only hope. No compromise with dishonor. Stand firm." The firm stance alienated many readers and almost broke the newspaper.)

White ultimately changed his mind about politics, about capital and about labor, a change whose seed was planted not long afterward when he first met and listened to Theodore Roosevelt.

"Perhaps if I had known the real significance of that election, perhaps if I had realized that it was the beginning of a long fight for distributive justice, the opening of a campaign to bring to the common man — the man lacking the acquisitive virtues, the man of one talent — a larger and more equitable share in the common wealth of our country, I should have been more consciously ashamed of my political attitude than I was," he wrote toward the end of his life.

Yet his ego wouldn't concede. All those years he kept framed above his desk a note from the speaker of the House of Representatives that said: "I haven't seen as much sense in one column in a dozen years."

Editors, it seems, save most of their vitriol for politicians — perhaps because there's a fine line between the two trades. The politician and the editor both profess to know what's best for the people. The politician and the editor both prosper on

Kansas state offices.) When McKinley was elected, the political boss Mark Hanna offered White anything he wanted. What did he want?

"Nothing, absolutely nothing. You couldn't give me an office if you wanted to, and I guess you do," the young editor replied. Hanna then sent him off to see the president-elect with a note that said, "He wants no office!"

White loved the fame, but he was as uncorruptible as he was — then — fat and egotistical.

"No matter how important Will gets to be, he

approval of the people. The politician and the editor both are men — and, these days, women — of no little ego. The politician and the editor — though the editor would deny it — both want to be loved.

But same or different, the editor and the politician pull no punches with each other in their love-hate relationships. In the 1840s, when John Tyler was president, Walt Whitman wrote an editorial in the *Aurora* that began: "Let no one be surprised when we utter our opinion that the high functionaries and chief officers of the American government, just now, are less distinguished for abilities than any executive or any cabinet the city of Washington ever held in its limits before. We imagine there are very few intelligent men who will not agree with us in this."

In 1884, *The* (New York) *World* assailed Republican presidential candidate James Blaine and the rich contributors who dined with him one evening at Delmonico's.

"It was a Feast of Fraud," the *World* wrote. "It meant danger to the Republic. Unless rebuked by the people it will mean death to the liberties of the people. Death to real republican government. Death to honor and integrity in public life. Death to confidence and honesty in business and private life. Death to the real protection of Labor from the insolent tyranny of Capital. Death to the Republic itself eventually!

"Shall Jay Gould rule this country? Shall he own the President? Is not his power too dangerous already?"

And in 1979, *The Louisville* (Ky.) *Times* had had it with Mayor William Stansbury and his "bumbling leadership." Noting he had lost the support of his own party, the *Times* wrote an editorial that ended: "He has worn out his welcome with everyone. His party wants him to go. The city's elected legislature wants him to go. According to the *Times'* recent poll, the public wants him to go. So git."

Nothing, though, can compare with the vitriol or passion — one man's vitriol is another's passion — that spewed forth from Grover Cleveland Hall in 1927. Hall had been editor of *The Montgomery* (Ala.) *Advertiser* for about a year when a black man was beaten by the Ku Klux Klan. With courage and passion, he wrote editorials attacking racial and religious intolerance in general, and the politically powerful Klan in particular.

"The fiery cross is not a permanent source of heat," he wrote. "It will burn out." And: "There are now but two classes of people in Alabama — those who condone flogging by masked cowards, and those who condemn such outrages."

Hall won the Pulitzer Prize for his editorials against gangsterism, floggings, and racial and religious intolerance. But he saved his most fierce, most sarcastic, most biting words for U.S. Sen. Tom Heflin, "a bully by nature, a mountebank by instinct," "a preposterous blob" and — apparently the reason for the editorial — a religious bigot. The editorial, "Our Tom," is a classic of vitriol — or passion.

No editorial passion could ever match the political passion on the floor of the U.S. Senate in May of 1856. Inflamed by the fight over slavery, Sen. Charles Sumner of Massachusetts gave a scalding speech, singling out the absent Sen. Andrew Butler of South Carolina. ("The Senator touches nothing which he does not disfigure — with error, sometimes of principle, sometimes of fact. He shows an incapacity of accuracy. ... He cannot open his mouth, but out there flies a blunder.")

After the speech, a relative of the senator, a congressman named Preston Brooks, viciously beat Sumner with a cane on the Senate floor. "It was expressly to avoid taking life that I used an ordinary cane," Brooks said. It took Sumner more than three years to recover. The uncontrite Brooks resigned. While *The New York Times* editorialized that "a more infamous crime has never been perpetrated even in Washington" (the "even in Washington" seems a nice touch), Brooks was defended in the South.

The relationship between editors and politicians is complicated by so-called endorsement editorials. Editors have the time to explore platforms, to interview candidates and to study issues, and many then tell readers whom they favor, and why — using their own editorial philosophies as the yardsticks. Usually, the endorsements are straightforward. Sometimes, though, the reasoning is tortured.

After calling Walter Mondale a wimp who was too closely tied to labor and who had an unqualified congresswoman as a running mate, the *Chicago Tribune* in 1984 then ticked off a series of complaints against incumbent Ronald Reagan: He was threatening to bankrupt America; he was ignorant about the Soviet Union and used "air-headed rhetoric" in talking about foreign affairs. He was a "cue-card President," and he was so insensitive to First Amendment rights that an endorsement of him would be a "bitter pill for any newspaper to swallow." It then endorsed him.

And in 1988, the *Courier-Journal* was none too happy with incumbent U.S. Rep. Carroll Hubbard.

"Yes, Rep. Hubbard would soon be forgotten if it weren't for the congressional franking privilege, which enables him to fill his constituents' mailboxes with seed catalogues, calendars and congratulatory notes," editor David Hawpe wrote. "And, yes, his voting record in Congress shows little sign of independence — of a willingness to rise above the perceived prejudices of his constituents, the blandishments of well heeled lobbyists, or the wishes of the House Democratic leadership. But his opponent is Lacey Smith. Therefore, we endorse Carroll Hubbard."

The Des Moines Register continued to endorse one politician after he lost. "Best Man Lost," was the headline on a 1978 editorial bemoaning the victory of Senate candidate Roger Jepsen over incumbent Dick Clark. It repeated a bill of particulars against him, making the paper look — in the eyes of the publisher — like a "sore loser."

The situation was compounded a few days later when the senator-elect told the newspaper's editor, "I haven't yet met a person who voted against me." The editor shook his hand and said, "Then, let me be the first."

H.L. Mencken was equally as unsubtle in 1938, when, fed up with Franklin Roosevelt and the growing government, he ran what looked to readers like an almost blank editorial page in *The* (Baltimore) *Evening Sun.* In fact, as a short editorial next to the blank space explained, the space was filled with just over a million tiny dots, each representing one federal jobholder — "a graphic representation of the Federal Government's immense corps of jobholders."

The *Keene* (N.H.) *Sentinel* didn't even bother to put dots in the white space that ran after its editorial, "A Dry Brow": "We thought about publishing an editorial today concerning Japanese Prime Minister Kiichi Miyazawa's outrageous remark that Americans 'lack a work ethic . . . to live by the sweat of their brow.' But we decided to knock off early and watch a little TV."

But, just as in wartime, editors put aside partisanship in times of political crises.

In 1868, when President Andrew Johnson was impeached — but, ultimately, not convicted — *The New York Times* editorialized about calmness and fairness, not right and wrong. Noting that everyday life was going on in its everyday fashion, the *Times* said:

> "Why is this? What is the cause of all this repose? It is not indifference, for everybody is deeply interested. The dignity of the nation is at stake, and all feel that a great event is at hand which is pregnant with serious consequences, for good or evil, in regard to which passion is folly. All patriotic people, of all parties, feel that republican institutions are on trial, — that we cannot afford to make a great political blunder, or institute dangerous precedents; nor are people prepared to accept either a Mexico or a revolutionary France. The eyes of the whole world are upon us, and posterity will sift the matter with impartial scrutiny."

Similarly, when President Richard Nixon resigned in 1974 to avoid impeachment, the *St. Petersburg Times* wrote: "Our country's political institutions are stronger than ever. 'Separation of powers' and 'checks and balances' are not academic concepts to the Watergate generation. We have taken the Constitution out of the attic, dusted it off, and seen it work majestically. Our political system faced its severest test — a president who abused the vast power and prestige of this office to deceive the people and to violate the law — and emerged with renewed strength."

Leave the last word, again, to William Allen White, the man who changed his mind more than once after taking a political stand.

In 1910, he editorialized that "of all the fool things under the sun, talk of a third party in this country, or in any state in this country, is the foolest thing." Two years later, he was supporting the third-party presidential bid of Theodore Roosevelt. Similarly, he changed his mind after "What's the Matter With Kansas?," probably the most influential political editorial in American history.

Years later, looking back at some of his editorials and at how he changed his mind, he wrote: "An editor who can re-read his daily work with pride and satisfaction must be a sad spectacle; either too stupid to think and write frankly or too proud to admit he was wrong. . . . News is a chameleon. What seems red to-day may look green to-morrow and turn blue next week. And it's the editorial writer's job to keep his eyes on the changeling and do the best he can with it. At the end he can be proud if he was honest according to his lights, brave without being cruel, and as wise as a man may be who peeps at the world through a crack in the door." ꙮ

WHAT'S THE MATTER WITH KANSAS?

William Allen White, *The Emporia Daily Gazette*, Aug. 15, 1896

Today the Kansas department of agriculture sent out a statement which indicates that Kansas has gained less than 2,000 people in the past year. There are about 125,000 families in the state and there were about 10,000 babies born in Kansas, and yet so many people have left the state that the natural increase is cut down to less than 2,000 net.

This has been going on for eight years.

If there had been a high brick wall around the state eight years ago and not a soul had been admitted or permitted to leave, Kansas would be half a million souls better off than she is today. And yet the nation has increased in population. In five years ten million people have been added to the national population, yet instead of gaining a share of this — say half a million — Kansas has apparently been a plague spot, and in the very garden of the world, has lost population by the ten thousands every year.

Not only has she lost population, but she has lost wealth. Every moneyed man in the state who could get out without great loss has gone. Every month in every community sees someone who has a little money pick up and leave the state. This has been going on for eight years. Money is being drained out all the time. In towns where ten years ago there were three or four or half a dozen money lending concerns stimulating industry by furnishing capital there is now none or one or two

Kansas students and teachers during the 19th century stand in front of the last sod schoolhouse in the country.

that are looking after the interest and principal already out standing.

No one brings any money into Kansas any more. What community knows over one or two men who have moved in with more than $5,000 in the past three years. And what community cannot count half a score of men in that time who have left, taking all the money they could scrape together.

Yet the nation has grown rich. Other states have increased in population and wealth — other neighboring states. Missouri has gained nearly two million while Kansas has been losing a half a million. Nebraska has gained in wealth and in population while Kansas has gone downhill. Colorado has gained in every way while Kansas has lost in every way since 1888.

What is the matter with Kansas?

There is no substantial city in the state. Every big town save one has lost in population. Yet Kansas City, Omaha, Lincoln, St. Louis, Denver, Colorado Springs, Sedalia, Des Moines, the cities of the Dakotas, St. Paul and Minneapolis — all cities and towns in the West, have steadily grown.

Take up the Government Blue Book and you will see that Kansas is virtually off the map. Two or three little scrubby consular places in yellow fever stricken communities that do not aggregate $10,000 a year, is all the recognition Kansas has Nebraska draws about $100,000; little old North Dakota draws about $50,000; Oklahoma doubles Kansas; Missouri leaves her a thousand miles behind; Colorado is almost seven times greater than Kansas — the whole West is ahead of Kansas.

Take it by any standard you please, Kansas is not in it. Go east and you hear them laugh at Kansas, go west and they sneer at her, go south and they "cuss" her, go north and they have forgotten her. Go into any crowd of intelligent people gathered anywhere on the globe and you will find the Kansas man on the defensive. The newspaper columns and magazine pages once devoted to praise of the state, to boastful facts and startling figures concerning her resources, now are filled with cartoons, jibes and Pefferian speeches. Kansas just naturally isn't in the civilized world. She has traded places with Arkansas and Timbuctoo.

What's the matter with Kansas?

We all know; yet here we are at it again. We have an old moss-back Jacksonian who snorts and howls because there is a bath-tub in the State house; we are running that old jay for governor. We have another shabby, wild-eyed, rattle-brained fanatic who has said openly in a dozen speeches that "the rights of the user are paramount to the rights of the owner;" we are running him for chief justice, so that capital will come tumbling over itself to get into the state. We have raked the ash heap of human failure in the state and have found an old hoop skirt of a man who has failed as a business man, who has failed as an editor, who has failed as a preacher, and we are going to run him for congressman-at-large. He will help the looks of the Kansas delegation in Washington. Then we have discovered a kid without a law practice, and have decided to vote for him as attorney general. Then for fear some hint that the state had become respectable might percolate through the civilized portions of the nation, we have decided to send three or four harpies out lecturing, telling the people that Kansas is raising hell and letting corn go to weeds.

Oh, this is a state to be proud of! We are a people

who can hold up our heads. What we need here is less money, less capital, fewer white shirts and brains, fewer men with business judgment, and more of these fellows who boast that they are "just ordinary old clodhoppers, but that they know more in a minute about finance than John Sherman"; we need more men who are "posted," who can bellow about the crime of '73, who hate prosperity, and who think that because a man believes in national honor, that he is a tool of Wall street. We have had a few of them; some 150,000 — but we want more. We need several thousand gibbering idiots to scream about the "Great Red Dragon" of Lombard street. We don't need population, we don't need wealth, we don't need well dressed men on the streets; we don't need standing in the nation; we don't need cities on these fertile prairies; you bet we don't! What we are after is the money power. Because we have become poorer and ornerier and meaner than a spavined, distempered mule, we, the people of Kansas, propose to kick; we don't care to build up, we wish to tear down.

"There are two ideas of government," said our noble Bryan at Chicago. "There are those who believe that if you just legislate to make the well-to-do prosperous this prosperity will leak through on those below. The Democratic idea has been that if you legislate to make the masses prosperous their prosperity will find its way up and through every class and rest upon us."

That's the stuff. Give the prosperous man the dickens. Legislate the thriftless into ease, whack the stuffing out of the creditors, and tell debtors who borrowed money five years ago when the money in circulation was greater than it is now, that the con- traction of the currency gives him a right to repudiate.

Whoop it up for the ragged trousers; put the lazy, greasy fizzle, who can't pay his debts, on an altar, and bow down and worship him. Let the state ideal be high. What we need is not the respect of our fellow men, but a chance to get something for nothing.

Oh yes, Kansas is a great state. Here are people fleeing from it by the score every day, capital going out of the state by the hundreds of dollars; and every industry except farming paralyzed; and that crippled because its products have to go across the ocean before they can find a laboring man at work who can afford to buy them. Let's don't stop this year. Let's drive all the decent, self respecting men out of the state. Let's keep the old clodhoppers who know it all. Let's encourage the man who is "posted." He can talk, and what we need is not mill hands to eat our meat, nor factory hands to eat our wheat, nor cities to oppress the farmer by consuming his butter and eggs and chickens and produce; what Kansas needs is men who can talk, who have large leisure to argue the currency question while their wives wait at home for that nickel's worth of bluing.

What's the matter with Kansas?

Nothing under the shining sun. She is losing wealth, population and standing. She has got her statesmen and the money power is afraid of her. Kansas is all right. She has started in to raise hell as Mrs. Lease advised and she seems to have an over production. But that doesn't matter. Kansas never did believe in diversified crops. Kansas is all right. There is absolutely nothing wrong with Kansas. "Every prospect pleases and only man is vile." ❧

OPPOSITE: *Immigrants traveling through Kansas in the 1800s.*

OUR TOM

GROVER CLEVELAND HALL, *The Montgomery (Ala.) Advertiser*, Aug. 19, 1927

Sen. Tom Heflin. "A bully by nature, a mountebank by instinct."

I. BECAUSE WE HAVE NO MEANS OF OUR OWN OF KNOWING positively whether Heflin is sane or insane, and because we believe it to be in the public interest to clear up the doubt once and for all, we hereby make the following proposition to him:

Heflin shall agree to undergo an examination to determine whether he is rational, the examination to be conducted by a commission of three accred-ited psychiatrists, one of whom shall be nominated by The Advertiser, one by Dr. William Dempsey Partlow of Tuscaloosa, and one by Heflin, all nominations to be subject to review by the board of governors of the American Psychiatric Association, to determine the qualifications of the nominees.

If this commission reports against Heflin he must pledge himself to make no speeches any more forever; if, however, it should report in his favor, The Advertiser pledges itself here and now to support him for re-election against any man whom the Pope may decide to run against him next time.

Heflin may retort that he is also in doubt whether we are sane and that the proposition should provide for a lunacy commission to examine the writer of this editorial. We should not object to this, but we do not anticipate that Tom will question our sanity. Tom will no doubt admit that we are sane, as sanity goes, but that we are wanting in honor, decency and elemental morality. Very well, we agree here and now, if it will make Tom feel any better as he consents to take the witness chair, to have our morals put to the same test that we propose for his sanity. Sauce for the goose is sauce for the gander.

As we say, we do not know whether Tom is out of his head, or whether he is merely a simpleton. He is one or the other. In proof of the justice of this judgment we cite his Abbeville address delivered Wednesday, a liberal synopsis of which was published in The Advertiser yesterday. This is one of the most astounding speeches ever delivered by a responsible public man; yet it is characteristic of Heflin and shows him at his best, or worst, according to your point of view. It is appalling to realize that Alabama is partially dependent upon such a shameless man to uphold its dignity in the United States Senate.

II. Heflin spoke entirely without restraint at Abbeville. He spewed his filthy lava on Roman Catholics, insulting them by questioning their honor and patriotism. He repeated an anonymous tale from Missouri about Catholics tearing the American flag from the body of a dead soldier of the Catholic faith. This is an insult to every gold-star Catholic mother in the republic. What a monstrous thing it is to do for Heflin to attack the patriotism shown by American Catholics in the wars fought since Heflin became a mature man when in that period he has escaped military service in every war fought by his country!

Heflin made his usual attack on the press. Of the editor of the Wiregrass Farmer at Headland, Henry county, Heflin said he was a "hickory-nut headed little editor" — all because this fearless newspaper man had written an uncomplimentary editorial about Tom. Nevertheless, the editor of The Wiregrass Farmer is a gentleman of splendid intellectual attainments, fine moral courage, and would make a far more creditable United States Senator than his insulter.

Of the Hanson newspapers, Heflin said they had persistently suppressed news of the Catholic conspiracy to assassinate him. This is absurd, of course. The Advertiser never hears of any threats to Kill Tom until Tom makes a speech, in which case we faithfully chronicle the depressing tale. Witness Atticus Mullin's report of the Henry county speech as published yesterday. But we have never taken Tom's scares seriously, nor does anybody else. However, we want Tom to feel that he is safe in the land that he has saved from ruin so many times, and so if he will agree to it we will employ a body guard from among the inmates of the Woman's Home to accompany him and shoo the Jesuits off with a broom.

III. Tom continued by saying the "money from New York" was used to buy the three newspapers owned by Victor Hanson, saying in another place that "the money of the interests" bought these papers. This is a lie out of the whole cloth. There is no mystery about the ownership of these papers. The names of shareholders and bondholders are published twice a year in compliance with Federal law. Mr. Hanson owns a large majority of the shares in his papers. He is a man of ample means, all of which he earned here in Alabama. If he wants a loan he floats it with an Alabama banker and pays the usual rate of interest. Tom knows this or should know it, but he prefers to bear false witness about it.

Tom says that he single-handed and alone kept the United States out of war with Mexico, in spite of the Knights of Columbus. The only patriot in Congress! The other 95 Senators were about to betray the republic until Tom intervened. Anybody who believes this is gullible. The prevention of a war as big as that one would have been is quite beyond the slender talents and negligible influence of this utterly commonplace man. It is not possible that the least influential member of the United States Senate should have accomplished so much without assistance.

IV. Tom even employed the magic name of Lindbergh to enforce his indignities upon Catholics and to excite the prejudices of his hearers. He implied that Lindbergh, a Protestant and a Mason, would not observe the amenities in the presence of a Cardinal that Mayor Walker and Governor Smith observed. But Tom's hearers may ask him to reconcile this story, first brought to light by him, with the following statement in the August number of the Holy Cross, a monthly church paper published by Catholics in Russell county, Alabama:

Capt. Charles Lindbergh, as he was leaving Curtiss Field for his New York-Paris flight, was given a Christopher Medal by a Catholic lady of Brooklyn. He expressed grateful thanks to the donor for her thoughtfulness.

Christopher was the patron saint of travelers. Heflin attacked Oscar Underwood on the ground that Underwood is pro-Catholic in his views. Yet in Underwood's two races for the Presidency, Heflin made stump speeches in his behalf and twice voted for Underwood for Senator. The same Underwood that he is today—but a good enough Oscar for Tom, because at that time Tom had not become a Catholic baiter. Indeed, in those dear, dead days of old, Tom was not unfriendly to the Catholics and was not averse to making an occasional Fourth of July speech before Knights of Columbus audiences.

Please do not understand us to be trying to reason with Heflin. It is futile to argue with Tom, notwithstanding Abe Martin's recent observation to the effect that "it's funny how quick a fact will break up an argument." Tom does not recognize facts, except those manufactured by his own primitive imagination. And so we do not argue.

V. A bully by nature, a mountebank by instinct, a Senator by choice. Conceited and vain as the peacock is, but not proud as the nobleman is, for a choicer spirit would be too proud to assail the weak. He is bombastic and blustery, but is wanting in high courage; certainly he is wanting in that valor which scorns advantage, otherwise he would not select

Sen. Tom Heflin speaking at a Ku Klux Klan rally in New York.

the class with the fewest votes in Alabama on which to heap contumely and indignities. The Roman Catholics cast less than 2 per cent of the total vote in Alabama. If they had political power in this State Tom would be afraid of them, for he is quite the biggest 'fraid cat in the United States Senate, even as he is about the grossest demagogue there. Tom has spent a lifetime studying the art of dodging dangerous issues and otherwise playing safe.

Heflin hates and suspects the personal honor of all men who oppose his boundless ambition. In controversy he is intellectually without scruples, he is slanderous, cruel, goatish, cheap and absurd, and without a generous emotion. The monkeyshine is the only light he is capable of casting on any serious public question. Dressed like an Al Field tenor, Tom is gifted with the humor of mimickry, as Bert Swor is, but is entirely wanting in the higher quality of wit, for while the sight of an audience is to him the signal to release a deluge of words, an art long practiced by him, Tom never in his life fashioned an epigram. His diction is too sloppy even if his intelligence could provide the thought on which to hang the dainty language that adorns and distinguishes the epigram. He is a ham actor metamorphosed into a United States Senator by a sorry trick of fate that invested Tom with lofty aspiration and immense gall. He is a clown on the platform and only as an entertainer is he interesting, for he is ill-informed, inaccurate in thought and unreliable in statement. But a hero to thousands nevertheless! Yet all of his daring has been spent in killing phantom dragons and doing battle with armored straw knights.

Good taste? Sense of propriety? Such terms merely amuse Tom. Fairness? Courtesy? Such qualities under the Heflin code are signs of weakness in men and need not be respected by a gent with a mission and without a muzzle.

VI. Thus this preposterous blob excites our pity if not our respect, and we leave him to his conscience in order that he may be entirely alone and meditate over the life of a charlatan whose personal interest and personal vanity are always of paramount concern to him. ❧

OBJECT LESSON

H.L. Mencken, *The* (Baltimore) *Evening Sun,* Feb. 10, 1938

In the six adjoining columns *The Evening Sun* presents today a graphic representation of the Federal Government's immense corps of jobholders.

Each dot stands for one jobholder, and there are 1,000,000 odd of them. The actual enrollment, at 10 o'clock this morning, was reported to be 999,264 head, but additions were being made at the rate of more than one hundred an hour, so the million mark will no doubt be passed before the last edition of *The Evening Sun* is on the streets.

This is the first time in human history, so far as can be ascertained, that a million dots have ever been printed on one page of a daily newspaper. Indeed, it is probably the first time in history that a million objects of any sort have been assembled in so convenient and succinct a way that the whole number could be taken in at a glance.

All of us talk about millions, and hear about them, and read about them, and maybe dream of them, but who has ever seen one? Well, here is a chance to enjoy that instructive experience. There are 825 dots in each row counting from side to side, and 1,213 in each row counting from top to bottom. That makes 1,000,725 in all. The extra 725 are thrown in as makeweight for any dots that may be worn off in the course of printing the paper.

The dots, unfortunately, had to be made very small. There are, in fact, more than 3,500 to the square inch. Even so, the chart is too large for the taxpayer to paste in his hat. Let him hang it, instead, on his parlor wall, between "The American's Creed" and the portrait of Mr. Roosevelt.

It may not be beautiful, but it will be the most costly picture, at least symbolically, in his house. If there were no Federal jobholders every American taxpayer could afford to buy a hand painted oil painting by a more or less old master, real or bogus. If there were no jobholders at all every taxpayer's income would be increased twenty-seven per cent.

Such is the bill for being saved from revolution and ruin by Wonder Men. If it were not for the corps of Federal jobholders, so we are told, millions of Americans would be starving, and next-door neighbors would be shooting off machine guns at one another over the backyard fence. As it is, every American has a fat and easy job, wages are increasing everywhere, and market and store bills are going down steadily.

The chart, as we have intimated, shows the cost of these great boons in jobholders. It may serve also to show the cost in money. If each of its dots is taken to represent a dollar, then the Federal jobholders wipe the chart clean every twenty-two minutes. In the course of every day of eight hours, Sundays and holidays included, they knock off twenty-two charts. In the course of every week they knock off more than 150. In the course of a year they knock off more than 8,000.

Counting a dot to a dollar, the Federal jobholders have consumed nearly 85,000 charts since the New Deal began. The taxpayer, during that time, has supplied the dots for nearly 19,000. The rest have been filed away for future reference. ❧

OPPOSITE: *Each of the more than one million dots on the page represented a federal worker, according to H.L. Mencken.*

	1938—	1937—	
...ng	142,548	141,377	Gain 1,172
...g	157,833	153,274	Gain 4,559
...y	212,144	208,804	Gain 3,340

Member of the Associated Press

Associated Press is exclusively entitled
... use for publication of all news dis-
... credited to it or not otherwise
...ed in this paper and also the local news
...hed herein. All rights of republication
...cial dispatches herein are also reserved

Object Lesson

... the six adjoining columns *The
...ing Sun* presents today a graphic
...sentation of the Federal Govern-
... immense corps of jobholders.

...ch dot stands for one jobholder, and
... are 1,000,000-odd of them. The ac-
... enrollment, at 10 o'clock this morn-
...was reported to be 999,264 head, but
...ions were being made at the rate of
... than one hundred an hour, so the
...on mark will no doubt be passed be-
... the last edition of *The Evening Sun*
... the streets.

...s is the first time in human his-
...so far as can be ascertained, that a
...on dots have ever been printed on
...age of a daily newspaper. Indeed, it
...obably the first time in history that
...llion objects of any sort have been
...abled in so convenient and succinct
... that the whole number could be
... in at a glance.

... of us talk about millions, and hear
... them, and read about them, and
... dream of them, but who has ever
...one? Well, here is a chance to enjoy
... instructive experience. There are
...ots in each row counting from side
...le, and 1,213 in each row counting
... top to bottom. That makes 1,000,725.
... The extra 725 are thrown in as
...weight for any dots that may be
... off in the course of printing the

... dots, unfortunately, had to be
... very small. There are, in fact,
... than 3,500 to the square inch. Even
...he chart is too large for the tax-
...' to paste in his hat. Let him hang
...stead, on his parlor wall, between
...American's Creed" and the portrait
... Roosevelt.

...may not be beautiful, but it will
... most costly picture, at least sym-
...ally, in his house. If there were no
...ral jobholders every American tax-
... could afford to buy a hand-painted
...ainting by a more or less old
...er, real or bogus. If there were no
...lders at all every taxpayer's in-
...would be increased twenty-seven
...ent.

...h is the bill for being saved from
...ation and ruin by Wonder Men. If
...re not for the corps of Federal job-
...rs, so we are told, millions of
...icans would be starving, and next-
...neighbors would be shooting off
...ine guns at one another over the
...ard fence. As it is, every American
... fat and easy job, wages are in-
...ng everywhere, and market and
...bills are going down steadily.

... chart, as we have intimated,
...s the cost of these great boons in
...lders. It may serve also to show the
... money. If each of its dots is taken
...present a dollar, then the Federal
...lders wipe the chart clean every
...y-two minutes. In the course of
... day of eight hours, Sundays and
...ays included, they knock off twenty-
...harts. In the course of every week
...knock off more than 150. In the
... of a year they knock off more
...8,000.

...ating a dot to a dollar, the Fed-
...jobholders have consumed nearly
... charts since the New Deal began.
...taxpayer, during that time, has sup-
...the dots for nearly 19,000. The rest
...een filed away for future reference.

The Perfect Campaign

... Caroline County Commissioners
...just appropriated $850 for a cam-
...against the Japanese beetle. State
...ederal governments will match this
...The commissioners of Worcester
...omerset counties have already ap-
...ated funds for this fight.

...of which is encouraging. The Japa-
...eetle is obviously a menace of the
...rategory. And this campaign will
...comfort to those who think some-
...should be done about it.

...ng, no really effective method of
...ng the beetles has been found.
...g at them with baited traps is like
...g to bail out an ocean liner with a
...poon. Lead arsenate is death to
... but it cannot be used in the lavish
...es that would be necessary to ex-
...nate the beetles without risking
...xtermination of the people of Mary-
...as well.

...m the jobholders' point of view,
... the campaign is almost ideal.

BEST MAN LOST

GIL CRANBERG, *The Des Moines Register*, Nov. 9, 1978

THE DEFEAT OF IOWA'S DEMOCRATIC SENATOR DICK Clark by Republican Roger Jepsen is inexplicable. By all measures, Clark should have won—and deserved to win—a second term.

He was a hard-working, capable and creative lawmaker. He was in a key position to influence legislation favorable to Iowa agriculture. He kept in close touch with constituents. He built a large campaign fund and campaigned extensively. He was well-informed and eager to debate the issues with his challenger.

Jepsen evaded debates. He sidestepped more issues than he confronted. When he did speak out, he often was uninformed. His campaign consisted for the most part of simplistic catchwords and slogans.

But Jepsen trounced Clark in four-fifths of Iowa's counties and won most of the urban areas.

Incumbency is supposed to be a big political advantage, but in this case it may have been disadvantageous. Clark's courageous votes on the Panama Canal treaties and abortion made him vulnerable to voters who felt strongly about these issues. Jepsen's pitch on these emotional subjects evidently paid off.

Clark barely was able to carry heavily Democratic—and Catholic—Dubuque. Anti-abortionists alone may have accounted for much or all of Jepsen's 25,000-vote margin.

Jepsen hammered hard at Clark's liberalism. It probably is true that Clark is more liberal than most Iowans. But Jepsen undoubtedly is more conservative than most Iowans. We are perplexed how Iowans could, in the space of six years, make a 180-degree turn in their choice of U.S. senator.

Jepsen will need to develop a much better grasp than he has demonstrated of the national and international issues he will have to grapple with in Congress. He would be wise also not to construe his victory as a sure-fire sign that middle-of-the-road Iowa has been converted to far-right conservatism.

Dick Clark served Iowa and the nation with intelligence and dedication. We hope that his defeat does not mark his retirement from public life. ❧

THE LATEST OUTRAGE

New York Daily Times, May 23, 1856

SENATOR SUMNER, WHILE SITTING IN HIS SEAT IN the United States Senate yesterday, was brutally assaulted by one Brooks, aided by Keitt of South Carolina, — both members of Congress from that State. Brooks struck Sumner upon the head with a heavy cane several times, — knocking him down, and injuring him very seriously. A more infamous crime has never been perpetrated

Frank Leslie's Illustrated Newspaper
*depicted Rep. Preston Brooks striking
Sen. Charles Sumner in the head with a cane.*

THE IMPEACHMENT AND THE PEOPLE

The New York Times, April 5, 1868

O NE OF THE MOST REMARKABLE FACTS IN THE history of this country is the calmness with which the impending trial of Andrew Johnson is generally viewed. There is no unusual excitement. Gold falls rather than rises. No extraordinary violence is seen or apprehended. No threats are heard. The voice of passion in most quarters is hushed, and all patiently await the issue, be it what it may, and pursue their daily duties unruffled and serene.

Why is this? What is the cause of all this repose? It is not indifference, for everybody is deeply interested. The dignity of the nation is at stake, and all feel that a great event is at hand which is pregnant with serious consequences, for good or evil, in regard to which passion is folly. All patriotic people, of all parties, feel that republican institutions are on trial, — that we cannot afford to make a great political blunder, or institute dangerous precedents; nor are people prepared to accept either a Mexico or a revolutionary France. The eyes of the whole world are upon us, and posterity will sift the matter with impartial scrutiny.

We know all this — everybody knows it, and therefore we fall back on justice, and are willing that justice shall have its course. It is too serious and important a matter for passion. We feel that the gravity of the occasion, the dignity of the high court, the cause of liberty, the ability of the prosecuting party, the still greater ability of the counsel in defence, and the acknowledged

even in Washington. It remains to be seen whether the Senate of the United States will take any steps to punish this most flagrant and disgraceful breach of its privileges. That a man capable of so ruffianlike and cowardly an act, is at all sensitive to the opinion that decent men everywhere will entertain of his conduct, is not likely. But Brooks has certainly earned for himself universal contempt and detestation. ❧

Rep. Preston Brooks (left) and Sen. Charles Sumner.

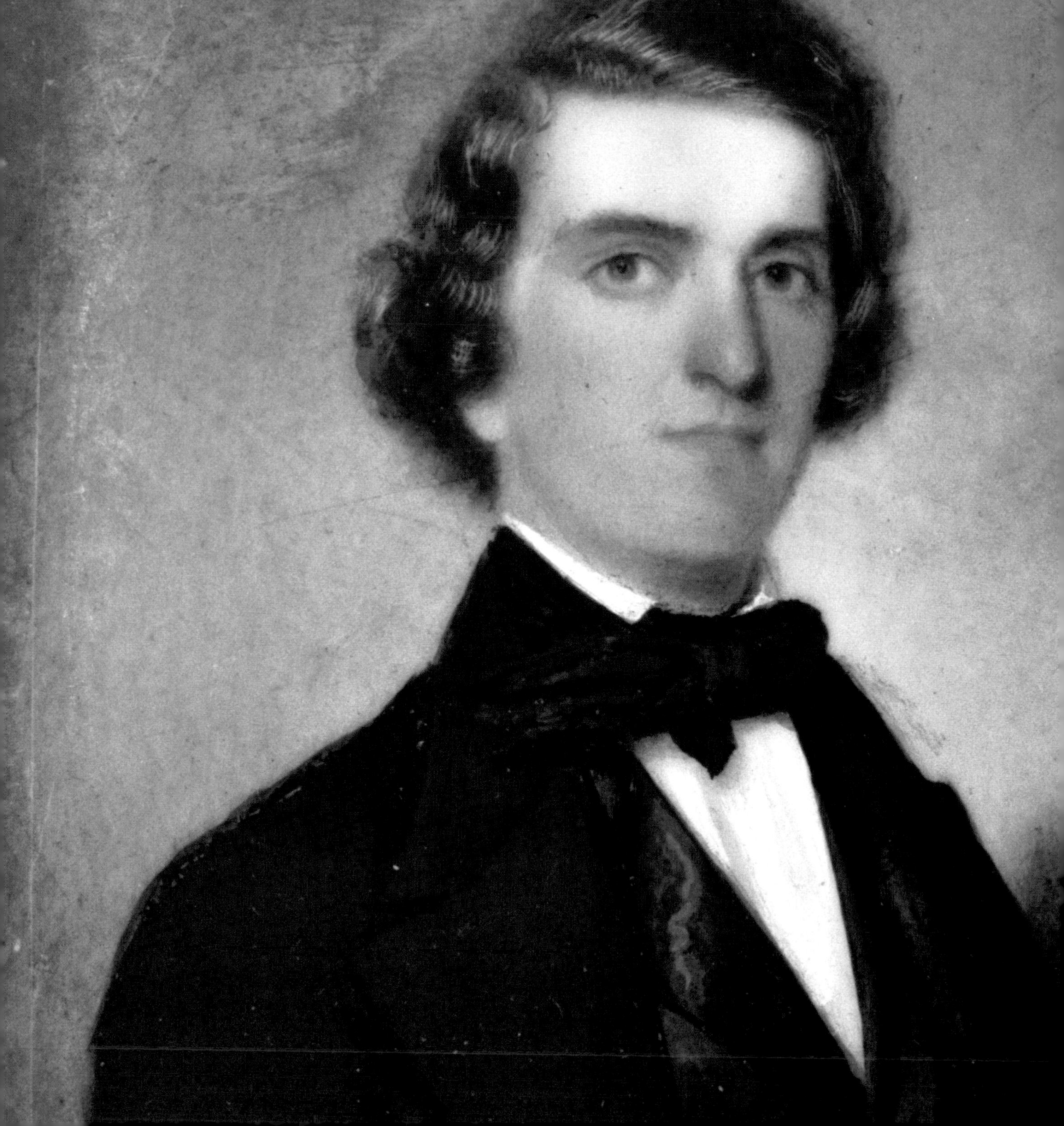

integrity and legal wisdom of the presiding Judge, will secure a just trial. And we are therefore calm and ready to accept any decision which may be made, as best for the country, and in accordance with enlightened interests. Sympathy for the President is suppressed in the greater interest we feel in justice and truth.

We know, that if the President is tried, and acquitted, on the ground that he is not guilty of high crimes and misdemeanors, the only ground on which he can be justly tried, however obnoxious he may be to the dominant party, or however open he may be to censure for mistakes and follies, patriotic people will rejoice, because no one but an angry partisan wishes to see the Chief Magistrate degraded, if he has committed no crime known to the laws. And all naturally love to see justice done, and to feel that men are not so bad as they are represented. If the President is acquitted in a fair and honorable trial, when the great questions at issue are settled by a manly appeal to established constitutional principles, and not to legal quibbles unworthy of the country, the Senate, and the cause of free institutions, then the dignity of the country is preserved and freedom gains by the trial, for the whole nation will become enlightened on the principles by which power is exercised. It is believed that the trial will be just, for the Senate cannot afford to be other than just, and no party can afford to make a blunder or be vindictive.

We know, further, that if the President is convicted of high crimes and misdemeanors, in a just and honorable trial, before such a court, with the eyes of the civilized world and all posterity upon it, then that every patriot, of all parties, will accept the judgment. Then no dangerous precedent will be established, for it is right to remove lawbreakers, however high their rank. Then a good precedent will be established, that no man can trifle with the laws of this great country, and that, if guilty, he will be punished. Then justice is established and the country is safe. Neither the laws, nor our institutions, nor public opinion, here or in Congress, will receive a shock. The nation will move on in dignity to fulfill its destiny.

But if the President is removed merely for a mistake, or because he is in the way of party triumphs, or from partisan hatreds, having committed no crime or misdemeanor in the opinion of the nation, when it reads the testimony and arguments, *even then* the people will be calm, because they will fall back on justice, and know that wickedness and passion will be avenged. Then the perpetrators of injustice will lose all their *prestige*, and no other harm will come than a wound to a party which cannot rule but by passion.

We take it for granted that, whatever the verdict, there is patriotism and intelligence enough left to the nation to see the right ultimately vindicated. What is *any* party, to the eye of a patriot, compared with the dominion of truth, and the integrity of free institutions?

If there be not patriotism and wisdom and intelligence in the nation sufficient to see justice vindicated on lofty and honorable grounds, and if a wrong be done, on the Jesuit principle that the end justifies the means, then we must expect revolution — anarchy — military despotism — all political evils combined, and the progress of constitutional liberty delayed for generations to come.

But nobody anticipates such calamities, because there is faith still in justice, and enlightened patriotism, and even far-reaching views of policy. A political blunder in this case is worse than crime. It is suicide. ➷

OPPOSITE: *President Andrew Johnson being served with the indictment for impeachment.*

U. S. SENATE

No.

MAIN ENTRANCE

To be taken up at

U. S. Impeac

ADMIT

MA

Philp & Solomons, Wash.

A ticket to President Andrew Johnson's impeachment in 1868.

SENATE

ment OF THE President

THE BEARER

RCH 13. 1868

Brown
Sergeant-at-Arms.

Wounded troops observe Christmas in Montmedy, France, in 1917.

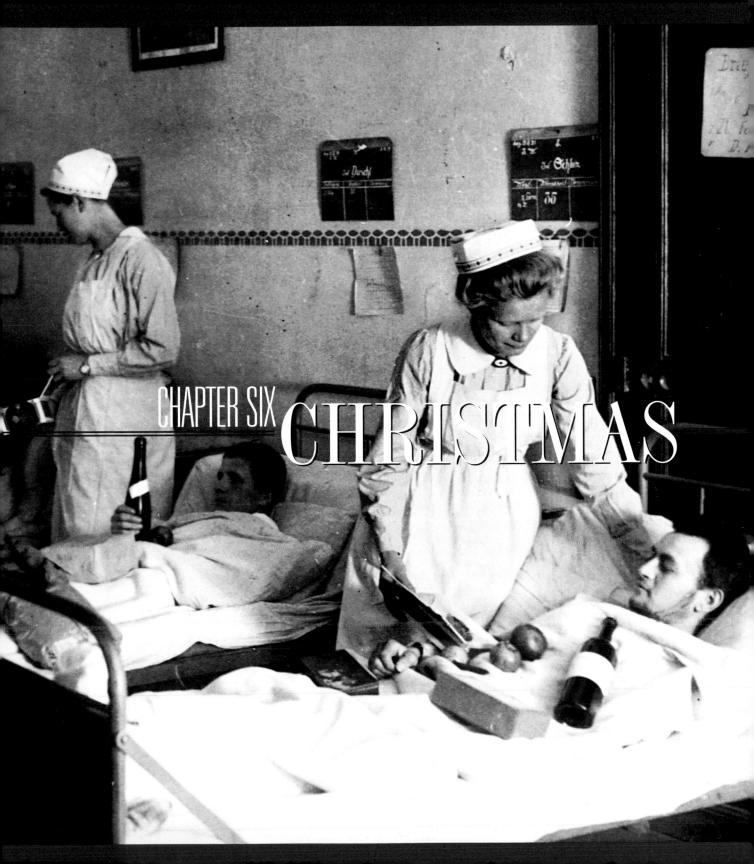

CHAPTER SIX CHRISTMAS

"YES, VIRGINIA, THERE IS A SANTA CLAUS."

OR, AT LEAST, THERE WAS ONE IN SEPTEMBER OF 1897 WHEN AN EDITORIAL WRITER NAMED FRANCIS P. CHURCH DASHED OFF AN EDITORIAL IN *THE* (NEW YORK) *SUN* IN RESPONSE TO A LETTER FROM THE YOUNG DAUGHTER OF A NEW YORK CITY SURGEON. ✑ "DEAR EDITOR: I AM 8 YEARS OLD," BEGAN THE LETTER FROM VIRGINIA O'HANLON OF WEST 95TH STREET IN NEW YORK. "SOME OF MY LITTLE FRIENDS SAY THERE IS NO SANTA CLAUS. PAPA SAYS 'IF YOU SEE IT IN The Sun, it's so.' Please tell me the truth; is there a Santa Claus?"

Francis Church, the editorial writer, was a former Civil War correspondent for *The New York Times* who had been writing editorials for the *Sun* for more than 20 years when Virginia's letter arrived in the middle of summer. For one reason or another, it was weeks before Church answered the letter with an editorial. The editorial itself caused little stir at the time.

But people remembered it, and they talked about it, especially about the second paragraph: "Yes, Virginia, there is a Santa Claus. He exists as certainly as love and generosity and devotion exist, and you know that they abound and give to your life its highest beauty and joy. Alas! how dreary would be the world if there were no Santa Claus. It would be as dreary as if there were no Virginias."

Eventually — but not right away — the *Sun* began reprinting the editorial each year at Christmastime, and by 1913 the *Sun* immodestly compared the editorial to the Gettysburg Address — "respecting the number of those who know its phrases and regard affectionately its sentiment and teachings."

Francis Church died in 1906, and Virginia O'Hanlon, who grew up to be a principal in the New York City school system, died in 1971. The editorial, it seems, will live forever.

"Yes, Virginia, there is a Santa Claus" remains the most famous line ever to appear in an editorial in an American newspaper. That editorial is full of joy and optimism, emotions that editorial writers seem to call up every year at Christmas, even in wartime.

"It is impossible to be very harsh of heart as we sit before the glowing Christmas fire or moralize beneath the happy shadows of the flaming Christmas tree," Henry Watterson wrote on Christmas Day of 1869 when the nation was still torn by the aftereffects of the Civil War and when families were still grieving the losses of more than 500,000 sons and brothers and fathers and husbands — and daughters and sisters and mothers and wives — in that war.

It was the same in 1917, when World War I was raging, and *The Chicago Daily Tribune* saw "an inextinguishable hope that out of the fire of suffering now blazing in the world there will come a better, wiser life for all peoples."

The same theme prevailed at *The New York Times* in that Christmas right after Pearl Harbor was bombed in 1941.

OPPOSITE: *Virginia O'Hanlon at 78. "Please tell me the truth; is there a Santa Claus?" she asked when she was 8. Editorial writer Francis P. Church answered her in print.*

U.S. troops celebrate a wartime Christmas. "The tears may come indeed and blind us. … But they are happy, ennobling, purifying tears, and bless Christmas for them with all its other blessings!" Henry Watterson said.

"We can, in the spirit of Christmas, try not to let the future be blackened and poisoned by hate. We can try to hate the deed more than the doer," the paper said on that Christmas morning.

Christmastime, too, seems the time for editorial writers to open up their Bibles. In 1946, the *St. Petersburg Times* editorialized about "That Christmas Message of Long Ago."

"Throughout a world still dazed by war, still unable to resolve difficulties between nations and individuals without bitter quarrels, there are countless tokens of gentleness, kindness and unselfishness," the paper noted. And, harking back to the words of the angel to the shepherds frightened by the light on the night Christ was born, the editorial ended: "Be not afraid."

Since 1949, *The Wall Street Journal* has each Christmastime run a biblical editorial written by the scholarly Vermont Royster and headlined "In Hoc Anno Domini" ("In This Year of Our Lord"). First published when the Cold War with the Soviet Union was heating up, it tells the story of Saul, or Paul, of Tarsus, about how the truth will set us free, and it concludes: "Stand fast therefore in the liberty wherewith Christ has made us free and be not entangled again with the yoke of bondage."

If holiday editorials often sound like sermons, it's because "the relation of the editor to his subscribers in a small American community is partly pastoral," William Allen White wrote in 1924, as he looked back at some of the editorials he had written over the years. The only thing wrong with that sentence is that the words "in a small American community" should be deleted.

Indeed, a preacher today could do worse on a Christmas morning than to say: "Through the glow which spreads over our inner life as we look out upon the day and the objects it discloses; as we look into ways that have been; as we look into faces that were; as we see hands stretched to us from shadowy depths, and feel strong grasps of love and tenderness meet our own, and kisses, pure and trusting, fall upon our lips, the tears may come indeed and blind us. … But they are happy, ennobling, purifying tears, and bless Christmas for them with all its other blessings!"

Those words were preached—printed, actually —on Dec. 25, 1869, in *The Courier-Journal*. They were in that editorial written by Henry Watterson. It was called, appropriately, "A Gush of Christmas." ❧

CHRISTMAS, 1917

The Chicago Daily Tribune, Dec. 25, 1917

ON THIS CHRISTMAS DAY OF 1917 SOMETHING NEW and poignant enters into the familiar emotions of the season. Everywhere among the holiday throngs of the days before there has run a new thread, the thread of khaki. In our windows hung with the holly wreaths of beloved tradition is the service flag. At the Christmas table, whether there be a chair vacant or none, there is a new figure, the figure of sacrifice.

Two thousand years ago there was born a child who was to stand in the ages to come for that idea, that a man shall save himself by losing himself, that man's life rises highest when it regards itself least. However men and nations of the western world have fallen below the message of Christ, it has been a light before their stumbling feet, and we live today in the dream of its fulfillment in the soul of man.

For three years America has lived in the shadow of the great war, and this year the shadow deepens and incloses us also. This generation of Americans has not known such a Christmas, but our fathers and mothers knew. We are feeling today something of what the men and women of 1861 felt, and the meaning and emotion are to grow in intensity.

We must pray today that the cup of supreme sacrifice be not placed at our lips, but that if we are to taste its bitterness that we be given strength not to shrink from it. In the ages which have gone before, men and women, fathers, mothers, and

Have you answered the Red Cross Christmas Roll Call?

A Red Cross poster at Christmastime in 1917. "The shadow deepens and incloses us," said The Chicago Daily Tribune.

wives innumerable, have paid the great price. They have done what they could to pass on to us what seemed precious to them, and we in our time cannot repudiate the debt.

Certainly, if there are sorrow and anxiety mingling in the thoughts of this Christmas day, there is also an inextinguishable hope that out of the fire of suffering now blazing in the world there will come a better, wiser life for all peoples. We may not be sure of this, but we may hope, and what is better, work and fight for it. ☙

THIS WARTIME CHRISTMAS

The New York Times, Dec. 25, 1941

IT IS NOT EASY TO KEEP THE SPIRIT OF CHRISTMAS IN time of war. The sad and ancient problem of the evil in men's hearts, and of the difficulty that all men meet with in trying to find a course of action that has no evil at all in it, seems this year further than ever from solution. Against our will we are part of a great and very dreadful war. Many who are innocent, as well as some who are deeply guilty, will die before this war ends. Each one of us will be in some degree responsible. This is the burden that circumstances in this generation have placed upon us. It is a burden we do not like to think about at Christmas time—but we must.

We can each do something to make it lighter, and to prepare for that day when the prayers that go up for a just peace, in churches, in congregations and in men's hearts, will at last be answered. We can, in the spirit of Christmas, try not to let the future be blackened and poisoned by hate. We can try to hate the deed more than the doer. Stand up against the deed we must, do our best we must to see that it is halted. Yet it is of equal necessity to bear in mind that in any civilization we can foresee on this planet our present enemies, if not their present leaders, must have a place. The evil wills that have taken possession of them must be destroyed, but to believe that we must either destroy whole nations or must forever hate them is the tragic credo of despair.

It is our duty to fight. We shall not fight the worse because as civilized people we recognize that it is better to build and to protect than it is to tear down and kill. We can bring a little Christmas into the stern scenes of war. We can give help, and some good cheer, to the sick, the weary and the wounded. We can sing old German and Italian songs that are bound up with the Christmas story, and we can remember that there has been, and can be again, a gracious and spiritual aspect of Japan.

But mostly, in the midst of this grim business that does not stop even for the Christmas holidays, we can think that one of our war aims — the very central one of them, perhaps — is to make a world that will be safe for the spirit of Christmas. For if we could be sure that after the firing stops there would be happiness and security for the world's children; if we could be sure that families would no longer be torn apart, or starved, or fearful; if travelers could go safely on their lawful errands all over the world and come home at holiday time to those who love them — if we were certain of these things, would not that be victory?

In the end it will come. The firmer and cooler our determination, the more of the Christmas mood we can keep even while we strike our hardest blows at evil, the readier we shall be for that kind of victory. ❧

OPPOSITE: *Soldiers in Italy take a break to hand out candy on a Christmas during World War II.*

IN HOC ANNO DOMINI

Vermont Royster, *The Wall Street Journal*, Dec. 24, 1949

WHEN SAUL OF TARSUS SET OUT ON HIS JOURNEY TO Damascus the whole of the known world lay in bondage. There was one state, and it was Rome. There was one master for it all, and he was Tiberius Caesar.

Everywhere there was civil order, for the arm of the Roman law was long. Everywhere there was stability, in government and in society, for the centurions saw that it was so.

But everywhere there was something else, too. There was oppression — for those who were not the friends of Tiberius Caesar. There was the tax gatherer to take the grain from the fields and the flax from the spindle to feed the legions or to fill the hungry treasury from which divine Caesar gave largess to the people. There was the impressor to find recruits for the circuses. There were executioners to quiet those whom the Emperor proscribed. What was a man for but to serve Caesar?

There was the persecution of men who dared think differently, who heard strange voices or read strange manuscripts. There was enslavement of men whose tribes came not from Rome, disdain for those who did not have the familiar visage. And most of all, there was everywhere a contempt for human life. What, to the strong, was one man more or less in a crowded world?

Then, all of a sudden, there was a light in the world, and a man from Galilee saying, Render unto Caesar the things which are Caesar's and unto God the things that are God's.

And the voice from Galilee, which would defy Caesar, offered a new Kingdom in which each man could walk upright and bow to none but his God. Inasmuch as ye have done it unto one of the least of these my brethren, ye have done it unto me. And he sent this gospel of the Kingdom of Man into the uttermost ends of the earth.

So the light came into the world and the men who lived in darkness were afraid, and they tried to lower a curtain so that man would still believe salvation lay with the leaders.

But it came to pass for a while in divers places that the truth did set man free, although the men of darkness were offended and they tried to put out the light. The voice said, Haste ye. Walk while you have the light, lest darkness come upon you, for he that walketh in darkness knoweth not whither he goeth.

Along the road to Damascus the light shone brightly. But afterward Paul of Tarsus, too, was sore afraid. He feared that other Caesars, other prophets, might one day persuade men that man was nothing save a servant unto them, that men might yield up their birthright from God for pottage and walk no more in freedom.

Then might it come to pass that darkness would settle again over the lands and there would be a burning of books and men would think only of what they should eat and what they should wear, and would give heed only to new Caesars and to false prophets. Then might it come to pass that men would not look upward to see even a winter's star in the East, and once more, there would be no light at all in the darkness.

And so Paul, the apostle of the Son of Man, spoke to his brethren, the Galatians, the words he would have us remember afterward in each of the years of his Lord:

Stand fast therefore in the liberty wherewith Christ has made us free and be not entangled again with the yoke of bondage. ❧

The Wall Street Journal *has published this editorial annually since 1949.*

Vermont Royster wrote to shed light. "For he that walketh in darkness knoweth not whither he goest."

HOLIDAY MESSAGE TUCKED AWAY IN PARK

MICHAEL G. GARTNER, *The (Ames, Iowa) Daily Tribune*, Dec. 23, 1996

WE HAVE MORE THAN A PASSING INTEREST, OF course, in Christopher Gartner Memorial Park in west Ames. We stopped by, throughout the fall, and watched the children playing on the little playground or romping on the two acres of lawn. We smiled when we saw a mother or father with a youngster — pushing a swing, perhaps, or tossing a ball, or just sitting and watching. We grinned, especially, the day we saw a little boy with a big dog, each watching out for the other. We laughed out loud when we saw two little boys getting into harmless mischief.

The park, just a few months old, is already serving its purpose, we thought.

That purpose is to provide joy unbounded — joy for little kids, joy for their parents, joy for their dogs.

For Christopher Carl Gartner was the most joyous boy that ever lived.

He was born grinning, and the grin only got bigger as he grew — and grew and grew and grew. He

The little boy, Christopher, loved the otter hound, Finnegan, "because his ears are so big you can wipe your tears on them."

laughed at everything — when he was little, at his grandpa's wild stories; when he was bigger, at his pals' wild escapades. By the time he was 15, he was an exuberant story-teller, regaling his pals with the latest funny thing his friend Andrew said, the latest crazy thing his friend Joey did. His grin and his laughter were infectious. Life for him was fun, and he wanted his friends and his mom and his dad and his grandparents to have fun, too. (He was genuinely kind, as well as cheerful, and early on he figured out that was an advantage. "You know," he once clued in his little brother, "if you're nice to your teachers you don't have to study nearly as hard," something he liked because being nice was a lot easier for him than studying.)

Life for him was love, too. By his early teens, he was a bear of a boy, probably six-feet three-inches or so, and he would almost have to bend over double to kiss his tiny grandma, whom he stopped by to see almost every day. But he never had that reticence or shyness that boys sometimes develop. He was an unabashed hugger from the day he was born in 1976 till the day he died in 1994. His last words to his father, as he lay in the hospital early in the morning of the summer day he died so suddenly and unexpectedly were, "I love you, too, dad."

We tell you this today, with more joy than sadness, for a couple of reasons. The first is just a technical one. The deed to the park was turned over to the city the other evening, so Christopher Gartner Memorial Park is now an official city park, and we just thought we'd tell you a bit about the boy the park is named after. (We could tell you much more — about how he goofily learned to walk with the help of a big unruly dog, who cushioned every fall; about how he drove his mother's new convertible into a tree the very day he got his driver's license — it was the tree's fault, he laughingly argued; about how he'd wake his parents at midnight to report in — and then tell them funny stories of what happened at the game or the party or wherever he'd been. All those or the million other happy memories that vie for space against the grieving a hundred times a day.)

The second reason we tell all this is because this is the Christmas season, the time of joy and of families and of fun and of love. We thought there was no better way to wish you a merry Christmas than to tell you the story of a boy who embodied laughter and love and giving, a boy who brought so much joy to so many people in just 17 years.

Our purpose surely is evident: to urge you to have fun this holiday season with your kids or your parents — or both. To urge you to sit around and tell family stories as two or three or sometimes four generations gather at the table — to share in the laughter. And to urge you to tell one another, the young and the old and the very old, that your family is a pretty nice family — to share in the love.

Finally, if it's a nice day tomorrow, you might want to wander over to Christopher Gartner Park — it's tucked away at the dead end of Abraham Drive — and toss a ball around or romp with a dog or push a swing. And think nice thoughts about the cheerful boy who has lent it his name.

It's too bad you never knew him.

You'd have loved his laugh.

You'd have loved him. ❧

IS THERE A SANTA CLAUS?

Francis P. Church, *The* (New York) *Sun*, Sept. 21, 1897

WE TAKE PLEASURE IN ANSWERING AT ONCE AND thus prominently the communication below, expressing at the same time our great gratification that its faithful author is numbered among the friends of The Sun:

"Dear Editor: I am 8 years old. Some of my little friends say there is no Santa Claus. Papa says 'If you see it in The Sun it's so.' Please tell me the truth; is there a Santa Claus?"

Virginia O'Hanlon
115 West Ninety-Fifth Street

Virginia, your little friends are wrong. They have been affected by the skepticism of a skeptical age. They do not believe, except they see. They think that nothing can be which is not comprehensible by their little minds. All minds, Virginia, whether they be men's or children's, are little. In this great universe of ours man is a mere insect, an ant, in his intellect, as compared with the boundless world about him, as measured by the intelligence capable of grasping the whole of truth and knowledge.

Yes, Virginia, there is a Santa Claus. He exists as certainly as love and generosity and devotion exist, and you know that they abound and give to your life its highest beauty and joy. Alas! how dreary would be the world if there were no Santa Claus. It would be as dreary as if there were no Virginias. There would be no child-like faith then, no poetry, no romance to make tolerable this existence. We should have no enjoyment, except in sense and sight. The eternal light with which childhood fills the world would be extinguished.

Not believe in Santa Claus! You might as well not believe in fairies! You might get your papa to hire men to watch in all the chimneys on Christmas Eve to catch Santa Claus, but even if they did not see Santa Claus coming down, what would that prove? Nobody sees Santa Claus, but that is no sign that there is no Santa Claus. The most real things in the world are those that neither children nor men can see. Did you ever see fairies dancing on the lawn? Of course not, but that's no proof that they are not there. Nobody can conceive or imagine all the wonders there are unseen and unseeable in the world.

You may tear apart the baby's rattle and see what makes the noise inside, but there is a veil covering the unseen world which not the strongest man, nor even the united strength of all the strongest men that ever lived, could tear apart. Only faith, fancy, poetry, love, romance, can push aside that curtain and view and picture the supernal beauty and glory beyond. Is it all real? Ah, Virginia, in all this world there is nothing else real and abiding.

No Santa Claus! Thank God! he lives, and he lives forever. A thousand years from now, Virginia, nay, ten times ten thousand years from now, he will continue to make glad the heart of childhood. ❧

OPPOSITE: *A young Virginia O'Hanlon. "Not believe in Santa Claus! You might as well not believe in fairies!" Francis P. Church told her.*

Children dreaming of Christmas in the 1900s. "How dreary would be the world if there were no Santa Claus. It would be as dreary as if there were no Virginias. . . . Is it all real? Ah, Virginia, in all this world there is nothing else real and abiding."

CHAPTER SEVEN

PASSIONS

"THE PEOPLE OF THIS CITY EMINENTLY NEED AND ARDENTLY DESIRE CLEAN STREETS."

THE YEAR WAS 1854, AND HORACE GREELEY WAS OFF ON ANOTHER TEAR IN HIS *NEW YORK TRIBUNE*. NEW YORK, HE WROTE, HAD BECOME "THE FILTHIEST AND MOST NOISOME CITY OF CHRISTENDOM." ❧ THE IMMEDIATE PROBLEM WAS HORSE MANURE, BUT THE LARGER PROBLEM WAS CORRUPTION. CONTRACTS WERE LET, AND "THE PEOPLE AND THE COUNCIL SUPPOSED [THE CONTRACTORS] WERE TO SWEEP THE STREETS; *THEIR* UNDERSTANDING, ON THE CONTRARY, SEEMED to be that they were to sweep only the Treasury."

To prove his point, Greeley waded through documents as well as manure to become knowledgeable about the issue. The next week, or perhaps the next day, he had to be knowledgeable on another issue.

"Assuming journalism, equally with medicine and law, to be a profession, it is the only profession in which versatility is not a disadvantage," Henry Watterson wrote in his autobiography in 1919.

"Editorial writing … is a peculiar occupation," Vermont Royster wrote some 65 years later. The editorial writer is a "professional amateur. He is rarely an expert on anything but he is forced to learn a little about many things — economics, law, science, government, sociology, and so forth." And then "he must be able to compress his thoughts into a few words" without losing sight "of the basic principles involved nor of the line of the argument."

And, of course, the editorial writer must write those facts and argue those thoughts with grace and style. Reporters use facts to inform, but editorial writers must use facts to persuade as well as to inform. Not every journalist can do that.

"Most journalists come to [editorial writing] because they have been good reporters," Royster noted, "and it is assumed that because they are knowledgeable about, let us say, government or foreign affairs they will have opinions worth listening to. Sometimes it's true, often not. Many a good reporter has been ruined by asking him to think."

What's more, there's no guarantee to the reader that the editorial writer's reporting is sound or opinion is valid. Thus, *The Washington Post* confidently ended an editorial as Prohibition loomed: "Will the country ever repeal the dry laws? That is a query frequently propounded in these days, and sometimes with most heartfelt interest. … In fact, it may be stated as the consensus of unprejudiced opinion, from either wet or dry sources, that alcoholic liquor is gone for good and all."

Looked at as a whole, an editorial writer's work is a collection "of vagrant fancies, passing wishes, hopes that died a-borning," William Allen White wrote some 30 years into his long career. "It is like a record of the emanations of a subconscious mind curious, heterogeneous, helter-skelter, mad."

OPPOSITE: *The streets of New York were often the topic of editorials in Horace Greeley's* New York Tribune. *Greeley (pictured on the previous pages) wrote with passion and precision about everything from politics in the halls of Washington to horse manure on the streets of New York.*

The curiosity — or perhaps the helter-skelterness, or the madness — knows no bounds. That's why readers of an editorial in Iowa — where people know the size of a cow but have a hard time imagining the tininess of a hummingbird — one day came across this line in an editorial about spring and the return of birds from their winter journeys: "In case anyone ever asks you, it would take 288,000 hummingbirds to outweigh a cow."

The editorial writer has an opinion on everything.

"We are glad to see that several of the most respectable ladies of our village possess sufficient independence to show their disregard of the imperious mandates of Fashion, and consult comfort and convenience in the matter of dress," the *Seneca County* (N.Y.) *Courier* editorialized in 1851. "It is now quite common to see the short dress and pantalettes in our streets, and it is admitted by nearly all that they are a decided improvement upon the *draggling* style. Indeed, they are very generally admired, and we hope that occasional rude and insulting remarks from blackguards, and the annoying conduct of ill-mannered boys, will not discourage the ladies in their attempt to introduce a wholesome and much needed reform."

(An aside: "Reform," incidentally, is an editorial word. It means a change for the better, and the good reporter doesn't let the spinning politician get away with such phrases as "tax reform" or "welfare reform" or "election reform.")

Issues abound, and they can always be turned to an editorial writer's advantage.

In 1995, when baseball team owners and baseball players were in a labor dispute, Dan Henninger

of *The Wall Street Journal* wrote an editorial suggesting that the sport be nationalized. An editorial in the *Journal* urging the nationalization of anything oozes with irony, of course, but it was a clever way of taking yet another shot at President Clinton, his wife and the administration man pushing a health-revision plan the *Journal* found particularly odious.

Irony. Compassion. Lyricism. Dismay. Despair. Editorial writers haul out all the devices.

Compassion? Read "Cecilia Cooney," written by Walter Lippmann in *The* (New York) *World* in 1924. It's about a woman portrayed in the papers as the "bobbed-hair bandit." On investigation, though, "there in the place of the dashing bandit was a pitiable girl; instead of an amusing tale, a dark and mean tragedy; instead of a lovely adventure, a terrible accusation."

Lyricism? Read "My Country 'Tis of Thee," written by Ronald G. Callvert in the Portland *Oregonian* in 1938. It's about the blessings of liberty, and how we must embrace those blessings and fight for them as war begins to engulf the world. The editorial concluded: "If you cherish this liberty, this equality, this peace that is peace material and peace spiritual — then defend with all your might the American ideal of government."

Dismay? Read "Exit John Barleycorn," which appeared in *The Washington Post* in 1918. Prohibition was just around the corner, and Congress was adding insult to injury. The *Post* lamented: "If the House accepts the bone dry rider adopted by the Senate — which no doubt it will — Washington will have the unique distinction of being the only dry capital in the world, so far as appears in all annals that survive. … It's all over but the shouting," *The Post* bemoaned. "All hope is gone."

Despair? Read "The House of a Hundred Sorrows," written by Edward M. Kingsbury in *The New York Times* as Christmas approached in 1925. Chronicling the woes of people in tenements, he concluded: "But you need no guide. Once in The House of a Hundred Sorrows you will visit every sad chamber in it. If your heart be made of penetrable stuff, you will do the most you can to bring hope and comfort to its inmates."

Finally, there is smugness. Read "To Intending Female Voters," written — clearly by a man — in *The New York Times* for the day in 1915 when men in New York, Massachusetts and Pennsylvania were voting on women's suffrage. Those parlous times — the events of the war and the "economic, financial, and commercial readjustments and reconstructions which it has caused" — "tax the intelligence of the male electorate." "And when thoughtful men are perplexed … the suffragists come, in all innocence, and ask to have the economic and political wisdom, not too high already, of the electorate diluted by the infusion of unpracticed, uninstructed feminism!" Note the exclamation point. "At this time of all times the poetizing and enfeebling of the practical instincts, experience, and capability of the State by the admission of women as voters would be a perilous venture."

In fact, men in all three states voted against suffrage on that November day, and the *Times* could barely suppress its glee the next day. Calling the vote a "memorable day's work," the *Times* man said: "The men of the mighty industrial States voted it down for the good of the State and the good of the women. The essential American conservatism, the old-fashioned notion of the position and duties of women, prevailed."

In 2001, the *Times* named Gail Collins — author of a book called *America's Women: Four Hundred Years of Dolls, Drudges, Helpmates and Heroines*— as editor of its editorial pages. ❧

"There are old reasons enough against woman suffrage, and it would be futile to cite them now," The New York Times *editorialized in 1915.*

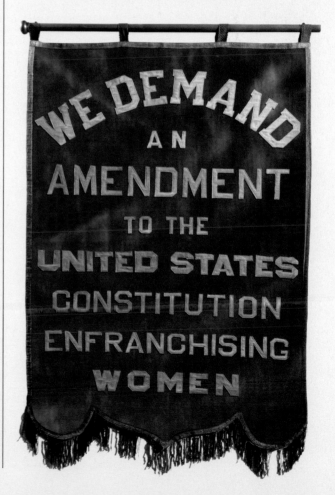

THE NATIONALIZED PASTIME

Dan Henninger, *The Wall Street Journal*, Feb. 9, 1995

The trouble with baseball is it ain't a railroad. Back in the good old days — when men were men, the Oval Office had a spittoon and Babe Ruth thought the President was just a fella who made less money than he did — the person who sits where Bill Clinton sits would have known how to deal with a bunch of oligopolists and their strikers.

He would've ordered those railroad magnates into his office, whomped them across their gold watch chains with a copy of the Railway Labor Act

The Wall Street Journal *used the 1995 major league baseball labor dispute to criticize President Bill Clinton and his policies while calling for the nationalization of the sport.*

of 1926, locked them in a room with a referee from the National Mediation Board, and dadgummit if that didn't work, he'd order the Army out to get the railroads running again.

Golly, but the times have changed. Today the President calls the oligopolists of baseball into his office and "sets a deadline" for the two sides to settle their strike. That deadline passes — strike one! Then the President sets another deadline, and it passes — strike two! But Bill Clinton's not about to strike out completely with a third deadline, so he tells Congress to go in and bat for him.

It figures. We'll bet Bill Clinton managed to never actually strike out in a childhood baseball game. Oops, gettin' late; gotta get home for dinner; too dark; looks like rain; got something in my eye; I think that plane's gonna crash!

But seriously, we sympathize with the President on this one. Look what he's dealing with. Here's one of the President's player negotiators quoted in yesterday's Washington Post: "This is not about getting $10 million a year or $6 million a year. I'd be willing to play this game for $3 million." If memory serves, Cornelius Vanderbilt once said exactly that about the New York Central (with appropriate inflation adjustments).

Now, when Mr. Clinton this week tried to send Congress into the game, Tris "Speaker" Gingrich refused to leave the bench: "I'm not sure Congress is the right place to try to organize the national pastime."

Organize the national pastime. What an intriguing phrase. When you consider that radical Republicans now run the country, that communism's been overrun by McDonald's and that Hillary's health care plan is dead, chances are we'll never see another bona fide state-run industry in our lifetimes. In a way that's sad, because viewed from a certain perspective, state-run industries are kind of fun: They're extravagant, showing up for work isn't that important, the bosses are toothless tyrants, they support the local economy into eternity.

Why not? Let's nationalize the national pastime. Seriously. Who cares whether baseball is run by Bud Selig or Ira Magaziner? That's right; we think the structure of the United States Baseball Agency (USBA) is perfectly suited to Mr. Magaziner's arcane skills. Admittedly, the distances between the bases and home might go metric under Mr. Magaziner, not to mention the probable pooling of salaries and a cap on hotdog prices. Also, all the games — well, some of them — would be broadcast on public television. Also the Dole-Gingrich Baseball Reorganization Act of 1995 makes Little Rock one of the new USBA franchises in 1996, and Secretary of Baseball Magaziner gets to appoint Bill Clinton as its general manager. Oh yes, the first Latin American franchise goes to Havana, provided Fidel steps down from his present job to run the club. So what's the problem? Tell George Steinbrenner and Marge Schott to get lost and tell Ricky Henderson and the rest of them to show up for their Civil Service exams this Monday at 8 a.m., Department of Labor, Building C, 10th floor, Section C-3, the Reich Auditorium. ❧

CECILIA COONEY

WALTER LIPPMANN, *The* (New York) *World*, May 8, 1924

FOR SOME MONTHS NOW we have been vastly entertained by the bobbed-haired bandit. Knowing nothing about her, we created a perfect story standardized according to the rules laid down by the movies and the short-story magazines. The story had, as the press agents say, everything. It had a flapper and a bandit who baffled the police; it had sex and money, crime and mystery. And then yesterday we read in the probation officer's report the story of Cecilia Cooney's life. It was not in the least entertaining. For there in the place of the dashing bandit was a pitiable girl; instead of an amusing tale, a dark and mean tragedy; instead of a lovely adventure, a terrible accusation.

In the twenty years she has lived in this city she has come at one time or another within the reach of all the agencies of righteousness. Five years before she was born her father was summoned to court for drunkenness and neglect; the Charities Department recommended then that her older brothers and sisters be committed to an institution. That did not prevent her parents bringing, with the full consent of the law, three or four more children into the world. Cecilia herself, the youngest of eight, came at four years of age into the custody of the Children's Society. Six months later, on the recommendation of the Department of Public Charity, she was turned back to her mother, who promptly deserted her.

NEXT PAGES: *Cecilia Cooney, the "bobbed-haired bandit," had been the source of countless New York newspaper headlines. "There in the place of the dashing bandit was a pitiable girl,"* The *(New York)* World *said.*

attack wrong, whether by predatory plutocracy or predatory poverty."

CECILIA COONEY.

For some months now we have been vastly entertained by the bobbed-haired bandit. Knowing nothing about her, we created a perfect story standardized according to the rules laid down by the movies and the short-story magazines. The story had, as the press agents say, everything. It had a flapper and a bandit who baffled the police; it had sex and money, crime and mystery. And then yesterday we read in the probation officer's report the story of Cecilia Cooney's life. It was not in the least entertaining. For there in the place of the dashing bandit was a pitiable girl; instead of an amusing tale, a dark and mean tragedy; instead of a lovely adventure, a terrible accusation.

In the twenty years she has lived in this city she has come at one time or another within the ——— —— ——————————. Five years before she was born her father was summoned to court for drunkenness and neglect; the Charities Department recommended then that her older brothers and sisters be committed to an institution. That did not prevent her parents bringing, with the full consent of the law, three or four more children into the world. Cecilia herself, the youngest of eight, came at four years of age into the custody of the Children's Society. Six months later, on the recommendation of the Department of Public Charity, she was turned back to her mother, who promptly deserted her.

She was next taken to Brooklyn by her aunt and for ten years or so attended parochial school. At the age of fourteen her mother brought her back to New York, took her to a furnished room, stole her clothes and deserted her. A year later, aged fifteen, Cecilia became a child-laborer in a brush factory in Brooklyn, and was associating at night with sailors picked up on the water-front. At sixteen Cecilia was back in New York, living with her mother, working as laundress for a few months at a stretch in various hospitals. At twenty she was married, had borne a child, had committed a series of robberies, and is condemned to spend the rest of her youth in prison.

This is what twentieth-century civilization in New York achieved in the case of Cecilia Cooney. Fully warned by the behavior of her parents long before her birth, the law allowed her parents to reproduce their kind. Fully warned when she was still an infant, society allowed her to drift out of its hands into a life of dirt, neglect, dark basements, begging, stealing, ignorance, poor little tawdry excitements and twisted romance. The courts had their chance and they missed it. Charity had its chance and missed it. Schools had their chance and missed it. The church had its chance and missed it. The absent-minded routine of all that is well-meaning and respectable did not deflect by an inch her inexorable progress from the basement where she was born to the jail where she will expiate her crimes and ours.

For her crimes are on our heads too. No record could be clearer or more eloquent. None could leave less room for doubt that Cecilia Cooney is a product of this city, of its neglect and its carelessness, of its indifference and its undercurrents of misery. We recommend her story to the pulpits of New York, to the school men of New York, to the lawmakers of New York, to the social workers of New York, to those who are tempted to boast of its wealth, its magnificence and its power.

———

a band of foreigners, meaning New York and New Jersey State officials, to exercise "the terrorism of a Spanish inquisition" in New York streets and make "mothers hug their children to their breasts" when (and if) the railroads send "their iron horses roaring and snorting along the highways." This is more than mere flubdub about a useful public-improvement plan. The man simply cannot know what he is talking about.

New York has got along after a fashion for the past six years by the impetus of a huge organization, and by the faithful work of intelligent men in the boroughs and departments. It has had no co-ordinating head; no City Government capable of attacking its very pressing problems; no Mayor even interested in those problems except for campaign purposes. It is evident that there is no hope of progress in schools, in sewage disposal, in cheapening the cost of living by better market and terminal arrangements, in rapid transit, until there is installed what the ——————— so sadly needs—a success.

THE SOLDIER IN THE WHITE HOUSE.

What happened to Mr. Coolidge's convictions about the right way to avoid an insult to Japan? Mr. Coolidge was opposed to the Senate's way of breaking off the gentlemen's agreement. He had said as much to the newspaper men in Washington, and his Secretary of State had publicly opposed the method which the Senate followed.

But California is solid for Japanese exclusion, and there is every apparent reason for believing that Tuesday's primaries explain why Mr. Coolidge hadn't a word to say of the Senate's action.

Either the President changed his own convictions under fire and said nothing to show the reason why, or he dodged the issue for the sake of votes. That is political expediency of the sort American opinion often humors. But it is not courage. It is not the straightforward New Englander speaking from the shoulder. It is the cautious politician playing safe.

MR. CANBY RESIGNS.

Henry Seidel Canby's resignation from the editorship of the New York Evening Post's Literary Review will be regretted by all readers of the Review who are aware of his part in shaping its policy. Since the days of the original Dial no magazine has occupied quite so influential a place in the world of books and criticism as was attained by the Review.

To what extent literature is guided by criticism is of course a matter of doubt, yet it is fairly certain that the critic's power to set standards for the creative artist is vastly underestimated in the United States. Mr. Canby and the group of associates of his own quality about him knew what they wanted, and were able to exercise a very large influence on American writers and book buyers. His resignation takes the heart out of a hopeful enterprise.

THE CITY IN THE TELEPHONE CASE.

To the Federal-injunction proceedings by which the New York Telephone Company has been enabled to raise its charges 10 per cent. pending full judicial inquiry, the city is an important party in interest. It is itself a large user of the service. It is proper that it should become representative of the great mass of private users of the service within the city. Judge Knox's grant of the city's petition to intervene was thus to be expected.

Questions of fact alone are at issue. What is a fair valuation of the company's property and were the old rates hopeless of earning a reasonable

———

tions of that Government whose equal benefits they would deny to particular groups of citizens. It puts both Democratic and Republican National Conventions on notice and makes it even more imperative that they, as party spokesmen, disavow and repudiate the Klan in their national platforms, as urged by The World.

Those Republican strategists who hoped to persuade the voters in great cities outside the South that the Klan was a Southern Democratic organization are brought sharply about by the Indiana primaries to inspect their own party structure. The sooner honorable political leaders realize that votes which may be manipulated by secret understandings with the Klan can only be obtained at the cost of public order and individual liberty the sooner will the Klan be thrust out of politics. And that is a necessity, at once.

THOSE TIRESOME INVESTIGATIONS.

Several weeks since Mr. Coolidge entered his "solemn protest" against the Senate's methods of investigation and read it a sharp lecture on its "constitutional and legal rights" because of the employment of Mr. Heney at Senator Couzens's expense. April 11 was a momentous occasion, celebrated in the Senate by a number of speeches lending weight to the President's warning.

Now that the thunder has died down, the Senate is going about its business as usual. The only attention paid to Mr. Coolidge's message takes the form of a routine resolution authorizing the committee investigating the Internal Revenue Bureau "in its discretion to employ counsel and such other agents, experts and accountants as in its judgment may be necessary to aid in the investigation." Senator Couzens will not pay for Mr. Heney's services. That's all—except that the committee is now free to engage as large a staff of assistants as it may see fit.

The Senate has digested Mr. Coolidge's message, and it has done nothing to halt any of the investigations or to limit their freedom of inquiry. In spite of the partisan pretense that the country is tired of investigations, in spite of the President's best efforts to stop them, the Senate, Republican no less than Democratic, does not dare not to investigate any departments under criticism or to drop the work half finished. Considering that the Senate is composed of politicians thinking just now of the elections and little else, that is eloquent evidence of what the country really thinks. It is a pretty good demonstration that the people who are so tired of the investigations are the people who have been hurt by them.

A CALL TO SERVE.

To the Editor of The World:

The editorial "Blind Reaction" is good and true. The Democratic Party is confronted to-day with a splendid opportunity to be of real service to the Nation and to mankind, to lift us up from the slough into which we have fallen and to consecrate this Nation once more to earnest endeavor and high achievement.

We as a Nation have fallen backward during these last four years, but with nations, as with individuals, falls are but stepping-stones to new heights. The reaction that set in after the war, the delusions and the prejudices have somewhat subsided. America is once more ready to stride forward. To lead her forward is the Democratic Party's opportunity. It is that party's, and that party's alone, for the Republican Party is incapable of it. I do not mean that the rank and file of the Republican Party are incapable of it. Man for man and woman for woman, the Republican Party is fully as patriotic as the Democratic, fully as loyal and fully as able. But there is a controlling group in the Republican Party

THE LARGEST DAILY CIRCULATION IN AMERICA

DAILY NEWS

NEW YORK'S PICTURE NEWSPAPER

HOME EDITION

Vol. 5. No. 259.   28 Pages   New York, Tuesday, April 22, 1924   2 Cents

BOBBED BANDIT ADMITS GUILT

NEARS DECISION.—Harry K. Thaw (right) talked with Attorney Cohen in Philadelphia yesterday as testimony in proceedings to determine whether Thaw is now sane ended. His sanity will be determined by jury tomorrow.—*Story on page 1*

CAUGHT.—Celia Cooney (above), much-sought gungirl, yesterday with her husband and partner in crime was captured in Jacksonville, Fla. The couple, almost penniless, surrendered without the slightest resistance and admitted participation in fourteen Brooklyn robberies. They will be brought back here today.—*Story on page 3.*

STORY ENDS.—Marie Corelli (above), English novelist, author of a score of romances, died yesterday in England of a heart attack, aged sixty.—*Story on page 3.*

LAST CALL.—This is the last photo of Mme. Eleonora Duse, the world's greatest tragedienne, who died yesterday of influenza in Pittsburgh.—*Story on page 2.*

She was next taken to Brooklyn by her aunt and for ten years or so attended parochial school. At the age of fourteen her mother brought her back to New York, took her to a furnished room, stole her clothes and deserted her. A year later, aged fifteen, Cecilia became a child-laborer in a brush factory in Brooklyn, and was associating at night with sailors picked up on the water-front. At sixteen Cecilia was back in New York, living with her mother, working as laundress for a few months at a stretch in various hospitals. At twenty she was married, had borne a child, had committed a series of robberies, and is condemned to spend the rest of her youth in prison.

This is what twentieth-century civilization in New York achieved in the case of Cecilia Cooney. Fully warned by the behavior of her parents long before her birth, the law allowed her parents to reproduce their kind. Fully warned when she was still an infant, society allowed her to drift out of its hands into a life of dirt, neglect, dark basements, begging, stealing, ignorance, poor little tawdry excitements and twisted romance. The courts had their chance and they missed it. Charity had its chance and missed it. Schools had their chance and missed it. The church had its chance and missed it. The absent-minded routine of all that is well-meaning and respectable did not deflect by an inch her inexorable progress from the basement where she was born to the jail where she will expiate her crimes and ours.

For her crimes are on our hands too. No record could be clearer or more eloquent. None could have less room for doubt that Cecilia Cooney is a product of this city, of its neglect and it carelessness, of its indifference and its undercurrents of misery. We recommend her story to the pulpits of New York, to the school-men of New York, to the lawmakers of New York, to the social workers of New York, to those who are tempted to boast of its wealth, its magnificence and its power. ➤

EXIT JOHN BARLEYCORN

The Washington Post, Dec. 25, 1918

Old John Barleycorn, who has been battered from pillar to post for the past five years or more, is now making his last stand in the rear trench, with about as much chance of surviving as Bill Hohenzollern has of occupying his former residence at Potsdam. To recapitulate:

A prohibition amendment to the Federal Constitution is now pending for ratification by the States, with the prospect that the necessary 36 States will have taken favorable action on it by February 1.

A bill has passed Congress and has been signed by the President forbidding the manufacture and sale of intoxicating liquor after July 1 for the period of the war.

And now — oh, crowning act of autocratic oppression! — the Senate has hooked a rider on to

SACRED TO THE
MEMORY
OF
JOHN BARLEYCORN
DIED JULY 1,
1919

OLD
NOKEM
COLD

WHISKY
RING

*"John Barleycorn" has been the personification of
liquor since the 1600s. The character was widely used
by cartoonists as Prohibition approached.*

WEBSTER

"So old John Barleycorn may go down fighting to the last, but he is doomed," The Washington Post *wrote. "All hope is gone."*

the war revenue bill making the Reed bone dry provision apply to the District of Columbia.

All this in addition to the fact that the distilling of liquor and the brewing of beer have been interdicted as war measures.

Hence the absolute hopelessness of the plight in which O.J.B. finds himself. If the House accepts the bone dry rider adopted by the Senate — which no doubt it will — Washington will have the unique distinction of being the only dry capital in the world, so far as appears in all annals that survive. True, it has been dry nominally since November 1, 1917 when the Sheppard law wiped out all the grog shops

and closed the club lockers but its aridity was relieved by the refreshing rivulets which poured in over the Baltimore boulevard, the booze special and the American Railway Express. There was no legal objection to bringing in liquor for one's own personal use, and it was not difficult to find some one willing to divide his supply with a *dry* friend for a consideration. There was balm in Gilead, and available at a very fair price, considering the war tax.

But this Reed amendment — what a paradox that such a provision should emanate from Missouri! — is an absolute blight upon a thirsty community. Under a penalty of $1,000 fine and six months behind the bars — iron bars — it prohibits the shipment of liquor into the District, the solicitation of purchases and the introduction through the mails of any advertising matter relating to liquor. Not only is Washington to be cut off from getting booze, but it is prevented from reading about it or looking at the current price lists. At the very least the Smithsonian Institution — the object of which is the diffusion of knowledge among men — might cache a bock beer sign among its relics for the enlightenment of future generations.

It's all over but the shouting. Before six months have passed it is evident that there will be a legal ban upon the manufacture, sale, purchase, transportation, giving away, advertising, solicitation or reading about liquor. So Old John Barleycorn may go down fighting to the last, but he is doomed. All hope is gone. The cohorts of prohibition have him surrounded, hemmed in, enfiladed and pocketed, and they are closing in with deadly purpose. Even Sahara has its oases, but — well, what's the use! ❧

MY COUNTRY 'TIS OF THEE

Ronald G. Callvert, *The Sunday Oregonian*, Oct. 2, 1938

In this land of ours, this America, the man we choose as leader dons at no time uniform or insignia to denote his constitutional position as commander-in-chief of armed forces. No member of his cabinet, no civil subordinate, ever attires himself in garments significant of military power.

In this land of ours, this America, the average citizen sees so little of the army that he has not learned to distinguish between a major and a lieutenant from his shoulder straps. When the chief executive addresses his fellow countrymen they gather about him within handclasp distance. Goose-stepping regiments are not paraded before him. When he speaks to the civilian population it is not over rank upon rank of helmeted heads.

In this land of ours, this America, there is no tramp of military boots to entertain the visiting statesman. There is no effort to affright him with display of mobile cannon or of facility for mass production of aerial bombers.

In this land of ours, this America, there is no fortification along the several thousand miles of the

"If you cherish this liberty . . . then defend with all your might the American ideal of government."

northern border. In the great fresh water seas that partly separate it from another dominion no naval craft plies the waters. Along its southern border there are no forts, no show of martial strength.

In this land of ours, this America, no youth is conscripted to labor on devices of defense; military training he may take or leave at option. There is no armed force consistent with a policy of aggression. The navy is built against no menace from the western hemisphere, but wholly for defense against that which may threaten from Europe or Asia.

In this land of ours, this America, one-third of the population is foreign born, or native born of foreign or mixed parentage. Our more numerous "minorities" come from fourteen nations. The native born, whatever his descent, has all political and other rights possessed by him who traces his ancestry to the founding fathers. The foreign born of races that are assimilable are admitted to all these privileges if they want them. We have "minorities" but no minority problem.

In this land of ours, this America, the common citizen may criticise without restraint the policies of his government or the aims of the chief executive. He may vote as his judgment or his conscience advises and not as a ruler dictates.

In this land of ours, this America, our songs are dedicated to love and romance, the blue of the night, sails in the sunset, and not to might or to a martyrdom to political cause. Our national anthem has martial words; difficult air. But if you want to hear the organ roll give the people its companion — "America ... of thee I sing." In lighter patriotism we are nationally cosmopolitan.

Unitedly we sing of Dixie or of Ioway, where the tall corn grows, of springtime in the Rockies, or of California here I come.

In this land of ours, this America, there is not a bomb-proof shelter, and a gas mask is a curiosity. It is not needed that we teach our children where to run when death-hawks darken the sky.

In this land of ours, this America, our troubles present or prospective come from within — come from our own mistakes, and injure us alone. Our pledges of peace toward our neighbors are stronger than ruler's promise or written treaty. We guarantee them by devoting our resources, greater than the resources of any other nations, to upbuilding the industries of peace. We strut no armed might that could be ours. We cause no nation in our half of the world to fear us. None does fear us, nor arm against us.

In this land of ours, this America, we have illuminated the true road to permanent peace. But that is not the sole moral sought herein to be drawn. Rather it is that the blessings of liberty and equality and peace that have been herein recounted are possessed nowhere in the same measure in Europe or Asia and wane or disappear as one nears or enters a land of dictatorship of whatever brand. This liberty, this equality, this peace, are imbedded in the American form of government. We shall ever retain them if foreign isms that would dig them out and destroy them are barred from our shores. If you cherish this liberty, this equality, this peace that is peace material and peace spiritual — then defend with all your might the American ideal of government. ❧

THE HOUSE OF A HUNDRED SORROWS

Edward M. Kingsbury, *The New York Times*, Dec. 14, 1925

THE WALLS ARE GRIMY and discolored. The uneven floors creak and yield under foot. Staircases and landings are rickety and black. The door of every room is open. Walk along these corridors. Walk into this room. Here is a sickly boy of five, deserted by his mother, underfed, solitary in the awful solitude of starved, neglected childhood. "Seldom talks." Strange, isn't it? Some, many children, never "prattle" like your darlings. They are already old. They are full, perhaps, of long, hopeless thoughts. There are plenty of other "kids" in this tenement. Here is one, only three. Never saw his father. His mother spurned and abused him. He is weak and "backward." How wicked of him when he has been so encouraged and coddled! Doesn't know any games. How should he? Do children play? Not his kind. They live to suffer.

In Room 24 is Rose, a housemother of 10. Father is in the hospital. Mother is crippled with rheumatism. Rose does all the work. You would love Rose if she came out of Dickens. Well, there she is, mothering her mother in Room 24. In Room 20 age has been toiling for youth. Grandmother has been taking care of three granddaughters who lost their mother. A brave old woman; but what with rheumatism and heart weakness, threescore-and-ten can't go out to work any more. What's going to happen to her and her charges? Thinking of that, she is ill on top of her physical illness. A very interesting house, isn't it, Sir? Decidedly "a rum sort of place," Madam? Come into Room 23. Simon, the dollmaker — but handmade dolls are "out" — lives, if you call it living, here. Eighty years old, his wife of about the same age. Their eyesight is mostly gone. Otherwise they would still be sewing on buttons and earning a scanty livelihood for themselves and two little girls, their grandchildren. The girls object to going to an orphan home. Some children are like that.

You must see those twin sisters of 65 in Room 47. True, they are doing better than usual on account of the coming holidays; making as much as $10 a month, whereas their average is but $6. Still, rents are a bit high; and the twins, have been so long together that they would like to stay so. In Room — but you need no guide. Once in The House of a Hundred Sorrows you will visit every sad chamber in it. If your heart be made of penetrable stuff, you will do the most you can to bring hope and comfort to its inmates, to bring them Christmas and the Christ:

"For I was a hungered, and ye gave me meat; I was thirsty, and ye gave me drink; I was a stranger, and ye took me in.

"Naked, and ye clothed me; I was sick, and ye visited me; I was in prison, and ye came unto me." ❧

In a December 1925 editorial about the plight of tenement dwellers, The New York Times urged its readers to bring "hope and comfort" during the Christmas season to those who lived in the "House of a Hundred Sorrows."

RETURN FROM PRODIGALS

William Allen White, *The Emporia Daily Gazette*, Dec. 12, 1922

Henry L. Mencken has returned from Europe to this nation of "third raters and boobs" and upon the whole he is glad to get home. He declares that even if we are a lousy lot, he "likes the show" we put up. And it really is a great show — the greatest show on earth.

What a gorgeous and exciting panorama flies across the pages of an American newspaper every day in the year. Here one faces all the "beasts at Ephesus," the impassioned booster, the crazy lover, the paranoac trader, the seer of visions, the shallow pated babbler, the bandits that would shame Ali Baba's 40 thieves, magicians that make music come out of the air and genii that direct power in machines a hundred miles distant. Fools caper across the pages of the papers and wise men hide in lonesome corners; dreams come true and well laid plans run wild. The dramatis personae throws into the cast of the mad drama, heroes, villains, clowns, gentlemen, ladies, servants, oafs, trolls, little knaves and big ones, angels and devils, the mob, its victim and its conqueror.

No wonder Mencken is glad to come back from the lamentable comedy of Europe and take his seat before the pageant of American life. He snorts and grunts more or less at it. He affects to despise most of its aspects, and some of its phrases are dispiriting, but it is the greatest show under God's mundane heaven, because the thing is alive. It means something because it has vitality. No one knows what it means. But it is significant of

"He sometimes opens his pig's mouth, fanged and ugly, and lets out the voice of God," William Allen White wrote of Mencken.

something — the Heaven only knows what. But, say, man, how it holds us! Those who have to pass out between the acts must give a wistful and lingering look back, no matter what phantasmagoria may flare before their eyes in the offing of eternity.

And one of the most engaging figures on the American scene is this same Mencken who comes back to the spectacle with interest renewed after looking at the debacle of Europe. With a pig's eyes that never look up, with a pig's snout that loves muck, with a pig's brain that knows only the sty, and a pig's squeal that cries only when he is hurt, he sometimes opens his pig's mouth, fanged and ugly, and lets out the voice of God — railing at the whitewash that covers the manure about his habitat. In all our American letters we have produced no more capable Caliban than Henry L. Mencken. And so long as he is a part of the American show, it will be worth the price.

Here's a welcome home to the porker who has been living among the prodigals! ❧

TO INTENDING FEMALE VOTERS

The New York Times, Nov. 2, 1915

Of the enthusiasm, energy, ingenuity, vocal persistence, the aesthetic and decorative effect of the woman suffragists, there can be but one opinion. They have been diligent. They have been devoted. Their ardor, their proselyting passion, their variety of attack, have been beautiful to see. They must have convinced themselves more strongly than they were convinced before. But if to their own they added the tongues of men and angels they could hardly persuade the majority of voters at this time.

The eyes and thoughts of men are busied with events of the war and problems which it has forced on the United States. The economic, financial, and commercial readjustments and reconstructions which it has caused, the transformation of this country into a creditor nation, the new legislation that will be required to meet new situations — a host of difficult problems has arisen. They are of a nature that demands the gravest steady attention and study. They will tax the intelligence of the male electorate. They are not sentimental, moral, humanitarian. They are matters of national self-defense, of business self-preservation and enlargement. And when thoughtful men are perplexed, seeing so many thorny questions, so many contingencies, so much dependent on the war, such possibilities of swift transitions of trade after the war, the suffragists come, in all innocence, and ask to have the economic and political wisdom, not too high already, of the electorate diluted by the infusion of unpracticed, uninstructed feminism!

There are old reasons enough against woman suffrage, and it would be futile to cite them now. Men's minds are made up. At this time of all times the poetizing and enfeebling of the practical instincts, experience, and capability of the State by the admission of women as voters would be a perilous venture. Aside from that, a certain recoil from radicalism, a return toward conservatism, natural after a long, continuous forward movement, is discernible in the public temper. The old notion about the position of women may be outworn, but our friends, the suffragists, having seen it so strong even in a nursery of reform like Wisconsin, may, perhaps, count on finding it stronger in New York, Pennsylvania, Massachusetts. ❧

OPPOSITE: *A program from a 1913 suffrage parade. As far back as 1878,* The Washington Post *editorialized:* "It would be folly to deny that in almost every instance in history where [woman] has been clothed with power, she has outrivaled men in the commission of deeds of cruelty and crime." THIS PAGE: *Amelia Bloomer was anything but content with her lot. A stirring suffragette, she also lent her name to the loose trousers she popularized.*

CHAPTER EIGHT
FREEDOMS

Seven Hollywood writers and directors who refused to testify
at the House Un-American Activities Committee
hearings arrive at District Court in Washington, D.C.,
where they will be tried for contempt of Congress.

Drawn on Stone by Hoffmann from a Daguerr.

Printed by Nagel & Weingärtner, N.Y.

Entered according to act of Congress in the year 1852 by Nagel & Weingärtner, in the Clerks Office of the District Court of the Southern District of New York.

R.t Rev.d D.r Hughes.

"WE SORROW FOR OUR NATIVE LAND."

WALT WHITMAN, STILL IN HIS EARLY 20S, WAS JUST WARMING UP WITH THAT LINE. THE DATE WAS MARCH 17, 1842, A YEAR WHITMAN WAS WRITING EDITORIALS FOR THE *AURORA*, A NEW YORK NEWSPAPER. HE WAS INCENSED OVER A GREAT ISSUE OF FREEDOM: WHETHER PUBLIC FUNDS IN NEW YORK SHOULD BE USED TO FINANCE CATHOLIC EDUCATION — IN PARTICULAR, EDUCATION FOR WAVES OF CHILDREN OF IRISH IMMIGRANTS. ❧ IT WAS A GREAT AND GRAND FIGHT over a great and grand principle, and it lasted for years. New York's public schools were, in theory, nonreligious, though they apparently had enough of an anti-Catholic and anti-Irish flavor to incense the Irish-born Bishop John Joseph Hughes. Hughes, who later became the first archbishop of New York, knew his politics as well as his religion, and he launched a campaign to get state funding to set up schools for Catholics.

It divided the city, the politicians and the newspapers. Two of the greatest editorial writers of the day, Walt Whitman and Horace Greeley, lined up against him. One was vitriolic, the other calm. But both were unyielding. Whitman called the bishop a "hypocritical scoundrel," "that reverend villain," a man with "corrupt and selfish motives." When a critic assailed Whitman for editorials showing "the fiercest invective, and the hottest hate," he replied in print that "we are well aware that we used strong language; we *meant* to."

After an election in which Catholic schools were the issue, rioters attacked the bishop's house. "In the course of the evening, some of the windows of the priest Hughes' residence were broken by brickbats," Whitman wrote in the next day's editorial. "Had it been the reverend hypocrite's head, instead of his windows, we could hardly find it in our soul to be sorrowful."

Greeley appealed to logic and law, in an editorial published on Nov. 24, 1851:

"That we differ with the Bishop on certain points of Religious Faith, is quite true, but we have no wish to abridge his liberty on that account. ... We hold his right to Civil and Religious Freedom as precious as our own. ... He would have Religion form a part of every child's education. Very good — we concur in that view. But it is one thing to assume that each child should be taught Religion, and quite another to maintain that Religious dogmas should be taught in *common schools*. We desire and intend that our own children shall be taught Religion; we do *not* desire that it shall be taught them in Common Schools. For this we shall take them to Church, to Sunday School, to Bible Class, or wherever else they may be taught by those who we believe will teach them Divine Truth in its purity, while for the acquisition of Reading, Writing, Arithmetic, &c., we shall send them to Common or secular Schools. Why is not

OPPOSITE: *Archbishop John Hughes. "But it is one thing to assume that each child should be taught Religion, and quite another to maintain that Religious dogmas should be taught in common schools," Horace Greeley wrote in 1851.*

this distinction a natural and just one? How *can* a man so wise as the Archbishop speak of our Common School System as 'not calculated to meet the requirements which Catholic parents, at least, are bound to fulfill toward their Catholic offspring?' Why, Rev. Sir! it never *pretended* to do any such thing. You might as well object that it does not wash, dress and vaccinate them. ... Why should you find fault with the Schools for doing their own proper work and not attempting yours?"

Hughes ultimately lost his fight, and he went on to set up the nation's first Catholic school system. But versions of the fight have continued over the generations, as have fights over other freedoms guaranteed Americans in the Bill of Rights. Surprisingly, perhaps, the press—the great beneficiary of that Bill of Rights — has not always defended freedom for others. Indeed, when national crises arise, the press often sides with censoring and censuring.

Thus it was that in 1943, when some people were proposing that at least some of the 110,000 interned Japanese be freed, the *Los Angeles Times* was fervid, and racist, in its opposition. Not only would the release endanger the security of Americans, but also "few Americans would work with them."

Many of these Japanese were American citizens. But the *Times* was unswayed.

"As a race, the Japanese have made for themselves a record for conscienceless treachery unsurpassed in history," it concluded. "Whatever small theoretical advantages there might be in releasing those under restraint in this country would be enormously outweighed by the risks involved." (*The New York Times*, by contrast, a year earlier urged that "loyal aliens" be given an identification card and released. "It all boils down to the simple fact that loyalty or lack of loyalty is determined by character, not by place of birth," the paper said.)

And thus it was that in 1947 the *New York Herald Tribune* endorsed, in effect, loyalty oaths. It was a time when politicians were capitalizing on many Americans' fears that communism could get a hold in this country, and the motion picture industry blackballed 10 people after they were cited for contempt in refusing to answer questions of a congressional committee.

"It is hard to maintain that a mass-communication industry is powerless to deny employment on suspicion of secret membership in a subversive organization," the *Herald Tribune* editorialized.

That incensed E.B. White, one of the great essayists of the day, who wrote and told the newspaper that the suggestion "that employees should be required to state their beliefs in order to hold their jobs ... is inconsistent with our Constitutional theory and has been stubbornly opposed by watchful men since the early days of the Republic." He added, "I can only assume that your editorial writer, in a hurry to get home for Thanksgiving, tripped over the First Amendment and thought it was the office cat."

The entire exchange — two editorials, two letters from E.B. White and a we-have-the-last-word editor's note following the second letter — is one of the most wonderful and enlightening debates on freedom ever to appear in a newspaper. The exchanges are printed here in their entirety.

Before communism, it was socialism that upset the people. And the people's reaction upset William Allen White.

"Probably more bigotry and reaction just now are hiding under the phrase 'Americanism' than ever hid under one word before," he wrote in *The Emporia Daily Gazette* in 1920. "If Americanism means anything, it means freedom of speech, freedom of thought, freedom of press. Every wicked, greedy force in America to-day is trying to strangle discussion under the guise of promoting Americanism. And as a result of the repression every mad political folly is thriving. Socialism, which has no ground to stand on as a creed under free debate, to-day is spreading under repression. … Americanism of the genuine sort fears no idea enough to suppress it. Americanism does not strangle the press or stop any debate. The man who talks about hunting them out, standing them up and shooting them down, is not 100 per cent American. He is 99 per cent coward who is afraid his creed won't stand the tests of free speech and a free press."

It is in times of crisis — times of war, of paranoia, of terror, of political outrage — when freedom is most compromised, of course. Historically, most editors have acknowledged that censorship of war news is a fact, and often an acceptable fact.

"In war time military necessity has everywhere the right of way," Henry Watterson wrote in a *Courier-Journal* editorial in 1917. "Its censorship must be thorough and unquestioned."

But he was just as certain that there should not be, and could not be, censorship of editorials. Indeed, censorship of thought or opinion would be far worse than censorship of fact or act. You can argue that a law against burning the flag, or a law against lap-dancing, is not an infringement of speech. But you can't argue that a person cannot believe that such a law is an infringement.

So *The Washington Post* can argue that a flag-burning amendment "would, in effect, turn the 'no' in the hallowed phrase 'Congress shall make no law' into an 'almost no' — which is a singular erosion of the principle for which the First Amendment stands."

"You tell me that law is above freedom of utterance," William Allen White wrote in a Pulitzer Prize-winning editorial in 1922 entitled "To an Anxious Friend." "And I reply that you can have no wise laws nor free enforcement of wise laws unless there is free expression of the wisdom of the people — and, alas, their folly with it. But if there is freedom, folly will die of its own poison, and the wisdom will survive. … You say that freedom of utterance is not for time of stress, and I reply with the sad truth that only in time of stress is freedom of utterance in danger. No one questions it in calm days, because it is not needed."

It is an editorial that should be posted in every legislature, in every classroom and, most certainly, in every newsroom. And the final paragraph should be etched into the hearts of every American:

"So, dear friend, put fear out of your heart. This nation will survive, this state will prosper, the orderly business of life will go forward if only men can speak in whatever way given them to utter what their hearts hold — by voice, by posted card, by letter or by press. Reason never has failed men. Only force and repression have made the wrecks in the world." ❧

NATIVE AMERICANISM REPUDIATED

WALT WHITMAN, *The New York Aurora,* April 18, 1842

The Aurora has been roaring very loudly and ably, though somewhat savagely,
on behalf of the Native Americans, during the past week. The roar is a pleasant one
and sounds like an honest one. But the 'rora has a bad habit
of calling people names. Oh fie! — *Yesterday's Mercury.*

We see the danger, let us have the remedy. Let us have a Native American party.
Harsh as the word may sound, it is our only safeguard. — *Yesterday's News.*

ONE OF THE MOST ARDENT WISHES OF OUR soul is, to see the American people imbued with a feeling of respect for, and confidence in, *themselves* — a feeling that shall impel them to place their own kind, and their own merits *first.* Entertaining a sentiment of this sort, we cannot look round and behold timid servility to a factious gang of foreigners — or the fostering, in our own republic, of trashy and poisonous European literature — or the bending of knees to the dicta of old world critics, merely because their commands come "by authority" — or the influx among us of vapid English, Scotch, French, and German quacks — without lifting our voice, and, in our way, doing all that we can to denounce and condemn those things.

It becomes our people to have a decent and a proper pride in their government and their country. We possess the most glorious constitution, the most enviable freedom, the happiest and best educated mass of citizens, of any nation that ever existed on the face of the earth. It is well for us to exult in this. Travellers, to be sure, talk about the national vanity of the Americans — but we appeal to any observing man if, in our conduct, we do not show a lamentable want of self complacency, of reliance on our intrinsic worth, and of independence of foreign sway.

Yet with all our antipathy for every thing that may tend to assimilate our country to the kingdoms of Europe, we repudiate such doctrines as have characterised the "Native American" party. We could see no man disfranchised, because he happened to be born three thousand miles off. We go for the largest liberty — the widest extension of the immunities of the people, as well as the blessings of government. Let us receive these foreigners to our shores, and to our good offices. While it is unbecoming for us to fawn upon them and flatter their whims, it is equally unnecessary that we should draw the line of exclusiveness, and say, stand off, I am better than thou. ❧

OPPOSITE: *Walt Whitman. "It becomes our people to have a decent and a proper pride in their government and their country."*

PROPOSALS BY AN OFFICER

WHICH STRAIN OUR BELIEF IN FREE SPEECH EXCEEDINGLY CLOSE TO THE BREAKING POINT

W.J. CASH, *The Charlotte* (N.C.) *News,* April 9, 1939

WE ARE SO THOROUGHLY CONVINCED THAT FREE speech should be free speech that we believe the doctrine ought to be stretched to the last final limit even in the case of retired army officers.

So we think old General Van Horne Moseley was within his rights when he inveighed against the Jews in the true Hitler vein before a patrioteer woman's organization at Philadelphia the other evening, when he yelled that the next war would be fought for them,

Gen. Van Horne Moseley. "He passed over the line of free speech and came dangerously close to sedition."

when he screamed that the Roosevelt Administration is Red. Maybe he was even within his rights when he cried that Fascism was an excellent "antitoxin" for the United States, and that the best type of democracy was insured by its battle against Communism, which he saw as a very great menace to us.

But when he went on to say that the army would, very rightly, "demur" if a "Leftist Administration" (he clearly meant the Roosevelt Administration) ordered it to fight in a war against the Fascist powers, and that a patrioteer army ought to be organized to deal with "emergencies" at home (he constantly calls the Roosevelt Administration an "emergency"), he passed over the line of free speech and came dangerously close to sedition. Frank Gwynn, commander of the American Legion in Pennsylvania, indeed walked out on the address in disgust and said flatly that it proposed nothing less than rebellion against the United States. And this man Moseley, you understand, is still an officer in the army — draws pay as such. If war were declared, he would almost certainly be called back into active service — could profoundly influence his command. Indeed, there must be many thousands of men in the army right now who will be profoundly influenced by what he says. For he holds the great rank of Major-General.

Altogether, it seems about time that the War Department at least admonished the old General that there is such a thing as court-martial for retired officers. ❧

COMMUNISM AND HOLLYWOOD

New York Herald Tribune, Nov. 27, 1947

It is doubtful whether any one, with the exception of Mr. J. Parnell Thomas, will feel happy over the action of the motion-picture industry in firing the ten persons cited for contempt of the Thomas committee and in henceforth barring Communists from the industry's pay rolls. The industry's own unhappiness is evident enough from the tortured language of the announcement, in which respect for justice and civil liberty struggles both painfully and obviously with the desire to escape the embarrassments brought down by Mr. Thomas's hippodrome.

Many will observe that the motion-picture business seems to have got along very well in the past utilizing the services of the evasive ten without discovering Communist propaganda turning up in its products. Many will feel that it is simply a case of a gigantic industry, always notoriously timid and sensitive to any kind of mass reaction, running to cover from popular hysteria, at the expense of destroying the livelihoods of a few writers and directors against whom nothing has been proved except that they evaded answering as to their political beliefs. It is neither a heroic nor an inspiring attitude. But is it inadmissible?

One cannot blink the fact that this is another of the difficult questions forced upon us by Communism, by its nature, its aims and, in particular, its methods. Communist secrecy and infiltration are facts, and it is difficult to argue that an industry of mass communications is denied by democratic principles the right of protecting itself against them. The ten put on a show before the Un-American Activities Com-

Rep. J. Parnell Thomas and actor Robert Taylor at a House Un-American Activities Committee hearing.

mittee which was damaging to the industry. Now they have issued from Hollywood an answering blast, denouncing their dismissal not merely as an invasion of their liberties but as part of an "attempt to control films, books and science in order to facilitate the dissemination of anti-democratic, anti-Semitic, anti-Negro and war-inciting doctrines."

Here is a piece of politically inspired propagandist nonsense of a kind which Hollywood certainly cannot be required to protect or encourage. It is hard to maintain that a mass-communication industry is powerless to deny employment on suspicion of secret membership in a subversive organization. This newspaper believes the power must be conceded; but it certainly should be used as sparingly as possible, and one trusts that the motion-picture industry's insistence on fairness and moderation will be observed. ❧

Hollywood stars, including Humphrey Bogart,
Lauren Bacall, Gene Kelly and Danny Kaye,
board a plane for Washington to protest the House
Un-American Activities Committee hearings.

Some of the members of the House Un–American Activities Committee, including Rep. Richard M. Nixon (far right).

THE AGE OF FEAR

MR. WHITE THINKS WE FELL OVER THE CAT

E.B. White, *New York Herald Tribune*, Dec. 2, 1947

To the New York Herald Tribune:

I am a member of a party of one, and I live in an age of fear. Nothing lately has unsettled my party and raised my fears so much as your editorial, on Thanksgiving Day, suggesting that employees should be required to state their beliefs in order to hold their jobs. The idea is inconsistent with our Constitutional theory and has been stubbornly opposed by watchful men since the early days of the Republic. It's hard for me to believe that the Herald Tribune is backing away from the fight, and I can only assume that your editorial writer, in a hurry to get home for Thanksgiving, tripped over the First Amendment and thought it was the office cat.

The investigation of alleged Communists by the Thomas committee has been a confusing spectacle for all of us. I believe its implications are widely misunderstood and that the outcome is grave beyond exaggerating. The essence of our political theory in this country is that a man's conscience shall be a private not a public affair, and that only his deeds and words shall be open to survey, to censure and to punishment. The idea is a decent one, and it works. It is an idea that cannot safely be compromised with, lest it be utterly destroyed. It cannot be modified even under circumstances where, for security reasons, the temptation to modify it is great.

I think security in critical times takes care of itself if the people and the institutions take care of themselves. First in line is the press. Security, for me, took a tumble not when I read that there were Communists in Hollywood but when I read your editorial in praise of loyalty testing and thought control. If a man is in health, he doesn't need to take anybody else's temperature to know where he is going. If a newspaper or a motion picture company is in health, it can get rid of Communists and spies simply by reading proof and by watching previews.

I hold that it would be improper for any committee or any employer to examine my conscience. They wouldn't know how to get into it, they wouldn't know what to do when they got in there, and I wouldn't let them in anyway. Like other Americans, my acts and my words are open to inspection — not my thoughts or my political affiliation. (As I pointed out, I am a member of a party of one.) Your editorialist said he hoped the companies in checking for loyalty would use their powers sparingly and wisely. That is a wistful idea. One need only watch totalitarians at work to see that once men gain power over other men's minds that power is never used sparingly and wisely, but lavishly and brutally and with unspeakable results. If I must declare today that I am not a Communist, tomorrow I shall have to testify that I am not a Unitarian. And the day after that I have never belonged to a dahlia club.

It is not a crime to believe anything at all in America. To date it has not been declared illegal to belong to the Communist party. Yet ten men have been convicted not of wrongdoing but of wrong believing. That is news in this country, and if I have not misread history, it is bad news. ❧

THE PARTY OF ONE

New York Herald Tribune, Dec. 2, 1947

ELSEWHERE ON THIS PAGE WE PRESENT A LETTER FROM a favorite reader, Mr. E.B. White, laying bare in all its nakedness the fallacy from which most, if not all, liberals are suffering in these distressful times. Mr. White is a "member of a party of one," and he "lives in an age of fear." In these lonely and timorous surroundings he cannot understand how others may neither be particularly afraid nor particularly concerned because the problem of combating Communist subversion requires us to summon up new concepts and new principles of action in the defense of democracy against a threat which has over and over again announced its intention of destroying democracy root and branch, as soon as it gets the opportunity.

The "members of the party of one" have been with us since the dawn of civilization. They have always been highly valuable elements in our civilization and nearly always as destructive as they have been valuable. Typically, they have been those who will always support a good cause up to the point at which support becomes dangerous or difficult; they have been those who will shout for justice until justice comes in conflict, as sooner or later it always does, with what is right and possible. They are the people who cannot understand that history marches on by its own imperatives, that legal principles are always subject to revision by the necessities of the facts which confront us at any given time; who cannot understand that a Communist deliberately and astutely using the principles of democracy to destroy those principles is different from a Truman Democrat or a Taft Republican trying to utilize the democratic process in order to get himself into temporary power.

The "members of the party of one" who "live in an age of fear" are probably the most dangerous single elements in our confused and complicated society. Most of us, though reasonably and normally terrified by the prospects of atomic warfare and so on, do not live in an age of fear. We still feel that the democratic principle has an ultimate validity in the world. We still feel that those who, by every utterance they make, announce themselves as anti-democratic and as resolved to use whatever power they may achieve through the kindliness of the democratic world in order to overthrow that world, are invidious and dangerous elements in our society. We do not "trip over the First Amendment." We think that the First Amendment carried obligations as well as guaranties. We think those obligations have something to do with thoughts as well as with actions, and if the "party of one" finally takes its stand upon the inviolability of the Dahlia Club we shall respect its position; but if it takes its stand upon the necessity of protecting the individual to the point of destroying Western democratic civilization, we shall demand that it answer for the political consequences of its position. ❧

Essayist E.B. White. "I hold that it would be improper for any committee or any employer to examine my conscience."

THESE EDGY TIMES
MR. WHITE BELIEVES US NEEDLESSLY UNKIND

E.B. White, *New York Herald Tribune*, Dec. 9, 1947

To the New York Herald Tribune:

The editorial that you wrote about me illustrated what I meant about the loyalty check system and about what would happen if it got going in the industrial world. My letter, expressing a dissenting opinion, was a letter that any conscientious reader might write to his newspaper, and you answered it by saying that I belonged to "probably the most dangerous element in our society." Thus a difference of opinion became suddenly a mark of infamy. A man who disagreed with a Tribune editorial used to be called plucky — now he's called dangerous. By your own definition I already belong among the unemployables.

You said that in these times we need "new concepts and new principles" to combat subversion. It seems to me the loyalty check in industry is not a new principle at all. It is like the "new look," which is in reality the old, old look, slightly tinkered up. The principle of demanding an expression of political conformity as the price of a job is the principle of hundred percentism. It is not new and it is blood brother of witch burning.

I don't know why I should be bawling out the Herald Tribune or why the Herald Tribune should be bawling out me. I read those Bert Andrews pieces and got a new breath of fresh air. Then I turn in a dissenting opinion about an editorial and get hit over the head with a stick of wood. These times are too edgy. It is obvious to every one that the fuss about loyalty arises from fear of war with Soviet Russia, and from the natural feeling that we should clear our decks of doubtful characters. Well, I happen to believe that we can achieve reasonably clear decks if we continue to apply our civil rights and duties equally to all citizens, even to citizens of opposite belief. That may be a dangerous and false idea, but my holding it does not necessarily make me a dangerous and false man, and I wish that the Herald Tribune next time it sits down to write a piece about me and my party would be good enough to make the distinction. Right now, it's a pretty important distinction to make.

(Perhaps we were over emphatic in our disagreement with Mr. White, but since the same editorial which suggested that he belonged to a "dangerous element" also said that it was a "highly valuable" element, he can scarcely hold that we were attaching any badge of "infamy" to him. We regret it if Mr. White took as a reflection upon himself what was intended only as a reflection upon his argument, and are glad to express our high personal regard for him. The argument, however, remains. It is decidedly not an argument arising from any fear of war with Russia (we happen to think that a very remote possibility) but from the fact that Communism, exploiting toleration in order to destroy toleration, has forced upon us an issue much deeper than that of mere non-conformity within the frame of a free society. We may be misguided in our attempts to deal with it, but it seems to us that Mr. White fails to deal with it at all. — Ed.) ❧

BRILLIANT BUT DULL

The New York Times, Dec. 8, 1933

It is now judicially decided that the "Ulysses" of James Joyce is not an obscene or pornographic book. That will prevail, at least so far as permitting the work to be imported into the United States. In the carefully prepared opinion of Judge Woolsey, certain general principles are laid down. It is not fair to tear a phrase or paragraph from its context. Since it is a question of intent, the novel must be judged as a whole. So dealing with it, Judge Woolsey finds a good deal in "Ulysses" that is vulgar and offensive, yet does not fall within the statute relating to obscene publications. There is no delighting in dirt for the sake of dirt. The book is held by the judge to be a sincere piece of literature, not designed to corrupt morals.

Admitting that parts of "Ulysses" are brilliantly written, Judge Woolsey decides that other sections of it are dull reading. This will be a disappointment, or a challenge, to all-the-way admirers of Joyce. They can read the deepest symbolism into his most routine and jejune writing. They will probably be chagrined, also, to find that the public has no great interest in this long-banned novel. While under exclusion, it was furtively read with delight; now that it can be freely bought and sold, there will be less appetite for it, one imagines. It is like prohibition. If drinking is forbidden, thousands will manage to get a drink; but as soon as it is made legal, the thrill of romance is taken away from defying or evading the law.

As for literary criticism of "Ulysses," Judge

James Joyce (right), the author of Ulysses, *and his publisher Sylvia Beach. The judge ruled his book not obscene—but dull.*

Woolsey indulges in a bit of his own. He declares the attempt of Mr. Joyce to be

> to show how the screen of consciousness, with its ever-shifting kaleidoscopic impressions, carries, as it were on a plastic palimpsest, not only what is in the focus of each man's observation of the actual things about him, but also in a penumbral zone residua of past impressions, some recent and some drawn up by association from the domain of the subconscious.

Please remember that this is judicial. It cannot be attacked without danger of contempt of court. ❧

'AN ENLIGHTENED PEOPLE'

The New York Times, July 1, 1971

The historic decision of the Supreme Court in the case of the United States Government vs. The New York Times and The Washington Post is a ringing victory for freedom under law. By lifting the restraining order that had prevented this and other newspapers from publishing the hitherto secret Pentagon Papers, the nation's highest tribunal strongly reaffirmed the guarantee of the people's right to know, implicit in the First Amendment to the Constitution of the United States.

This was the essence of what The New York Times and other newspapers were fighting for and this is the essence of the Court's majority opinions. The basic question, which goes to the very core of the American political system, involved the weighing by the Court of the First Amendment's guarantee of freedom against the Government's power to restrict that freedom in the name of national security. The Supreme Court did not hold that the First Amendment gave an absolute right to publish anything under all circumstances. Nor did The Times seek that right. What The Times sought, and what the Court upheld, was the right to publish these particular documents at this particular time without prior Governmental restraint.

The crux of the problem lay indeed in this question of prior restraint. For the first time in the history of the United States, the Federal Government had sought through the courts to prevent publication of material that it maintained would do "irreparable injury" to the national security if spread before the public. The Times, supported in this instance by the overwhelming majority of the American press, held on the contrary that it was in the national interest to publish this information, which was of historic rather than current operational nature.

If the documents had involved troop movements, ship sailings, imminent military plans, the case might have been quite different; and in fact The Times would not have endeavored to publish such material. But this was not the case; the documents and accompanying analysis are historic, in no instance going beyond 1968, and incapable in 1971 of harming the life of a single human being or interfering with any current military operation. The majority of the Court clearly recognized that embarrassment of public officials in the past — or even in the present — is insufficient reason to overturn what Justice White described as "the concededly extraordinary protection against prior restraint under our constitutional system."

So far as the Government's classification of the material is concerned, it is quite true, as some of our critics have observed, that "no one elected The Times" to declassify it. But it is also true, as the Court implicitly recognizes, that the public interest is not served by classification and retention in secret form of vast amounts of information, 99.5 per cent of which a retired senior civil servant recently testified "could not be prejudicial to the defense interests of the nation."

Out of this case should surely come a total revision of governmental procedures and practice in the entire area of classification of documents. Everyone who has ever had anything to do with such documents knows that for many years the classification procedures have been hopelessly muddled by inertia, timidity and sometimes even stupidity and venality.

Beyond all this, one may hope that the entire exercise will induce the present Administration to re-examine its own attitudes toward secrecy, suppression and restriction of the liberties of free man in a free society. The issue the Supreme Court decided yesterday touched the heart of this republic; and we fully realize that this is not so much a victory for any particular newspaper as it is for the basic principles of freedom on which the American form of government rests. This is really the profound message of yesterday's decision, in which this newspaper rejoices with humility and with the consciousness that the freedom thus reaffirmed carries with it, as always, the reciprocal obligation to present the truth to the American public so far as it can be determined. That is, in fact, why the Pentagon material had to be published. It is only with the fullest possible understanding of the facts and of the background of any policy decision that the American people can be expected to play the role required of them in this democracy.

It would be well for the present Administration, in the light of yesterday's decision, to reconsider with far more care and understanding than it has in the past, the fundamental importance of individual freedoms — including especially freedom of speech, of the press, of assembly — to the life of the American democracy. "Without an informed and free press," as Justice Stewart said, "there cannot be an enlightened people." ❧

New York Times *staffers celebrate the*
publishing of the Pentagon Papers.

LAP-DANCING: IT'S FREE SPEECH; IT'S A BUSINESS; IT'S STILL ILLEGAL

Michael G. Gartner, *The* (Ames, Iowa) *Daily Tribune*, Aug. 11, 1997

WE USUALLY TRY TO GATHER FACTS FIRST-HAND before we write an editorial, figuring that you can't have opinions if you don't have facts.

But we confess — before we get into today's editorial — that we have never been to Blondie's. We have never lap-danced, at least as it is defined by the Ames Municipal Code. And we have never seen anyone else doing it. It's yet another of our limitations.

We've read quite a bit about it, though, and it seems to us that it's a business: A near-naked woman working in a bar sits on a customer's lap and grinds about for a while; he holds her, probably not by her hand; and then he gives her some money. There doesn't seem to be a lot of affection, as in love or respect. And it doesn't seem particularly sportive, as in playful or frolicsome. It seems, as we said, a simple business transaction, somber if not sober — kind of like buying a lottery ticket, a customer's hope of something that will never materialize.

So we were a little surprised that Summer Bernstauch and her lawyer conceded she violated the ordinance last Jan. 10 when police issued her a citation while she was working at Blondie's on South Duff Avenue. She and her lawyer said, yes, she had violated the law. But they argued that the law was unconstitutional. They said that since it applied only to entertainers and not to other bar employees, it violated the Equal Protection Clause of the 14th Amendment. And they said that lap-dancing was a form of expression and thus was protected by the First Amendment guarantee of free speech.

District Associate Judge Steven P. Van Marel disagreed. Then, District Court Judge Gary L. McMinimee upheld him.

So, for now at least, that's that. The lap-dancing law is valid, and any entertainer who concedes she has been lap-dancing in Ames can be given a citation that will hold up in court.

But we don't see how any woman can be convicted if she doesn't concede she was lap-dancing. For the ordinance requires a judge to determine the state of mind of the lap-dancer and to characterize her mood and motive. That seems impossible.

The law says an entertainer cannot "fondle, caress or sit on the lap of any customer" if the entertainer is nude or — in the sportive language of the ordinance — "so attired as to leave exposed the entertainer's genitals, or pubic hair, or anus, or buttocks, or female breast, or female breast with only the nipple covered." It goes on to say that "'fondle or caress' shall mean to bring any part of the body into contact with the body of another, in a sportive or affectionate manner, for the purpose of producing or experiencing sexual arousal or excitement."

So now that we know that the ordinance is constitutional — so far, at least — why can't a lap-dancer say, "Yes, judge, I was lap-dancing. But my purpose was to make money, not to excite the customer." Or, "Yes, judge, I was lap-dancing. But I think the customer was a slob. I have no affection for him." Or, "Yes, judge, I was lap-dancing. But I was serious. There wasn't an ounce of sportiveness in my gyrations."

And what can the judge say? "That was not your purpose?" "The customer was a nice and loving man?" "You were in a frolicsome mood?" How could the judge know? How could anyone know?

We mention all this today — as we did a year ago, when the law was under consideration — just to point out how absurd the whole thing is. We think the law is unconstitutional, that lap-dancing like flag-burning or protest-marching is a form of expression that is protected by the First Amendment. But even if the law is constitutional, it is idiotic. It was passed because Ames Police Chief Dennis Ballantine — who is, as we always note, a good guy and a good chief — thought it would help deal with prostitution.

Arrest records indicate prostitution isn't particularly high on the list of criminal activity around town. But even if it were, this lap-dancing law is no way to deal with it. You enforce laws by arresting the law-breakers, not by inventing silly or dangerous new ordinances that have no bearing on the real issue.

Actually, we suspect the automobile is more directly linked to prostitution than lap-dancing is.

So maybe we should ban driving.

Or, at least, driving in a sportive manner. ❧

NOT A BURNING ISSUE

The Washington Post, July 5, 1998

THE IDEA OF A CONSTITUTIONAL AMENDMENT TO ban flag burning is one of those long-smoldering non-solutions to non-problems that flare up when Congress has nothing better to think about. The non-problem is that giant rash of flag burnings around the country that — somewhat inconveniently for supporters of the amendment — isn't happening. This particular form of expression is, in fact, exceedingly rare. But even if the practice were widespread and corroding the populace's regard for America's symbols and values, the proposed one-line amendment to the Constitution would still be an affront to free speech. Over the loud objections of First Amendment advocates, the proposal would grant Congress "power to prohibit the physical desecration of the flag of the United States."

The nine lives of this unnecessary and wrong-headed amendment would be merely a case study in Congress's ability to waste time pursuing imagined public obsessions, except for the danger that one of these years it actually will pass. And this could be the year. The amendment has already passed the House of Representatives, and it received 63 votes in the Senate back in 1995 — only a few short of the two-thirds necessary to be sent on to the states for ratification. Recently, the Senate Judiciary Committee sent it to the floor by a vote of 11 to 7.

Yet the arguments for the amendment are no better than they ever were. *Of course*, the flag is still a precious symbol and still worthy of respect, and burning it is still an odious form of political expression. But none of this separates it from dozens of other expressive actions that are equally offensive to our way of life. We do not contemplate constitutional amendments to exempt from First Amendment protection cross burnings, swastikas or other symbolic expressions of bigotry. Having an exception for desecration of the flag would probably not eviscerate the broader protections of the First Amendment. But it would, in effect, turn the "no" in the hallowed phrase "Congress shall make no law" into an "almost no" — which is a singular erosion of the principle for which the First Amendment stands. This principle has survived and enriched this country through periods in which unfettered expression caused great political stresses. Why should it be compromised now to prevent Americans from burning flags that they weren't planning to ignite in the first place. ❧

J.F. COOPER

WALT WHITMAN, *The New York Aurora*, April 19, 1842

THIS GREAT GAWKY HAS BEEN MAKING A STILL greater ass of himself, if possible, lately, by procuring at the hands of juries certain small potato verdicts, against a poor devil of an editor, a poor devil of an author, and God only knows how many more poor devils beside. For our own part, we don't see how any twelve men of sense could be led to pronounce in favor of this enormous ape.

The grounds for founding a libel prosecution on are so flimsy, so utterly destitute of any reason, that who can but be filled with amaze at the result? Cooper is damning himself utterly in the estimation of all sensible men. ❧

James Fenimore Cooper sued editors and authors, angering editorial writer Walt Whitman.

TO AN ANXIOUS FRIEND

William Allen White, *The Emporia Daily Gazette,* July 27, 1922

You tell me that law is above freedom of utterance. And I reply that you can have no wise laws nor free enforcement of wise laws unless there is free expression of the wisdom of the people — and, alas, their folly with it. But if there is freedom, folly will die of its own poison, and the wisdom will survive. That is the history of the race. It is the proof of man's kinship with God. You say that freedom of utterance is not for time of stress, and I reply with the sad truth that only in time of stress is freedom of utterance in danger. No one questions it in calm days, because it is not needed. And the reverse is true also; only when free utterance is suppressed is it needed, and when it is needed, it is most vital to justice. Peace is good. But if you are interested in peace through force and without free discussion, that is to say, free utterance decently and in order — your interest in justice is slight. And peace without justice is tyranny, no matter how you may sugar coat it with expediency. This state today is in more danger from suppression than from violence, because in the end, suppression leads to violence. Violence, indeed, is the child of suppression. Whoever pleads for justice helps to keep the peace; and whoever tramples upon the plea for justice, temperately made in the name of peace, only outrages peace and kills something fine in the heart of man which God put there when we got our manhood. When that is killed, brute meets brute on each side of the line.

So, dear friend, put fear out of your heart. This nation will survive, this state will prosper, the orderly business of life will go forward if only men can speak in whatever way given them to utter what their hearts hold — by voice, by posted card, by letter or by press. Reason never has failed men. Only force and repression have made the wrecks in the world. ❧

William Allen White. "Only when free utterance is suppressed is it needed, and when it is needed, it is most vital to justice."

Anti-war demonstrators burn a flag in Chicago in 1991.

AFTERWORD

The Pueblo Star-Journal *rolls off the presses in Colorado circa 1910.*

"EDITORIAL WRITING IS A... PECULIAR OCCUPATION,"

VERMONT ROYSTER WROTE IN 1983 AFTER RETIRING FROM *THE WALL STREET JOURNAL* AS ONE OF HISTORY'S GREATEST EDITORIAL WRITERS. THE EDITORIAL WRITER IS A "PROFESSIONAL AMATEUR," ROYSTER WROTE. "HE IS RARELY AN EXPERT ON ANYTHING BUT HE IS FORCED TO LEARN A LITTLE ABOUT MANY THINGS — ECONOMICS, LAW, SCIENCE, GOVERNMENT, SOCIOLOGY, AND SO FORTH." ❧ BUT THAT BREADTH OF KNOWLEDGE DOESN'T EXPLAIN WHY ROYSTER WAS SO great — or why Horace Greeley or Henry Watterson or William Allen White were so great. Nor does it explain why editorials and editorial pages today are so bland.

Today's editorial writers are, often, true experts in their subjects. Many big newspapers have editorial writers who specialize in science or medicine or law or foreign affairs. Many little newspapers have editors and editorial writers who know everything that's happening in their towns.

But Greeley of the *New York Tribune*, Watterson of *The Courier-Journal*, White of *The Emporia Daily Gazette*, and Royster, and their newspapers, had something lacking in most of today's editorial writers and newspapers: personality. And that personality — personal and institutional — made the men voices to be listened to, and made the institutions forces to be reckoned with.

On any given day, the men and their newspapers could be outrageous, outlandish, outspoken or outstanding. The editorials of the young White helped elect a man to the White House. The edi-torials of an old Watterson helped stir a nation to war. Greeley, in his day, was as influential as any politician. Royster, in his way, set the political agenda for business leaders and the business agenda for political leaders. They wrote anonymously, but they were far from anonymous.

Now, the anonymous are truly anonymous. They are not men — or women — about town. Few people in any city could tell you the name of the editorial page editor of their local newspaper or the names of any of the editorial writers. That's one of the problems.

"Perhaps the anonymity of editorial writing is largely to blame for its flaccidity," H.L. Mencken wrote in 1923 in criticizing the thinking in the editorials of Watterson. Mencken, who gained journalistic fame for his signed writings, not his unsigned editorials, and who periodically criticized all editorial writers, said: "The man who has to take personal responsibility for what he writes is far more apt than the anonymous man to be frank. He cannot hedge and evade the facts as he sees them

---

OPPOSITE: *Los Angeles* Daily News *reporters work by desk lights to get the paper out during a blackout in 1941.*

without exposing himself to attack and ridicule." Though wrong about Watterson, he had a point.

But it's more than that.

Today's editorials — and of course there are exceptions — inform but do not inspire. Or inflame. Sometimes, they lack opinion. Usually, they lack passion.

"A lot of people don't have opinions," Richard Aregood, an opinionated and passionate editorial writer, told an interviewer in 1993. "That's where the passion comes from. You've got to believe in something. There are a lot of things I believe in, and strongly. And you've got to care about what you're writing, or," he laughingly told the interviewer, "it reads like an editorial."

Passion comes from love — or hate. You have to love your community to write stirringly about its issues. You have to hate oppression to write movingly about freedom. To write passionately, you have to have a stake in your community, a stake in democracy. That's why Greeley was so stirring. He loved his country and wanted to make it better. Hodding Carter Jr. and Hazel Brannon Smith and Harry Ashmore and Ralph McGill and others wrote passionately because they believed in America and its Constitution even more than they believed in the South and its traditions. Jimmy Ward wrote just as passionately out of hate. You can't be politically correct when you're fighting for democracy — or against it.

The Wall Street Journal right now probably has the best editorial page in America. It's as contentious as it is conservative. But whether you believe it to be profane or prophetic, it's always provocative. The page lost some grace and civility when Royster retired, but it lost none of its sense of purpose.

The page knows right — in every sense of that word — from wrong, or at least its definition of right from wrong (or, synonymously to the *Journal* editorial writers, right from left). The page is ringing in its defenses and righteous in its attacks.

In the days of Greeley and Watterson and White and Royster, news pages would teach, editorial pages would preach. Sometimes, they'd preach with hellfire and damnation, sometimes with calm and balm. But they didn't pull punches. What editor today would dare challenge his state's famous senator to take a sanity test, the way Grover Cleveland Hall challenged Alabama Sen. Tom Heflin in 1927? Today, the editor would be run out of town — or, more likely, transferred out of town by his corporate bosses.

And that's another difference. Today, most newspapers are owned by corporations based in far-off cities, and they move editors and publishers around as if they were branch managers at banks — which is the way some corporate owners look upon their very profitable empires. You can't write knowingly — let alone passionately — about your town if you are an itinerant writer or if you fear your absentee bosses.

When Henry Watterson died in 1921, William Allen White noted the passing of an era.

"It is not by accident that the newspaper business is developing no more editors like Henry Watterson," White wrote. "Young men as bright as Watterson have no million dollars, and no million dollar friends" to finance newspapers for them, he noted. "So the young men hire out their brains. They are naturally not given the liberty in their hired men's jobs that they would have on their own papers. So they get into other work, or shrivel up and die mentally. … The day of the big individual editor has passed. The day of the big corporation-owned paper is here."

White owned the *Emporia Daily Gazette* and thus had a very real stake in his town and his state as well as his nation. Ownership of the newspaper gave him the freedom to speak his mind; affection for his community gave him the desire to. It was both a business and a calling. Early on, he put up billboards that said: "All right! Cuss the Gazette, but read it!" People did both.

Today's owners — and today's editors — want you to read their newspapers, but not to cuss them. They want their papers to be "inclusive," to be "reader-friendly," to not offend, and that includes their editorial pages. Today's newspapers would never say "To Hell with the Hohenzollerns and the Hapsburgs" — or today's equivalent — and certainly wouldn't tell complaining churchmen that "we'll be hornswaggled if we don't repeat it six days in the week and twice on Sundays! There!" They don't want to lose the church-page advertising or have to take calls from the mothers of 6-year-olds who don't read the newspaper anyway.

As a result, many of today's newspapers — especially those owned by big corporations — put out editorial pages devoid of thought; others, devoid of controversy. They are, quite simply, boring.

"An editorial, to have any rationale at all, should say something. It should take a line," Mencken told a conference of editorial writers in 1947. He then went on to tell them how boring their pages were. Given the blandness and banality, he asked, "Why have editorials at all?"

Perhaps Mencken's dreary outlook was influenced by the Pulitzer Prize-winning editorials of William Waymack of *The Des Moines Register*. One 1936 editorial began: "It is announced that regional hearings will be held between the first and the middle of next month by the president's committee on farm tenancy — two meetings in the south, two in the middle west and one on the west coast. The one on the west coast is in a sense supplementary." It makes a person wonder whether anyone has ever read the second paragraph.

Mencken's refrain in 1947 about the decline of the editorial — as well as this afterword's similar refrain in 2005 — was not new.

In 1866, a man named James Parton wrote in *The North American Review*: "The prestige of the editorial is gone. Just as there is a party in England who propose the omission of the sermon from the church service as something no longer needed by the people, so there are journalists who think the time is at hand for the abolition of editorials, and the concentration of the whole force of journalism upon presenting to the public the history and picture of the day. ... Editorials neither make nor mar a daily paper." Two decades later, Joseph Pulitzer's *World* abandoned editorials.

In fact, editorials both make and mar a newspaper — and a town and a nation. They make it when they expose and inspire, they mar it when they're expedient and insipid. Today, in this age of instant news reported without interpretation or context, fractious television bellowers, fact-free radio talkers, Internet bloggers and political befoggers have cornered the market on passion and outrage. But not on thought. Now, strong editorials are more needed than ever.

Democracy needs their passion, their outrage and, especially, their uncommon sense. ❧

The Emporia Daily Gazette *newsroom circa 1937.*
"Nothing fails so rapidly as a cowardly paper,"
owner William Allen White said.

One of the first daily newspapers in New Mexico set up its operations underneath a juniper tree in the mid-1800s.

A newspaper office circa 1904.

ACKNOWLEDGMENTS

THIS BOOK HAS BEEN PRODUCED IN PARTNERSHIP WITH the Freedom Forum. It has been a true partnership.

Charles Overby, the chief executive of the Freedom Forum and a former editor himself, not only made the foundation's resources available but also added valuable suggestions, kept me from heading down one wrong path — and recalled and then found that most interesting editorial on Ben Butler. Similarly, Peter Prichard, until recently president of the Freedom Forum and still the president of its Newseum, read the drafts carefully and provided guidance. Joe Urschel, the executive director of the Newseum, was helpful as well.

Peggy Engel, the managing editor of the Newseum, a fountain of ideas and a whirlwind of enthusiasm, shepherded the book from the beginning, negotiating with the National Geographic Society, pointing us toward pictures and graphics, and gently reminding about deadlines.

Lisa Lytton, senior editor at National Geographic, championed the book from its inception and kept us all on track. Melissa Farris created an inspired design and found many great pictures.

And the book simply could not have been written without the work of Sharon Shahid, a senior writer at the Newseum. She was indefatigable in her research and unerring in her critiques, letter-perfect in her editing and, all the while, cheerful. She is wonderful.

Karen Wyatt, director of visual resources for the Newseum, added great ideas about the photos and graphics — and then along with Indira Williams Babic, Sarah Osborne and Martha Davidson — found great material.

Eleven other people at the Newseum and the Freedom Forum also lent their hands — and their eyes and their ears and their thoughts. They found obscure editorials and historic newspapers, checked elusive facts and pointed out glaring mistakes. These people are: Nancy Stewart, Jerrie Bethel, Rick Mastroianni, Kristi Conkle, Kathryn Zaharek, Sage Hulsebus, Max Brown, Angela Johnson, Jeff Schlosberg, Don Ross and Ann Rauscher. Political memorabilia collector Tony Lee generously made artifacts available, and Randall Hagadorn photographed them.

David Shedden, the director of the library at the Poynter Institute in St. Petersburg, Fla., was most helpful on my visit there and in subsequently finding material I sought. Mark Taflinger of the *Courier-Journal*'s library in Louisville found and photocopied some old, old editorials by Henry Watterson. Vincent Fitzpatrick, curator of the H.L. Mencken Collection at the Enoch Pratt Free Library in Baltimore, found and photocopied some old, old editorials by and about Mencken. Lottie Lindberg of Dow Jones was equally helpful in providing copies of editorials from *The Wall Street Journal*, and Sharon Schreiber of the University of Mississippi was unfailingly helpful. It goes without saying that the resources of the Library of Congress were indispensable.

My father, the best writer I've ever known, first made me aware of William Allen White, an awareness that has brightened my days for more than 50 years. Bill Ellison, a retired newsman in Louisville, first told me about Henry Watterson and gave me a collection of his editorials. I knew Vermont Royster from my days at *The Wall Street Journal* and saw his brilliance firsthand. And every newspaperman knows about Horace Greeley.

Sharon Shahid was the main editor of this book, but I prevailed upon three other great editors also to read drafts. They are Jim Soderlind, a retired managing editor of *The Wall Street Journal*; Irene Nolan, a former managing editor of *The Courier-Journal*, and my wife, Barbara McCoy Gartner, who in 1967 became the first woman hired since World War II for the national editing desk of *The Wall Street Journal*. All found mistakes. But any mistakes that made it into print are my fault, not theirs.

I should note, with some embarrassment, that this book contains two editorials that I wrote. This was done at the insistence of colleagues at the Freedom Forum. They were amused that anyone would defend lap-dancing as a form of protected speech, and they knew my son Christopher and were touched by his memory.

There is no one as single-minded and boring as someone reporting and writing a book, so I apologize now to my friends, my colleagues and my children — Mike and Melissa — and I promise to quit talking about it.

Michael Gartner

ILLUSTRATIONS

2: The New York Times. 4: Heritage Village of Pinewood Cultural Park. 8: White Family Collection, Emporia State University. 9: National Archives & Records Administration. 10: Courtesy Dow Jones & Company. 11: Look Magazine Collection, Library of Congress. 12-13: Mathew Brady, Library of Congress. 14: White Family Collection, Emporia State University. 18: Newseum Collection. 23: Library of Congress. 24-25: Bettmann/CORBIS. 27: Aspen Daily News. 29: Newseum Collection. 32-33: Division of Rare & Manuscript Collections, Cornell University. 34: Bettmann/CORBIS. 37: Newseum Collection. 38-39: Frank & Marie-Therese Wood Print Collections, Alexandria, Va. 41 (left): Newseum Collection. 41 (right): Courtesy Tony Lee. 42: Library of Congress. 43: Courtesy The Ellsworth American. 44-45: Courtesy Tony Lee. 46-47: Bettmann/CORBIS. 48: National Archives & Records Administration. 52, 55: Library of Congress. 57: Los Angeles Times. 58-59: Bancroft Library, University of California, Berkeley. 62: The Associated Press. 64-65: John Paul Filo. 66-67: Stan Stearns/Bettmann/CORBIS. 68: Library of Congress. 71: Bettmann/CORBIS. 72-75 (all): Library of Congress. 76: Bettmann/CORBIS. 78-79: Philadelphia Daily News. 80: White Family Collection, Emporia State University. 83: Bettmann/CORBIS. 84-85: The Associated Press. 86-87: Flip Schulke/CORBIS. 88: Bettmann/CORBIS. 91: The Granger Collection, N.Y. 92: Gordon Conner/Ohio State University Archives. 94 (left): Bettmann/CORBIS. 94 (right): Library of Congress. 95: The Granger Collection, N.Y. 96: National Archives & Records Administration. 100: CORBIS. 101: Newseum Collection. 103: Library of Congress. 105: CORBIS. 107, 110-111: Bettmann/CORBIS. 112-113: Brown Brothers. 114: CORBIS. 116: Courtesy Tony Lee. 120: CORBIS. 123: Bettmann/CORBIS. 124: George Grantham Bain Collection, Library of Congress. 127: Bettmann/CORBIS. 129: The Baltimore Evening Sun. 131: CORBIS. 132: Collection of McKissick Museum, University of South Carolina. 133: Mathew Brady, Library of Congress. 135: Library of Congress. 136-137: Bettmann/CORBIS. 138-139: CORBIS. 140: Bettmann/CORBIS. 142: CORBIS. 143: Swim Ink 2, LLC/CORBIS. 144: Bettmann/CORBIS. 147: The Associated Press. 148: Warren Taylor. 151: Courtesy James Temple. 152-153: Scheufler Collection/CORBIS. 154-155: CORBIS. 156: Library of Congress. 159: Museum of Connecticut History. 160: Robert Maass/CORBIS. 162: Library of Congress. 163: New York Daily News. 165: Art Wood Collection of Caricature & Cartoon, Library of Congress. 166: Library of Congress. 167: Bettmann/CORBIS. 170-171: The Granger Collection, NY. 172: Bettmann/CORBIS. 174: Library of Congress. 175: Seneca Falls Historical Society. 176-177: Bettmann/CORBIS. 178: Nagel & Weingaertner, Library of Congress. 183: Time Life Pictures/Getty Images. 184: BG Don F. Pratt Memorial Museum, Fort Campbell, Ky. 185-192 (all): Bettmann/CORBIS. 194-195: National Archives & Records Administration. 198: Library of Congress. 199: White Family Collection, Emporia State University. 200-201: Ralf-Finn Hestoft/CORBIS. 202-204 (all): Bettmann/CORBIS. 208-209: Bernard Hoffman/Time Life Pictures/Getty Images. 210-213 (all): Bettmann/CORBIS.

BIBLIOGRAPHY

Brenner, Marie. *House of Dreams: The Bingham Family of Louisville*. New York: Random House, 1988.

Carter, Hodding Jr. *Where Main Street Meets the River*. New York: Rinehart & Company, Inc., 1953.

Cockerill, John A. "Some Phases of Contemporary Journalism." *The Cosmopolitan Monthly Magazine*. October 1892.

Davies, David R., ed. *The Press and Race: Mississippi Journalists Confront the Movement*. Jackson: University Press of Mississippi, 2001.

Fry, Don, ed. *Best Newspaper Writing: 1993*. St. Petersburg, Fla.: Poynter Institute, 1993.

Gottlieb, Robert. *Thinking Big: The Story of the Los Angeles Times, Its Publishers, and Their Influence on Southern California*. New York: Putnam, 1977.

Greenfield, Meg. *Washington*. New York: Public Affairs, 2001.

Hale, William Harlan. *Horace Greeley: Voice of the People*. New York: Harper & Brothers, 1950.

Kluger, Richard. *The Paper: The Life and Death of the New York Herald Tribune*. New York: Alfred A. Knopf, 1986.

Krock, Arthur. *The Editorials of Henry Watterson*. New York: George H. Doran Company, 1923.

Lancaster, Paul. *Gentleman of the Press: The Life and Times of an Early Reporter, Julian Ralph of the Sun*. Syracuse, N.Y.: Syracuse University Press, 1992.

Library of America. *Reporting Civil Rights: American Journalism 1941–1963*. New York: Library of America, 2003. Distributed by Penguin Putnam.

Mahin, Helen Ogden. *The Editor and His People: Editorials by William Allen White*. New York: The MacMillan Company, 1924.

McDougal, Dennis. *Privileged Son: Otis Chandler and the Rise and Fall of the L.A. Times Dynasty*. Cambridge, Mass.: Perseus Publishing, 2001.

Mencken, H.L. *A Gang of Pecksniffs: And Other Comments on Newspaper Publishers, Editors and Reporters*. Edited by Theo Lippman Jr. New Rochelle, N.Y.: Arlington House Publishers, 1975.

Menckeniana: A Schimpflexicon. New York: Octagon Books, 1977.

Paine, Thomas. *Thomas Paine Reader*. Edited by Michael Foot and Isaac Kramnick. New York: Penguin Books, 1987.

Roberts, Chalmers. *The Washington Post: The First 100 Years*. Boston: Houghton Mifflin, 1977.

Rodgers, Marion Elizabeth. *The Impossible H.L. Mencken: A Selection of His Best Newspaper Stories*. New York: Anchor Books, 1991.

Royster, Vermont. *The Essential Royster: A Vermont Royster Reader*. Edited by Edmund Fuller. Chapel Hill, N.C.: Algonquin Books of Chapel Hill, 1985.

———. *My Own, My Country's Time: A Journalist's Journey*. Chapel Hill, N.C.: Algonquin Books of Chapel Hill, 1983.

———. *A Pride of Prejudices*. New York: Alfred A. Knopf, 1967.

Scharff, Edward E. *Worldly Power: The Making of the Wall Street Journal*. New York: Beaufort Books Publishers, 1986.

Sloan, William David, and Laird B. Anderson. *Pulitzer Prize Editorials: America's Best Writing 1917–2003*. Ames: Iowa State Press, 2003.

Stone, Geoffrey. *Perilous Times: Free Speech in Wartime*. New York: W.W. Norton, 2004.

Teachout, Terry. *The Skeptic: A Life of H.L. Mencken*. New York: HarperCollins, 2002.

Tifft, Susan E., and Alex S. Jones. *The Trust: The Private and Powerful Family Behind the New York Times*. Boston: Little, Brown and Company, 1999.

Van Deusen, Glyndon G. *Horace Greeley: Nineteenth-Century Crusader*. New York: Hill and Wang, 1953.

Waldron, Ann. *Hodding Carter: The Reconstruction of a Racist*. Chapel Hill, N.C.: Algonquin Books of Chapel Hill, 1993.

Watterson, Henry. *"Marse Henry": An Autobiography*. New York: George H. Doran Company, 1919.

Wendt, Lloyd. *The Wall Street Journal: The Story of Dow Jones & the Nation's Business Newspaper*. New York: Rand McNally, 1982.

White, E.B. *Essays of E.B. White*. New York: Harper & Row, 1977.

White, William Allen. *The Autobiography of William Allen White*. New York: The MacMillan Company, 1946.

Whitman, Walt. *Walt Whitman of the New York Aurora, Editor at Twenty-Two: A Collection of Recently Discovered Writings*. Edited by Joseph Jay Rubin and Charles H. Brown Jr. State College, Pa.: Bald Eagle Press, 1950.

INDEX

ABOUT THE AUTHOR

MICHAEL GARTNER was trained as a lawyer, spent his career as a journalist, owns a Triple-A baseball team and is president of the Iowa Board of Regents.

Over the years, he has been Page One editor of *The Wall Street Journal,* editor and president of *The Des Moines Register,* editor of the *Courier-Journal* and *Louisville Times,* general news executive of Gannett Co. and *USA Today,* and president of NBC News. He also has been an op-ed columnist for *The Wall Street Journal* and *USA Today.*

In 1997, he won the Pulitzer Prize for editorials he wrote for *The* (Ames, Iowa) *Daily Tribune,* of which he was editor and co-owner. The prize was given for his "common sense editorials about issues deeply affecting the lives of people in his community."

Gartner was born in Des Moines in 1938. He graduated from Carleton College, in Northfield, Minn., and received his law degree from New York University. In 1994, he was a Fellow at the Institute of Politics at Harvard University. He is a member of the bar of New York and Iowa.

He is a former president of the American Society of Newspaper Editors, and for 10 years in the 1980s and early 1990s was a member of the Pulitzer Prize Board. He is the only former board member to go on to win a Pulitzer Prize. He was a trustee of the Freedom Forum's First Amendment Center and now is a trustee of the Freedom Forum's Newseum in Washington, D.C.

Michael and Barbara Gartner have a daughter, Melissa, and a son, Mike, both of whom live in Des Moines. Their other son, Christopher, died of juvenile diabetes at age 17 in 1994.

ABOUT THE NEWSEUM

THE WORLD'S FIRST interactive museum of news — the Newseum — opened in Arlington, Va., in 1997. Its mission was simple: to help the public and the news media understand one another better.

The Newseum also celebrates the value of a unique American notion— the First Amendment. The First Amendment — a covenant between the government and the people — assures that no law will suppress the people's right to a free press, to speak freely, to worship, to assemble in public or to petition the government for redress of grievances. By assuring a free flow of information, the First Amendment helps ensure that Americans remain forever free. We believe that visitors will come to the Newseum as tourists, but leave as supporters of the First Amendment and the vital role a free press plays in a free society.

In 2007, the Newseum and its administrative offices will relocate to Washington, D.C., at Pennsylvania Avenue and Sixth Street, N.W., between the U.S. Capitol and the White House.

The Newseum is one of three priorities — along with First Amendment freedoms and newsroom diversity — of the Freedom Forum, a nonpartisan foundation dedicated to free press, free speech and free spirit for all people.

NEWSEUM STAFF FOR THIS BOOK: Sharon Shahid, editor; Karen Wyatt, illustrations editor; Ann Rauscher, copy editor; Indira Williams Babic and Sarah Osborne, illustrations assistants; staff of the Freedom Forum library; Margaret Engel, managing editor.

OUTRAGE PASSION & UNCOMMON SENSE

PUBLISHED BY THE NATIONAL GEOGRAPHIC SOCIETY

John M. Fahey, Jr.
President and Chief Executive Officer

Gilbert M. Grosvenor
Chairman of the Board

Nina D. Hoffman
Executive Vice President

PREPARED BY THE BOOK DIVISION

Kevin Mulroy
Senior Vice President and Publisher

Kristin Hanneman
Illustrations Director

Marianne R. Koszorus
Design Director

STAFF FOR THIS BOOK

Lisa Lytton
Project Editor

Melissa Farris
Art Director/Illustrations Editor

Meredith Wilcox
Illustrations Specialist

Gary Colbert
Production Director

Lewis Bassford
Production Project Manager

MANUFACTURING AND QUALITY CONTROL

Christopher A. Liedel
Chief Financial Officer

Phillip L. Schlosser
Managing Director

John T. Dunn
Technical Director

One of the world's largest nonprofit scientific and educational organizations, the National Geographic Society was founded in 1888 "for the increase and diffusion of geographic knowledge." Fulfilling this mission, the Society educates and inspires millions every day through its magazines, books, television programs, videos, maps and atlases, research grants, the National Geographic Bee, teacher workshops, and innovative classroom materials. The Society is supported through membership dues, charitable gifts, and income from the sale of its educational products. This support is vital to National Geographic's mission to increase global understanding and promote conservation of our planet through exploration, research, and education.

For more information, please call 1-800-NGS LINE (647-5463) or write to the following address:
National Geographic Society
1145 17th Street N.W.
Washington, D.C. 20036-4688 U.S.A.

Visit the Society's Web site at www.nationalgeographic.com.
Visit the Newseum's Web site at www.newseum.org.

Library of Congress Cataloging-in-Publication Data available upon request.

ISBN 0-7922-4197-5

Printed in China

The New York Times

Reg. U. S. Pat. Off.

"All the News That's Fit to Print."

Published Every Day in the Year by
THE NEW YORK TIMES COMPANY.

...PH S. OCHS, President and Publisher.

Godfrey N. Nelson, Secretary.

FRIDAY, DECEMBER 8, 1933.

OFFICES OF THE NEW YORK TIMES
...York City: Telephone LAckawanna 4-1000

... Bldg. .Times Square | Washington Hts. 585 W. 181st
...WARK........ Tel. Market 2-3900. 17-79 William St.
...te PLAINS. Tel. White Plains 9300. 26 Grand St.
...SHINGTON... Nexs. Albee Bldg. | Advts. Star Bldg.
...LTIMORE... Sun Building. Baltimore St. and Sun Sq.
...ICAGO, News, 435 N. Michigan; Bus., 360 N. Michigan
...LOUIS, Globe Dem. Bldg. DETROIT. Gen. Mot. Bldg.
...STON, 18 Tremont St. LOS ANGELES, 1151 S. B'way
... FRANCISCO.742 Market St. SEATTLE.610 Lloyd Bldg.
...XPON. News, Trist. House Sq.; Bus. 3 Salisbury Sq.
...RIS...18 rue de la Paix; ROME...53 Via dell' Arcina
...RLIN. Kochstrasse 22; COPENHAGEN...Politiken Bldg.
...NNA.5 Rosenburgerstrasse; BUDAPEST 29 Eotvos Utca
...VETA.45 Route de Florissant; DUBLIN 153 Castle Av.
...SCOW.... Bolshaya Ordinka 53. WARSAW.. Reabant 32
...WARDS.Skopinanska 18. BUENOS AIRES San Martin 214
...CHAREST. Delitreaza 21; JERUSALEM, Sionbn Bldg.
...NO. Al Atram House; LISBON. 21d Prea. Terreiro
...ANGKAI. Emb. De. Sachovek; TOKYO.13 Hatcazachi
...MIT. Claudio Cuello 17; MEXICO, D. F Independencia 13
...NAL ZONE. Balboa Hgts.; MANILA. 1589 F. B. Harrison

...SCRIPTION RATES: UNITED STATES,
POSSESSIONS AND TERRITORIES.

...dition.	1 Yr.	6 Mos.	3 Mos.	1 Mo.	2 Wks.	1 Wk.
...ry & S'nd'y.	$14.00	$7.50	$3.75	$1.25	$.70	$.48
...ekday	10.00	5.00	2.55	.85	.55	.35
...nday	5.00	2.60	1.40	.50	.30	.20

...anada, Cuba, Dominican Republic, Haiti, Mex-
...Newfoundland, Spain and colonies, Central
... South America, except British Honduras,
...tish, French and Dutch Guiana.

...dition	1 Yr.	6 Mos.	3 Mos.	1 Mo.
...ekday and Sunday....	$18.00	$9.60	$4.50	$1.80
...ekday	12.00	6.00	3.00	1.00
...nday	6.00	3.00	1.50	.50

Other Foreign Countries.

...dition	1 Yr.	6 Mos.	3 Mos.	1 Mo.
...ekday and Sunday...	$50.00	$25.00	$12.50	$4....
...ekday	32.00	16.00	8.00	2.75
...nday	18.00	9.00	5.50	1.50

...NALIST (Finance and Commerce). Fridays. A year.
...$7; Canada, Mexico, South and Central America.
...$7.50; other countries. $8.

...E NEW YORK TIMES BOOK REVIEW (weekly).
...a year, $3; Canada, $5; foreign, $5.50.

...O-WEEK PICTORIAL (rotogravure weekly). United
...States, Canada, Mexico, Central and South America.
...a year, $4; other countries, $6.

...RRENT HISTORY MAGAZINE (monthly). a year
...$3; Canada $3.75; foreign $4.25. A copy, 35c.

...E NEW YORK TIMES INDEX—12 monthly volumes.
...paper bound, $25; Annual Cumulative Index (rag
...paper), $25; by mail, $25; Monthly and Annual
...Cumulative Indexes, $52.50.

...E NEW YORK TIMES RAG PAPER edition for
...permanent preservation, cloth bound, 2 volumes per
...month, $170 per annum; semi-monthly bound volumes,
...regular newsprint, $72 per annum.

A TIMELY LEAD.

If only for one paragraph in his
...dress to the Federal Council of

loans, although the rate of the preceding September had been only 1⅛.

In the financial and investing community there was yesterday expression
of relief that, at the Treasury, the correct procedure was still being followed
of taking up maturing indebtedness
through new borrowings when the public finances rendered impossible its redemption from a Treasury surplus. In
reality, there had not been the slightest
reason to anticipate any other recourse.
The foolish clamor of certain misguided
public men, that maturing United
States bonds should be redeemed in flat
money issued under the Inflation Act's
discretionary provisions, fell absolutely
flat, and was treated by the Government with silent contempt.

The "agitation," if it can so be
called, may be renewed hereafter; it
was immediately incited by the Treasury's offer, last October, to exchange
new twelve-year government bonds for
the Fourth Liberty 4¼s, of which
$1,900,000,000 had been called for re-
demption next April. To some of our
legislators it seemed waste of good
money to issue a new loan in order to
provide for such redemption, when the
Government still had the printing-press
available and possessed the power to
declare its output "lawful money."
But it is not at all probable that the
next revival of that proposal will get
a reception any different from what
was given it last October.

MR. FLYNN ON BRIDGE-CROSSING.

Edward J. Flynn, who pontificates
in the Bronx, must speak with authority on all matters relating to bridges.
So long as he occupies his throne he
won't let the Tammany Tiger cross
"the Harlem River bridges." Politically considered, these are to be one-way
structures. Mr. Flynn made ample
use of them in his war against Mr.
Curry this Fall. Presumably he will
continue to do so, since he is to go forward with his operations against the
somewhat shaky monarchy in Union
Square. He will cross and recross at
his pleasure, but Tammany must keep
its feet off!

Certain persons in Mr. Flynn's
satrapy who have the impudence to call
themselves Tammany Democrats have
proclaimed their intention to nominate
a candidate for State Senator in the
special election on Dec. 28 in the
Twenty-first district. True to his principle of unilateral autonomy, Mr. Flynn
artfully blends with it the issue of party

book is held by the judge to be a sincere piece of literature, not designed to
corrupt morals.

Admitting that parts of "Ulysses"
are brilliantly written, Judge Woolsey
decides that other sections of it are
dull reading. This will be a disappointment, or a challenge, to all-the-way
admirers of Joyce. They can read the
deepest symbolism into his most routine
and jejune writing. They will probably
be chagrined, also, to find that the
public has no great interest in this
long-banned novel. While under exclusion, it was furtively read with delight;
now that it can be freely bought and
sold, there will be less appetite for it,
one imagines. It is like prohibition.
If drinking is forbidden, thousands will
manage to get a drink; but as soon as
it is made legal, the thrill of romance
is taken away from defying or evading
the law.

As for literary criticism of "Ulysses,"
Judge Woolsey indulges in a bit of his
own. He declares the attempt of Mr.
Joyce to be

> to show how the screen of con-
> sciousness, with its ever-shifting ka-
> leidoscopic impressions, carries, as it
> were on a plastic palimpsest, not
> only what is in the focus of each
> man's observation of the actual
> things about him, but also in a pe-
> numbral zone residua of past impres-
> sions, some recent and some drawn
> up by association from the domain
> of the subconscious.

Please remember that this is judicial.
It cannot be attacked without danger
of contempt of court.

RIFT IN THE AAA.

The AAA, or Agricultural Adjust-
ment Administration, has its Right
Wing and its Left. On some points
they disagree—most immediately on
the question of codes dealing with products manufactured from farm com-
modities. The Right, represented by
Mr. Peek, is described as favoring a
minimum of regulation, particularly
with respect to profits. It believes
that millers, packers and other proc-
essors should be permitted to earn
what they can, so long as the farmer
himself receives a fair price. The Left,
with the university economists in the
van, favors regulation all along the
line, with a strict curb on profits.

Disagreement on these points can be
traced partly to a general difference of
opinion regarding the proper relations